PROFESSIONAL LIABILITY OF LAWYERS

PROFESSIONAL LIABILITY OF LAWYERS

General Editor
DENNIS CAMPBELL
B.A., J.D., LL.M.
Member, Iowa State Bar and New York State Bar

Editor
CHRISTIAN T. CAMPBELL
LL.B., LL.M.
Member, New York State Bar

PUBLISHED UNDER THE AUSPICES
OF THE
CENTER FOR INTERNATIONAL LEGAL STUDIES
Salzburg, Austria

LLP

LONDON NEW YORK HAMBURG HONG KONG
LLOYD'S OF LONDON PRESS LTD.
1995

Lloyd's of London Press Ltd.
Legal Publishing Division
27 Swinton Street, London WC1X 9NW

USA AND CANADA
Lloyd's of London Press Inc.
Suite 308, 611 Broadway
New York, NY 10012 USA

GERMANY
Lloyd's of London Press GmbH
59 Ehrenbergstrasse
2000 Hamburg 50, Germany

SOUTH EAST ASIA
Lloyd's of London Press (Far East) Ltd.
Room 1101, Hollywood Centre
233 Hollywood Road
Hong Kong

First Published 1995

British Library Cataloguing in Publication Data
A catalogue record for this book is available from the British Library

ISBN 1-85044-869-8

Text set in Sabon by
The Center for International Legal Studies
Salzburg, Austria
Printed in Great Britain by
WBC Print Ltd.
Bridgend, Mid Glamorgan

Preface

Lawyers have not only benefited from the trend toward greater compensation for ever widening concepts of "defective" products and services. They have also become a target. The present volume examines the current state of lawyers' professional liability in several major jurisdictions. This examination reveals that the development of the law has not been uniform despite international efforts at harmonisation, such as those of the International Bar Association and the European Community.

The proliferation of foreign-based practices suggests the relevance of understanding the risks of practice outside a lawyer's home jurisdiction — even, or especially, with regard to those jurisdictions where the extent of exposure to compensation claims arising out of legal practice has not fully crystallised. While a single multijurisdictional volume cannot be exhaustive of these issues, the reports here aim to convey such an understanding.

The chapters on each jurisdiction consider the current professional, civil, administrative and criminal rules applicable to the practice of law, in particular those relating to litigation conduct, general and specialist advice, conflicts of interest, confidentiality, the applicable standards of professional performance and the available compensatory remedies for their breach. The reports also indicate aspects of liability coverage required of and available to legal practitioners and special issues of transnational practice.

Christian Campbell

Center for International Legal Studies
Salzburg, Austria
September 1994

CONTENTS

CHAPTER 8. IRELAND

CHAPTER 9. ITALY

CHAPTER 10. NEW ZEALAND

CHAPTER 11. SPAIN

The Contributors

Rebecca Brunner-Peters, United States resident counsel to the Zurich firm Umbrich Badertscher & Roesle, is the holder of degrees from Colby College, University of Rochester and University of Pennsylvania Law School and is admitted to practice in Pennsylvania and the District of Columbia. She completed a fellowship at the University of Zurich Law Faculty in 1989 and has specialised in corporate, banking, tax and securities law. She has previously co-authored articles on Federal tax law, money laundering, hostile take-over and turn-arounds and workouts.

Louis B. Buchman is a partner with the Paris firm Caubet Buchman Spalter. The holder of degrees from the University of Paris, he has been certified by the Paris Bar as a specialist of European Law and of the Law of International Relations. He is a member of the Paris and New York Bars.

Edmund Butler is a partner with the Dublin law firm of L. K. Shields & Partners. A law graduate of University College Dublin and a fellow of the Chartered Institute of Arbitrators, he specialises in commercial litigation.

Gregory C. Everard is a partner with the national firm Kensington Swan in Auckland. A graduate of University of Auckland he specialises in professional indemnity insurance law and has been admitted to practice in New Zealand and Victoria, Australia.

Vanessa Fenton, a law graduate and holder of a Master's Degree in Law from University College Cork, is employed in the Dublin Law Firm of L. K. Shields & Partners.

Michael R. Goldman is litigation partner with the commercial firm of Rudnick & Wolfe in Chicago, Illinois. A graduate of DePaul Law School and Ohio Wesleyan University, he specialises in commercial litigation and professional liability in numerous jurisdictions throughout the United States.

Ferdinand Graf, an attorney-at-law admitted in Austria (Vienna) and New York, is a graduate of Vienna University and New York University School of Law. He is the author of several publications in the field of attorney's liability in Austrian and international publications. He published a text book on attorney's liability in 1991.

Peter Kalichman is an associate with the firm McDougall, Caron in Montreal. A graduate of the Université de Montréal and of McGill University, he specialises in civil and commercial litigation.

John Lapraik is a partner with Mills & Reeve Solicitors in Cambridge. A graduate of the University of Reading, he specialises in commercial litigation with a particular emphasis on professional negligence claims.

Thomas Lindemann is a partner with Boesebeck, Barz & Partner. As a graduate of the University of Göttingen in both law and economics, he specialises in corporate law, mergers and acquisitions and mutual funds.

Gianni Manca is the senior partner of Piergrossi Villa Manca Graziadei of Milan, Rome and Edinburgh. A 1948 graduate of the University of Rome he has served as President of the Council of European Bars and chaired its committee for the preparation of a Code of Conduct for European lawyers.

Christos A. Papachristou is a senior partner with the Athens firm of lawyers, Christos Papachristou & Associates. A graduate of Southampton University, England (LL. M.), he specialises in corporate and commercial law.

Simon Reich is a partner with the Antwerp firm, De Roy, Demets & Reich. A graduate of Antwerp University, he is a member of the Executive Committee and President of the Publications Commission of the European Lawyers' Union.

Héctor Rodríguez Molnar is a partner with the Madrid law firmof Membrillera & Rodriguez Molnar. The holder of degrees in law from the Argentine Catholic University of Buenos Aires, the Complutense University in Madrid, and the University Pennsylvania (LL.M.), he has served as Vice Chairman of the Committee on International Environmental Law of the International Bar Association (IBA) and is currently a member of the IBA's Council of the Section on Business Law.

Lars Sandberg is an associate of Advokatfirman Södermark in Stockholm, Sweden. He is a graduate of the University of Uppsala (LL.B.) and has studied at the University of Minnesota Law School.

Thomas Tendorf is a partner with Advokatfirman Södemark in Stockholm, Sweden. He is a graduate of the Universities of Uppsala (LL.B.) and London (LL.M.) and specialises in Swedish and international commercial litigation and arbitration.

Contributors' Contact List

Austria
Ferdinand Graf
Preslmayr & Partner
Dr. Karl-Lueger-Ring 12
1010 Vienna 1
Austria
Tel: (+431) 533 16 95
Fax: (+431) 535 56 86

Belgium
Simon Reich
De Roy, Demets &Reich
Schermersstraat 1
2000 Antwerpen
Belgium
Tel: (03) 226 6386
Fax: (03) 226 8630

Canada
Peter Kalichman
McDougall, Caron
1000, rue de la Gauchetière Ouest,
Bureau 2600
Montréal, Québec H3B 4W5
Canada
Tel: (514) 399 1000
Fax: (514) 399 1026

England and Wales
John Lapraik
Mills & Reeve
Francis House
112 Hills Road
Cambridge CB2 1PH
England
Tel: (0223) 644 22
Fax: (0223) 355 848

France
Louis B. Buchman
Caubet Buchman Spalter
31, Boulevard Malesherbes
75008 Paris
France
Tel: (1) 42 65 60 60
Fax: (1) 42 65 38 38

Germany
Thomas Lindemann
Boesebeck, Barz & Partner
Schlüterstraße 37
10629 Berlin
Germany
Tel: (030) 88 57 45 0
Fax: (030) 88 57 45 99

Greece
Christos A. Papachristou
Law Offices
104, Aeolou Street
Athens GR 105 64
Greece
Tel: (01) 321 1134
Fax: (01) 324 0727

Ireland
Edmund Butler and Vanessa Fenton
L.K. Shields & Partners
31 Merrion Square
Dublin 2
Ireland
Tel: (01) 661 0866
Fax: (01) 661 0883

Italy
Gianni Manca
Piergrossi Villa Manca Graziadei
Via Dei Gracchi 320
00192 Rome
Italy
Tel: 06-321 5901
Fax: 06-321 3218

New Zealand
Gregory C. Everard
Kensington Swan
22 Fanshawe Street
Private Bag
92101 Auckland
New Zealand
Tel: 0-9-379 4196
Fax: 0-9-309 4276

Spain
Héctor Rodríguez Molnar
Membrillera & Rodrigues Molnar
Velázquez, 78 - 5° Izda.
28001 Madrid
Spain
Tel: (34-1) 431 67 95
Fax: (34-1) 575 81 90

Sweden
Thomas Tendorf and Lars Sandberg
Advokatfirman Södermark
Strandvägen 1
Box 140 55
104 40 Stockholm
Sweden
Tel: (08) 670 5750
Fax: (08) 663 6720

Switzerland
Rebecca Brunner-Peters
Umbricht Badertscher & Roesle
Bahnhofstrasse 22
P.O. Box 4174
8022 Zürich
Switzerland
Tel: 01-211 2550
Fax: 01-221 2552

United States
Michael R. Goldman and Scott A. Semenek
Rudnick & Wolfe
Suite 1800
203 North LaSalle Street
Chicago, Illinois
U.S.A. 60601-1293
Tel: (312) 368-4000
Fax: (312) 236 7516

TABLE OF CASES

AUSTRIA

BELGIUM

CANADA

ENGLAND

FRANCE

GREECE

IRELAND

NEW ZEALAND

SWEDEN

SWITZERLAND

UNITED STATES

TABLE OF LEGISLATION

EUROPEAN COMMUNITY

FRANCE

GERMANY

GREECE

CHAPTER 1

AUSTRIA

FERDINAND GRAF
Preslmayr & Partner
Vienna, Austria

INTRODUCTION

Presently, approximately 3,000 attorneys are permitted to practice in Austria, a relatively small number when compared to the size of the bars of other European countries. The reason for this can in part be found in the Austrian bar's stringent admission requirements. Admission to the bar requires, following the completion of law studies, five years of practice besides passing the bar exam, which may be taken only after the applicant has completed three years of practice.

Members of the Austrian bar are called *Rechtsanwalt*. Unlike the English and Welsh system, there is no distinction between solicitors and barristers, and unlike the present, German system, Austrian attorneys are not limited as to the courts before which they may practice. The Austrian *Rechtsanwalt* is entitled to represent clients in all legal matters and before all courts.

Legal services

However, legal services in Austria may also be procured from other professionals. The *Notar* (notary public) serves as a judicial commissioner in probate and similar proceedings. He prepares a special form of document, that is, notarial deeds, and may also act as private counsel in contract and commercial matters. They are, as a general rule with some exceptions, not entitled to represent clients in court.

Another group of legal advisors is formed by *Wirtschaftstreuhänder und Steuerberater*, accountants and tax advisors. They provide financial accounting services and counsel clients in tax matters. They are entitled to represent clients in certain proceedings relating to tax law. In certain areas, such as labour law, other persons and/or organisations are permitted to give legal advice and represent clients in court.

The Austrian bar is organised on a federal basis with every province having its own bar (*Rechtsanwaltskammer*). The nine provincial bars form the federal *Rechtsanwaltskammertag*, which is the national representative body of Austrian attorneys.[1] Membership in the bar is mandatory and every attorney is a member of the bar of the province in which his office is located.[2]

The organisation of the bar, is regulated by statute, the *Rechtsanwaltsordnung* (RAO).[3] The procedural and substantive rules governing disciplinary actions are set forth by a statute known as the *Disziplinarstatut* (DSt).[4] The disciplinary measures range from a warning to a permanent ban from practice. The DSt created a disciplinary body, called the *Disziplinarrat*, which is authorised to take disciplinary measures against members of the bar and trainee attorneys, that is, those who have not completed their practice period for admission to the bar.

At present, membership in the Austrian bar is limited to Austrian citizens. However, following the formation of the European Economic Area (EEA) attorneys admitted to practice in any member state of the EEA will be permitted to practice in Austria upon passing an "entry exam" called the *Eignungsprüfung*. The requirements for this test were established by a recent statute, the EWR *Rechtsanwaltsgesetz* 1992.[5]

Practice structures

The majority of Austrian attorneys practice either alone or together, in other words, with one other attorney. Only recently have firm sizes expanded so that there are presently a number of firms consisting of five or more partners. Further structural changes in the practice of law are occuring as some Austrian firms have formed relationships with larger foreign law firms.

Law firms can only operate as partnerships or as professional corporations, called *Erwerbsgesellschaften*.[6] These professional corporations resemble partnerships, however, contrary to a partnership under Austrian law, they can hold title to property and can sue and be sued in court. Nonetheless, incorporation does not affect professional responsibility;[7] nor does it insulate the partners from malpractice actions. Austrian attorneys are not permitted to form corporations with limited liability.

1. See *Rechtsanwaltsordnung*, Section 35.
2. See *Rechtsanwaltsordnung*, Section 22.
3. *Gesetz vom* 6. Juli 1868, *RGBl* Nr. 96, *womit eine Rechtsanwaltsordnung eingeführt wird*.
4. *Gesetz vom* 1. April 1872, *RGBl* Nr. 40, *betreffend die Handhabung der Disziplinargewalt über Rechtsanwälte und Rechtsanwaltsanwärter*.
5. BGBl Nr. 21/1993.
6. See *Erwerbsgesellschaftengesetz*, *BGBl* 1990/257; statute regulating the formation of professional corporations.
7. See *Rechtsanwaltsordnung*, Section 21 (d).

GENERAL CAPACITIES

In the Austrian legal system, the attorney is the source of legal advice. He represents clients in criminal and civil proceedings at the courts and before administrative authorities. Attorneys also act as custodians and are frequently appointed as trustees in bankruptcy. Although attorneys, to a certain degree, do specialise, their power to represent is not affected or limited by such specialisation.

GENERAL DUTIES

The professional standards and duties of an attorney are defined by the RAO, the DSt and the general provisions of the Austrian Civil Code (ABGB).[8] The RAO and the DSt contain, *inter alia*, general provisions regarding an attorney's obligation to observe his professional duties,[9] to be faithful to his client and his client's interests,[10] to keep all information received confidential,[11] to avoid conflicts of interest,[12] and to protect the interests of his clients for a certain time period after the representation has terminated.[13] Furthermore, the attorney is obliged not to violate the honour and reputation of the bar.[14]

The bar oversees compliance with these rules.[15] Violations are prosecuted by the bar[16] before the *Disziplinarrat* in a proceeding similar to a criminal hearing. Two appellate bodies review the decisions of the *Disziplinarrat*. The *Disziplinarrat* has no power to award damages or to decide as to the civil liability of attorneys. These actions are within the jurisdiction of the public courts.

Civil courts are not bound by the decisions of the *Disziplinarrat* or by the other disciplinary bodies of the bar. In deciding malpractice cases, the courts do not apply the DSt and only rarely refer to the RAO; instead, they base their decisions on the general principles of the Austrian law of damages as they are set forth in the ABGB.

8. *Allgemeines bürgerliches Gesetzbuch*; 1 June 1811, JGS 946.
9. *Disziplinarstatut,* Section 1.
10. *Rechtsanwaltsordnung,* Section 9 (1).
11. *Rechtsanwaltsordnung,* Section 9 (2).
12. *Rechtsanwaltsordnung,* Section 10 (1).
13. *Rechtsanwaltsordnung,* Section 11.
14. "Ehre und Ansehen des Standes"; *Rechtsanwaltsordnung,* Section 10 (2) and *Disziplinarstatut,* Section 1.
15. *Disziplinarstatut,* Section 1.
16. *Disziplinarstatut,* Section 21.

PROFESSIONAL STANDARDS

There are no statutes or normative provisions defining the specific duties of an attorney, with which an attorney must be familiar, what advice must be given to a client in a specific situation, or which court decisions or legal publications have to be known. The specific duties an attorney has to comply with have been defined and specified by the courts.[17] Their decisions are based on Section 1299 and Section 1300 of the ABGB which set forth the standard of knowledge and diligence which is required from an expert in his field. Attorneys are such experts within the statutory meaning. Section 1299 and Section 1300 No. 1 of the ABGB read as follows:

"Section 1299:

A person who publicly claims an office, art, trade, or handicraft, or who voluntarily assumes, without necessity, a business which demands specialised knowledge or extraordinary diligence, thereby that he warrants the necessary diligence and extraordinary knowledge; therefore, such person is liable for the lack thereof."

"Section 1300 (first sentence):

An expert is liable when he gives, for consideration, negligently bad advice in matters of his art or science".[18]

Under Section 1299 and Section 1300 of the ABGB, an attorney, like any other expert, will be held liable if he fails to meet the standard of diligence and knowledge that would be required from an average and responsible member of his profession. In applying this rule, the courts compare the conduct of the attorney with that required from an average member of the profession. The comparison, it should be noted, is not to the actual conduct of most members of the same profession, but to the conduct which could and should be required from the average member. Thus, the comparison is not a question of fact but of law.

The standard of diligence and knowledge can be altered by an agreement between the parties. An attorney can agree to provide advice in fields of law which the average attorney would not be required to know. For example, although it is common that attorneys will advise the client to consult tax counsel in regard to specific questions concerning tax law, the attorney may agree that he will provide the client advice in all tax matters. In such circumstances, the attorney would be subject to the high standard of knowledge in this field of the law as well.

Courts will also impose a stricter standard upon attorneys who hold themselves out as being specialists in certain fields of the law. According

17. For a comprehensive survey, see Graf, *Anwaltshaftung*, pp. 41 *et seq*.

18. These are private translations based on the translation of P. Baeck, *The General Civil Code of Austria*, 1972. No official translations have been rendered to date.

to Sections 45 *et seq.* of the *Richtlinien zur Berufsausübung* (RL-BA),[19] attorneys may designate specific areas of law as specialties.[20] The local bar organisations keep a list of attorneys who have designated themselves as specialists. A client, justifiably relying on such a designation, can expect the attorney to be more knowledgeable in the area of specialisation than the average practitioner, and thus, lack of such knowledge may render the attorney liable.

However, the effect of the designation of areas of specialisation should not be overestimated. On the one hand, clients often do not know that an attorney holds himself out as a specialist in the field of law or that their cases touch such areas. It remains to be resolved whether, in such circumstances, an attorney will be subject to a stringent standard of knowledge required of a specialist, though the client did not actually rely on the attorney's specialisation. On the other hand, even attorneys who are not specialists are required to advise clients as to the fact that a matter involves certain legal issues they are not familiar with. Therefore, if a matter for which the attorney is retained requires special knowledge of tax law and the attorney takes the case without advising the client as to his lack of knowledge in this field, he will be held liable if he subsequently fails to see or solve tax law issues involved.

It will be no defence to argue that the knowledge of these tax law issues is beyond the standard of knowledge required from an average member of the profession. In this case, the "extraordinary knowledge" required under Section 1299 of the ABGB is not the knowledge of the tax law issues *per se,* but the knowledge that tax law issues the attorney is not familiar with will be involved. In other words, an attorney is required to know whether he has the necessary knowledge to take on a certain matter. Only when an attorney advises the client that he is not a specialist in the field of law in question and the client still wants him to pursue the matter, will the courts apply the lower standard of knowledge.

Austrian law on damages

To collect damages under Austrian law, three requirements must be satisfied. These requirements will be addressed in the context of an action by the client for breach of contract, out of which most legal malpractice suits arise. In a suit for damages based on a claim for breach of contract the client must prove that:

(1) He suffered a loss (for example, that he had to pay extra taxes or lost a trial);

19. A regulation issued by the bar regulating the exercise of the profession.
20. See *Richtlinien zur Berufsausübung,* Section 45 (2) lit g.

(2) The loss was caused by the attorneys breach of contract (i.e. that the loss would not have occurred had the attorney acted dutifully; that the attorney's failure was a *conditio sine qua non* for the loss); and

(3) The attorney violated his contractual obligations (for example, that the attorney did not give proper advice or failed to act in time).

If the client can satisfy this burden of proof, the attorney, in some cases, can avoid being liable if he can prove that he did not act negligently, that is, he did not act with fault.

Loss

The first requirement is more or less self-evident. A client may bring a suit only if he suffered a certain harm. Austrian law distinguishes between financial losses and non-monetary injury.[21]

In the field of legal malpractice, only claims for financial losses are relevant. The available remedies are restitution and monetary damages. A person causing a loss must either return the damaged property to its former state, that is, make restitution, or pay the estimated price thereof, that is, pay monetary damages.[22]

The amount of damages is the difference between the claimant's actual financial situation and the position in which he would have been had not the harmful event occurred.[23] The difference is the monetary value of the loss caused, and the amount that a claimant is entitled to recover.

21. Damages for non-material harm are granted only in a limited number of cases, so, for example, where a person has suffered personal injury the courts may award damages for the "suffering of the person", ABGB, Section 1325; similarly in the case of injury to personal freedom, ABGB, Section 1329; see OGH EvBl 1990/135, 27 March 1990, 5 Ob. 544/90. Non-material damages are of no practical importance in the field of legal malpractice. In Austria, not all decisions of the Supreme Court, the *Oberster Gerichtshof*, or the Courts of Appeal are reported; however, a substantial number of decisions appear in official court reports — for civil matters it is the "*Entscheidungs-sammlung des Österreichischen Obersten Gerichtshofes in Zivil- (und Justizverwaltungs) sachen*", cited as "SZ" — or private legal publications, such as the "*Anwaltsblatt*", cited as "AnwBl.", the "*Österreichische Juristenzeitung*", cited as "EvBl." or the "*Juristische Blätter*" cited as "JBl". Decisions of the Supreme Court in this paper are cited by publication either with the page or with the number within this publication, the official docket number and the date. Unreported decisions are cited with their docket number and the date and are referred to as "not reported". Unless indicated otherwise, all decisions cited are Supreme Court decisions. Contrary to the United States or England, decisions are not cited with the names of the parties.

22. See ABGB, Section 1323, first sentence: "In order to make amends for damages caused, the damaged property must be returned to the former state or, if this is not possible, the estimated price thereof must be paid."

23. See, Koziol-Welser, *Grundriß des bürgerlichen Rechts*, 9th ed., Vol. I, p. 423 ; SZ 55/29, 3 March 1982, 1 Ob. 829/81; SZ 53/107, 27 August 1980, 1 Ob. 636/80.

Causation

The second requirement concerns causation. The plaintiff may collect damages only if a certain act or omission of the defendant caused the loss. Further, the plaintiff will only be liable if his act or omission can be regarded as the adequate cause of the harm done to the plaintiff. In other words, there is no liability if the harm is the result of a highly uncommon and unlikely chain of causation.[24]

Whether a certain act caused an event is a question of whether the act was a *conditio sine qua non* for the event. Thus, if the event would have occurred even without the action in question, the action was not its cause. The same standard is used to determine whether an omission caused a certain event. In this circumstance, the court investigates whether the harming event would have taken place even if the defendant had acted dutifully.[25]

Breach of contract

A party to a contract will be held liable only if he acted "unlawfully".[26] A party to a contract acts unlawfully if he did not perform the contract in accordance with its terms. Therefore, the plaintiff must show either that the attorney violated the specific terms of the contract or that he did not perform his services as it would be required from an average and responsible member of the profession.

Fault

The basic presumption of the Austrian law of damages is that a person will only be held liable if he acted with fault. In the absence of an agreement to the contrary, there is no strict liability under Austrian contract law.[27] Therefore, liability will not only be based on the showing

24. The first requirement that the claimant's loss was caused by the defendant is a factual question; see 8 May 1990, 4 Ob. 512/90, not reported. On the other hand, the second requirement, whether the loss was an adequate consequence of a certain act, is a question of law; see Koziol-Welser, *Grundriß des bürgerlichen Rechts*, 9th ed., Vol. I, p. 413.

25. See, Koziol-Welser, *Grundriß des bürgerlichen Rechts*, 9th ed., Vol. I, p. 412; EvBl 1990/135, 27 March 1990, 5 Ob. 544/90.

26. See ABGB, Section 1294.

27. See ABGB, Section 1295(1), first sentence: "A person is entitled to demand indemnification for the damage from a person causing an injury by his fault; the damage may have been caused either by violation of a contractual duty or without regard to a contract."

that the defendant violated his duties, i.e. acted unlawfully; additionally, there must be proof that the defendant could have performed the contract. The test is whether an average and responsible person in the same situation as the defendant would and could have performed the contract.

The general rule in tort is that all conditions, damage, unlawfulness, fault, and causality have to be proven by the party claiming damages.[28] This rule is modified in contract cases. If the act causing the damage constitutes a breach of contract, then the party seeking recovery does not have to prove that the defendant acted with fault. Rather, the burden is on the defendant to prove otherwise.[29]

However, this defence is not available if the plaintiff's case is based on the allegation that the attorney did not have the necessary knowledge or diligence as required by Section 1299 of the ABGB. Under this provision, the attorney will be held liable for the lack of "necessary diligence and extraordinary knowledge".

Civil liabilities

The vast majority of legal malpractice cases involve the attorney's liability to his client for breach of contract. To prevail in such a suit, the client has to satisfy his burden of proof as to the requirements outlined in the previous section.

Not only is the client with whom the attorney has contracted entitled to claim damages for breach of contract, but third-party beneficiaries are as well. The attorney will be held liable to a third-party beneficiary if at the time he performed his services he knew or should have known that his services should benefit a certain individual or at least an easily identifiable person. In order to prevent unlimited liability, the courts apply the following rather strict requirement for a third party beneficiary to recover damages:

(1) The transaction must be intended to benefit the third person; and
(2) It must have been foreseeable for the attorney that his failure could harm the third party.

Sometimes the cases suggest, in addition to the aforementioned requirements, that there must be a special relationship between the contractual

28. See ABGB, Section 1296; Koziol-Welser, *Grundriß des bürgerlichen Rechts*, 9th ed., Vol. I, p. 421; OGH 27 February 1990, 4 OB 607/89, 1991 AnwBl 51.

29. See ABGB, Section 1298: "A person who asserts that he has been prevented from performing a contractual or legal obligation without any fault on his part must bear the burden of proof thereof."

party and the third party which justifies the intended benefit, however, it seems that the courts no longer require a third party beneficiary to establish this fact.[30]

For example, the intended beneficiary of a will that was drafted by an attorney has a recognised claim against the attorney for malpractice if the will due to the attorney's failure to properly perform was not valid and the intended beneficiary did not receive whatever he should have received.[31]

The claim for damages of the third party beneficiary is derived from and based on the contract between the attorney and client. The contract therefore, can limit the attorney's liability. So, for example, if the contract specifies that a legal document, such as a legal opinion rendered by the attorney, must not be given to third parties the courts will reject a claim by a third party who nevertheless received the legal opinion, relied on it, and suffered damages because the opinion was incorrect.[32]

It is unlikely that courts would find that a legal opinion is inherently drafted to benefit third persons and that such third persons could rely on the legal opinion even if the legal opinion expressly states that it is only intended for the use by certain persons. However, if there is no such provision, a court would probably find that those third parties who could be foreseen to rely on the legal opinion are entitled to claim damages for breach of contract as third-party beneficiaries.

Another area in which the question of an attorney's liability to third parties could arise concerns the representation of corporate clients. The general rule is that only the client, that is, the corporation, may sue for breach of contract. Consequently, shareholders who are not parties to the contract between the corporation and the attorney could only sue in tort. Theoretically, there remains the possibility that in a case in which a corporation hires an attorney to handle a matter in which only the shareholders and not the corporation would benefit, the shareholders could sue for damages in contract as third-party beneficiaries. However, no such cases have been decided by the Supreme Court as yet. The same holds true for other third parties such as directors.[33]

30. See, Koziol-Welser, *Grundriß des bürgerlichen Rechts*, 9th ed., Vol. I, p. 309.

31. See OGH SZ 59/106, 19 June 1986, 7 Ob. 568/86 regarding the liability of a notary public.

32. See SZ 43/236, 22 December 1970, 8 Ob. 281/70, regarding the liability of an accountant. To date, there have been no decisions of the Supreme Court dealing with an attorney's liability to third parties who relied on a formal legal opinion which later turned out to be wrong. However, the criteria applied in such a case would probably be the same.

33. In cases in which an attorney represented the corporation and later is asked to represent a director in a matter against the corporation, the attorney has to reject the second matter, as a conflict of interest would arise.

Attorney drafting a contract

The general rule is that an attorney owes his professional duties only to his client, but there is an exception of great practical importance. An attorney who drafts an agreement between his client and his client's business partner will usually be held liable not only to his client but also to the business partner(s). Most of the cases which reflect this doctrine involve real estate and loan transactions.[34]

A line of cases holds that it is not necessary that each party formally authorised the attorney to draft the contract.[35] It is sufficient that based on all the circumstances, the attorney knew or should have known that the parties to the contract were relying on him to draft the contract not only in the interests of one of the parties, but of all the parties.

To avoid this expanded liability, an attorney must explicitly state that he is representing only one of them. In such circumstances, the other parties will have been put on notice that their interests will not be represented by the attorney drafting the contract. However, the standard for an effective disclaimer is very high. If there is any doubt as to whether the attorney is representing the interests of a specific party, the courts will hold against the attorney. No liability arises in the case where the third party made it clear that he does not need the attorney's advice. For example, in one case, an attorney representing the buyer in a real estate transaction was not held liable to the seller who never contacted the attorney and where the circumstances made it clear that the seller was not relying on his advice.[36]

Similar reasoning should apply in cases in which the third party is represented by an attorney, since the third party has made it clear that he is relying on his own attorney. However, in a recent decision, the Supreme Court held that an attorney who drafts the sales contract in a real estate transaction could be liable to the other party even though the latter was represented by another attorney.[37]

It is not clear what the legal basis for the other party's claim against the attorney is. In most cases, there is no express agreement between the attorney and the third party. Some decisions find an implied contractual relationship between the attorney and the third party[38] and others simply state that the third party was entitled to rely on an attorney's general

34. See SZ 28/57, 23 February 1955, 7 Ob. 77/55; RZ (*Richterzeitung*) 1967, 202, 22 December 1966, 5 Ob. 209/66 (not reported) 26 January 1988, 8 Ob. 593/87, for further reference and a more detailed discussion, see Graf, *Anwaltshaftung*, pp. 96 *et seq.*

35. See EvBl. 1959/262; 3 June 1959, 5 Ob. 193/59; SZ 57/108, 13 June 1984, 3 Ob. 612/83.

36. NZ (*Notariatszeitung*) 1987, 284, 5 March 1987, 7 Ob. 534/87.

37. NRsp. 1988/185, 15 March 1988, 8 Ob. 645/87.

38. See, JBl 1962, 152, 20 September 1961, 6 Ob. 279/61.

standard of care.[39] Also, some legal writers suggest that the third party should be protected as a third-party beneficiary.[40]

None of these theories is particularly convincing. The basis for the protection of a third-party beneficiary is the contract between the original parties, that is, the attorney and the client. It is not very convincing to argue that the attorney and client intended to protect the third party's interests. Usually, quite the opposite is true, the client engaged the attorney to improve his position in contract negotiations and to protect his own rights. The same arguments apply in the case of implied contractual relations. The adverse interests of the client and his business partner conflict with the proposition that the attorney implicitly entered into a contract with this third party. As to the third argument involving the implied trust in the attorney's professional duties, it was already stated above that the attorney does not owe obligations to the general public. As a general rule, he is only responsible to his client. In the absence of such legal obligations to the general public, there is no basis for the courts to protect the general public's trust in such, non-existing, duties.

In some cases, an attorney's liability to a third party can be based on Section 1003 of the ABGB, which in effect requires an attorney to immediately notify a potential client who wanted to retain the attorney if he is not willing to handle the matter. Otherwise, the attorney will be held responsible for any damages suffered by the client because of this failure to notify. In the case of an attorney drafting contracts it can be argued that the failure to notify his client's business partner that he is drafting the contract only on behalf of his client falls within the scope of Section 1003 ABGB, that is, the attorney failed to notify that he is not willing to protect the business partner's interests, too.

Tort

An attorney's liability to third parties, who are not third-party beneficiaries, is of no practical importance. Under the Austrian law of damages, a financial loss that does not involve personal injury and/or damage to property is recoverable only:

(1) In the case of a breach of contractual duties;
(2) If the person causing the loss acted willfully; or
(3) If the loss was caused by an action that violated a specific statutory duty that was intended to protect the person suffering the loss.

39. See SZ 43/221, 2 December 1970, 6 Ob. 282/70 (not reported), 19 April 1983, 5 Ob. 613/82.

40. See Koziol, *Österreichisches Haftpflichtrecht*, 2nd ed., Vol. II, p. 87.

Besides these exceptions, the Austrian law of damages does not provide for recovery of mere financial losses in tort.

None of the three cases is relevant in the field of legal malpractice. Most of the malpractice cases involve negligent rather than willful action and the acts of attorneys usually do not result in personal injury or damage to property. Furthermore, statutory provisions prescribing an attorney's professional duties are usually interpreted as protecting only the attorney's client but not other third parties.[41]

Procedure

A malpractice action against an attorney must be brought in a court. Depending on the amount of damages claimed and the nature of the claim and the underlying transaction, either a district court (*Bezirksgericht*), a court for general civil matters (*Landesgericht*), or a commercial court (*Handelsgericht*) will have jurisdiction over the matter.

In the case of a violation of the rules of professional responsibility, there may also be a proceeding within the local bar organisation. In this disciplinary proceeding, only disciplinary measures against the attorney can be imposed. A person suffering damages would not be a party to such a disciplinary proceeding, and no damages can be awarded by the bar itself.

Recoverable damages

Under the Austrian legal system, the courts may award damages for breach of contract only in an amount equal to the actual damage suffered by the claimant, but no punitive damages are available. It is up to the claimant to prove the amount of damages suffered. Such damages can include: actual financial loss, additional costs incurred due to the attorney's failure, and expected gains which were not realised due to the attorney's failure.

SPECIFIC CIVIL LIABILITIES

The following section will provide a comprehensive overview of those areas of legal practice in which malpractice cases have frequently arisen.

As a general rule, it is up to the client to provide the attorney with all information necessary to handle the situation for which he has sought

41. Attorney malpractice can, theoretically, result in criminal liability as well. However, those cases are of no practical importance.

legal advice. However, the client, especially if inexperienced in legal matters, often will not know which factual details are of legal importance. The client often will inform the attorney only as to the facts he deems necessary and important. The attorney must be wary of this "selection of facts" by the client. He has to inquire actively as to all the additional facts significant and necessary to form a legal opinion in the matter to provide advice. An attorney's failure to inquire as to the relevant facts can result in liability.[42]

Once the attorney has satisfied this obligation and has instructed his client as to which additional information is relevant, it is the client's responsibility to provide him with all necessary information. The attorney need not check on the veracity of the information supplied by his client. With regard to factual information such as time and place of an accident or deficiencies of goods delivered, the attorney need not check whether the information received was correct. However, any legal inferences drawn by the client such as if and when a contract was formed or what kind of contract, may not be relied upon, since a layman is not competent to judge such matters.[43]

The attorney may also assume that the client would not intentionally supply misleading information. Therefore, no legal malpractice action may be based on the claim that the attorney should have suspected that the information received from the client was incorrect.

Knowledge of the law

Statutes, regulations, other normative provisions

Attorneys are presumed to know all statutes, regulations and other normative provisions.[44] Lack of such knowledge will constitute negligence. There are no exemptions for statutes or regulations which are used only rarely or which are outside the main areas of the attorney's practice.[45] Therefore, for practical purposes, the standard applied with respect to the requisite knowledge of the law is higher in degree than the one used to

42. See 26 April 1983; 4 Ob. 505/83, not reported.

43. See 26 April 1983, 4 Ob. 505/83, not reported: The attorney acts negligently if he relies only on the information of his client as to the person against whom a claim should be brought.

44. See EvBl. 1972/124, 11 November 1971; 1 Ob. 296/71; SZ 58/165, 7 November 1985, 7 Ob. 501/85; WBl ("*Wirtschaftsrechtliche Blätter*") 1989, 160, 2 February 1989, 7 Ob. 720/88.

45. See RdW ("*Recht der Wirtschaft*") 1989, 221, 1 March 1989, 1 Ob. 516/89; EvBl 1963/482, 4 September 1963, 1 Ob. 115/63; such a limitation was suggested for German law, see Vollkommer, *Anwaltshaftungsrecht* (1989) Rz., pp. 124 *et seq*.

determine negligence, that is, complete knowledge is required rather than the knowledge of the average and responsible member of the profession.

Knowledge of foreign law is required if such knowledge is necessary to handle a certain matter correctly. Therefore, the attorney must either gain the necessary knowledge by research, retain a foreign attorney, or advise his client that he is not competent to render an opinion as to the foreign law aspects of the matter. The client is then left to seek legal advice as to these questions from another source.

Though the requirements in respect of the knowledge of law are very strict, upon inspection, they seem reasonable. The risk of the attorney not applying a relevant normative provision must lie either with the attorney or the client. There are good reasons to impose this risk upon the attorney. First, an attorney is not required to take on a particular client, and as a general rule there is no obligation on the part of the attorney to take on every mandate.[46] Second, obviously only the attorney would be competent to judge what questions of law are involved and whether he is competent to answer these questions and take the case. The client generally would neither be able to judge which fields of the law are involved nor whether they are commonly used and understood by attorneys. He has to rely on the attorney.[47] Third, the attorney is in the best position to procure adequate insurance to cover the risk of legal malpractice. The costs for such insurance can be spread among all clients. The client has no possibility to cover or spread his risk. Thus, it is the attorney who is in a better position to recognise, to avoid, and finally to bear the risk that he is not competent to render advice on a particular matter.

An attorney may rely on the existing legal provisions in counselling his client. He is not required to investigate whether the normative provisions are, in fact, constitutional. The Supreme Court has held that an attorney will not be liable if he has advised his client to follow a specific statutory provision which later is successfully challenged on the ground that it violated the Constitution.[48] Attorneys need not predict the likelihood of the client's case being a vehicle for change in the law.

It has to be stressed that these standards are imposed only if the attorney has sufficient time to properly research a certain matter. Thus, if advice must be immediately rendered, the standard of knowledge will be lower. However, an attorney's negligence could be found if the attorney does not point out to his client that this advice lacks the certainty of a more thoroughly examined expertise.

46. An exception applies in the case of attorneys' being required to act for indigent clients; in those cases there is an obligation to take a case. The attorney cannot reject the case arguing that it involves fields of the law he is not comfortable with. The basis for this is the legal presumption that an attorney has to know all the law and that there are no specialists.

47. See WBl. 1989, 280, 26 April 1989, 1 Ob. 529/89.

48. See 18 April 1989, 5 Ob. 555/89 (not reported).

Malpractice cases related to the lack of knowledge of the law seem to be the most frequent reasons for malpractice actions.[49]

Court decisions, professional literature

The standard of knowledge required of an attorney with respect to court decisions and academic legal opinions is less stringent. However, attorneys should keep up to date with the published decisions and professional literature. Attorneys are presumed to know rules of law that have been reaffirmed in a line of cases.[50] These holdings are readily obtainable through legal publications and have, even in a civil law country, great persuasive power.

There is no settled standard as to other decisions that turn out to be relevant to a certain matter but that are not part of such repeated holdings of the Supreme Court. However, as a general rule an attorney will not be held liable for negligence with respect to unsettled propositions of the law if his opinion is reasonable although subsequently not followed by the courts. There is no negligence if the attorney's opinion as to a certain question of law is reasonable and legally justifiable.[51]

ADVICE

One of the most important professional duties of an attorney is to give complete and full advice to his client.[52] The main objective of the attorney's work is to give his client advice as to the best and most advantageous way to proceed with his case.

Courts recognise that giving advice requires judgement and that many issues are often uncertain and are subject to disagreement. Therefore, it would be patently unfair to subject an attorney to liability simply because a judge later disagrees with the attorney's judgement. Because of this situation, it is generally accepted that an attorney is not liable for an error of judgement on an unsettled proposition of law.[53]

49. See, for example, EvBl. 1963/336, 30 April 1963, 8 Ob. 115/63; RdW 1989, 128, 15; 12 December 1988, 7 Ob. 661 – 665/88; RdW 19 86, 268, 9 April 1986, 1 Ob. 518/86.

50. See EvBl. 1972/124, 11 November 1971, 1 Ob. 296/71; WBl. 1989, 160; 2 February 1989, 7 Ob. 720/88.

51. See SZ 58/165, 7 November 1985, 7 Ob. 501/85.

52. See SZ 56/181, 30 November 1983, 1 Ob. 785/83; RdW. 1986, 268, 9 April 1986, 1 Ob. 518/86; NZ 1987, 148, 24 April 1986, 7 Ob. 550/86.

53. This rule is accepted in other jurisdictions as well, see Mallen, Smith, *Legal Malpractice*, Sections 14.1 *et seq.*, who trace the origins of this rule back to a 1767 decision of the House of Lords.

Points of law established in a line of Supreme Court decisions will be regarded as settled, and the attorney is obliged to know them. However, as to many legal issues, it is far from clear whether the courts will regard them as settled or unsettled. In advising his client, the attorney must research the various ways in which the client's case could proceed. The attorney has a duty to avoid involving the client in unsettled and potentially unfavourable areas of the law if research reveals alternative means as less problematic in achieving the same result.

Incorrect advice concerning the statute of limitations and other time bars or the special form requirements under Austrian law are a frequent basis for legal malpractice actions. If several statutes of limitations are applicable to a certain claim an attorney has to act according to whichever limitation expires earliest. An attorney may not rely on the fact that it is reasonable to conclude that the longer period of limitation is applicable. He must act in the safest way possible and must bring the claim within the shorter statute of limitations.[54]

The same reasoning applies to available remedies. If it is not clear in which period of time a claim for a particular remedy must be brought the attorney has to act in the shorter period. Similarly, if there are two remedies available, the attorney has to choose the remedy which is more likely to lead to a favourable result for the client.[55] All arguments which can be useful and helpful have to be incorporated.

There are also strict requirements as to the scope of the attorney's obligation to advise. Clients will often not see all the legal aspects of the factual situation. Their questions to the attorney will often be incomplete. Therefore, the attorney is not only required to give advice as to those points expressly addressed in the questions but also on other related aspects which the attorney believes to be important and has reason to believe that the client is not aware of. So, for example, when an attorney represents a client in a criminal matter, he has to advise the client of any civil claim his client may also have, such as a claim for damages connected to this matter, which could be barred by a statute of limitation. It is no defence for an attorney to argue that the client did not ask whether a claim connected to this criminal procedure would be barred by the statute of limitations.[56]

The obligation to give full and complete advice is somewhat limited as to clients who have legal knowledge or who are experienced in legal matters. Such clients are deemed to be able to formulate the questions put to the attorney, and the attorney may rely on the client being able to specifically address all the relevant issues. Therefore, with respect to

54. See EvBl. 1963/482, 4 September 1963, 1 Ob. 115/63; WBl. 1987, 212, 4 March 1987, 1 Ob. 710/86; JBl 1972, 426, 2 February 1972, 1 Ob. 11/72.

55. See JBl. 1956, 620, 7 March 1956, 3 Ob. 119/56.

56. See EvBl. 1963/482, 4 September 1963, 1 Ob. 115/63.

those clients, the attorney is not obliged to address issues not raised by the client. Whether the client has legal knowledge would be revealed by his occupation or profession. An attorney may reasonably presume that a bank in respect of a typical banking transaction will need his advice only as to those points specifically addressed in the questions. For example, a bank will be deemed knowledgeable as to legal issues associated with securing a loan. Thus, an attorney will not be held liable if he advises the bank only to those issues raised by the bank. The attorney need not advise on connected matters which he reasonably can assume to be known by a bank.[57]

Extended counselling will be required if an attorney knows or should know that the client is legally inexperienced or at least is not experienced with respect to the legal issues relevant to the matter he has brought before the attorney. A typical example would be a foreign client who is not familiar with the Austrian legal system. For example, the Supreme Court held an attorney liable for not apprising his foreign client as to the existence and special function of the Austrian *Grundbuch*, a public register in which many relevant facts as to real estate are entered. The Court held that the attorney could not rely on his foreign client being familiar with legal institutions that are specific to the Austrian legal system.[58] Similarly, advice as to other typical Austrian legal requirements has to be very detailed. For example, the Austrian *Gebührengesetz* is a statute that imposes a fee, i.e. a kind of tax, for the execution of certain documents. If an attorney does not advise his client of the fact that signing a document may trigger a fee, the attorney will violate his professional duty.

Malpractice actions are frequently brought by clients on the basis that their attorney did not advise them correctly as to the chances of succeeding in litigation.[59] Since the outcome of litigation is usually not predictable, the attorney is not required to specify the chances of winning a case in court. However, if *ab initio* there was no chance of winning a case, the attorney is obliged to apprise the client of this. The difficulty for the attorney is that in predicting whether the case may later be held as having had no chance of succeeding. Not all cases are as clear as the one decided by the Supreme Court in which an attorney brought a suit against the clear and unambiguous wording of a statute.[60] It was held that the attorney violated his professional duties because he failed to clearly advise the client that there was no chance of succeeding. In such a hopeless case, it did not suffice, and therefore was no defence, that the

57. See NZ 1987, 148, 24 April 1986, 7 Ob. 550/86.

58. Not reported, 26 January 1988, 8 Ob. 593/87.

59. See WBl. 1989, 160, 2 February 1989, 7 Ob. 720/88; SZ 58/165, 7 November 1985, 7 Ob. 501/85.

60. WBl 1989, 160, 2 February 1989, 7 Ob. 720/88.

attorney had told his client that there was "some risk" involved in the proceeding or that the "likelihood of succeeding was not great".

Generally, the burden is on the client to prove that the attorney failed to give correct advice. However, a *prima facie* case is made regarding an attorney's failure to inform the client of the likelihood that he would prevail where the action had no chance of succeeding. The presumption is that a reasonable client would not bring a claim in a hopeless action. It will be up to the attorney to prove that he gave correct advice or that there were specific reasons why the client wanted to bring an action even though there was no realistic chance of success. With respect to the latter argument, the attorney, for example, may show that the client wanted to improve his situation in settlement negotiations and therefore wanted to bring the claim, though he was advised that there was no chance of succeeding. It will then be up to the client to prove that the attorney's advice was incorrect.

INSTRUCTIONS BY THE CLIENT

The attorney is bound to follow the instructions given by his client.[61] If the attorney does not approve of a certain instruction he must either terminate his representation or follow the instruction. He may not simply disregard it.

The duty to follow the client's instructions, also implies that the attorney has to obtain the client's approval regarding material decisions. The attorney is the client's advisor and not his guardian; therefore, it is up to the client, for example, to decide whether to accept a settlement, or enter into a contract. However, the attorney is not obliged to obtain the client's approval for every minor step to be taken in a matter. Thus, decisions which do not materially alter the client's position, such as procedural questions, whether to offer a certain piece of evidence in a trial or what arguments to use in a brief may be made by the attorney alone.

If obtaining of a client's instruction as to a certain matter would cause delay, which could be harmful for the client's interests, the attorney may proceed without instruction, but must seek approval as soon as possible. If the attorney believes that following the client's instruction would be detrimental to his cause he must so inform and warn the client, to avoid liability.[62]

The issue whether an attorney has to advise his client as to possible malpractice claims that a client may have against the attorney has yet to

61. See Section 1009 ABGB; Section 9 RAO; RdW 1983, 106, 23 June 1983, 6 Ob. 610/83.

62. See Strasser in Rummel, ABGB, Rz., pp. 14 *et seq.* on Section 1009.

be decided by the courts. German courts have held that the attorney must advise his client as to such possible claims.[63] However, the legal situation in Germany and Austria in this regard is not comparable. Under the applicable German Statute,[64] a malpractice claim has to be brought within three years after the termination of the contractual relationship between the attorney and his client. In Austria, a claim against the attorney can be brought within three years after the client knows that he suffered a loss and that the loss was caused by the attorney,[65] but in any event no later than 30 years following the occurrence of the event from which the loss arose.[66] In other words, in Germany clients have to bring suit within three years whereas in Austria clients could have as much as thirty years. Therefore, the decisions of the German courts were intended to balance the adverse effects on clients' interests of the short statute of limitations.[67] In Austria, one could argue, there is no need to impose such a duty upon the attorney as the long statute of limitations provides sufficient protection for the client.[68]

DEFENCES

Elements of claim

As outlined in the previous sections, a claim for damages has to include proof that the act was unlawful, that there was a loss and that there was a causal link between the act and the loss. An attorney's fault, i.e. his negligence or wilful wrongdoing, will be presumed according to Section 1298 of the ABGB. The lack of either of these conditions provides a valid defence for the attorney.

In some cases, it may prove difficult for the client to establish that he suffered a loss due to an attorney's negligence. This arises where an unfavourable result was obtained in a proceeding brought by the attorney on behalf of the client, and the client later alleges that the loss was due to the attorney's negligent representation. In such cases, the client must prove that a decision more favourable to him would have been rendered if the attorney had not acted negligently. The same reasoning applies where an attorney negligently fails to appeal against an unfavourable decision.

63. See Vollkommer, *Anwaltshaftungsrecht* (1989), pp. 260 *et seq.*

64. *Bundesrechtsanwaltsordnung*, Section 51 — Federal Statute regulating the legal profession.

65. ABGB, Section 1489.

66. ABGB, Section 1489.

67. See, Vollkommer, *Anwaltshaftungsrecht*, pp. 255 *et seq.*

68. For further references, see Graf, *Anwaltshaftung* note 138 at p. 34.

A typical scenario involves a client who instructs his attorney to proceed with an appeal against an unfavourable court or administrative decision, the attorney then negligently fails to bring the appeal within the proper time period, and the adverse judgement, therefore, becomes final and conclusive, i.e. no further avenues for appeal remain. Subsequently, the client institutes a malpractice action against the attorney, claiming that the judgement would have been reversed by the appellate court provided an appeal had been filed.

Furthermore, the client claims entitlement to compensation from the attorney for adverse financial consequences suffered as a result of the attorney's error. To defend himself against the malpractice claim the attorney may show that the appellate court would have affirmed the lower court's decision and that the client, therefore, did not suffer a loss, but was actually spared the cost of an appeal. The burden of proof is on the plaintiff, i.e. the client.

In such a proceeding, a court must first decide which result the client would have obtained in the first suit had an appeal been filed in time. Based on this hypothetical decision, the court hearing the malpractice claim will decide whether the attorney's failure was the cause for the client losing the underlying suit. If the court finds that the client would have lost the first proceeding anyhow, then it will find for the attorney and will reject the client's malpractice action against the attorney. In the absence of proof as to how the hypothetical appeal would have ended, the court hearing the malpractice action will base its decision on how it would have decided the hypothetical appeal.[69]

The attorney, in his defence, may argue that the client acted negligently too, i.e. that the loss was partly caused by the attorney's failure but that it could either have been avoided or limited if the client had not also acted negligently. Under Section 1304 of the ABGB, negligence on the part of the client and which contributed to the loss reduces the recoverable damages to the extent attributable to the client.

However, according to a recent Supreme Court decision, a client may rely upon an attorney's competence and is not obliged to supervise an attorney's work. In that case, the attorney had to prepare an appeal. An argument which could have been successful was not included in the appeal. Before filing the appeal, the attorney sent a copy to the client who read the appeal and authorised the attorney to file it. The appeal was not successful. Later, in the malpractice action, the client argued that the attorney's failure to include the argument made him liable. The attorney argued that the client, who himself was legally knowledgeable, should have

69. For a detailed discussion of the problem of the "hypothetical appeal" and a suggested solution, see Graf, "The Hypothetical Appeal: Aspects of Legal Malpractice in Austria", *New York University Journal of International Law and Politics*, Summer 1992, Vol. 24; number 4 at 1651 *et seq.*

noticed that this argument was missing and further that the client's failure to do so should be considered as amounting to contributory negligence, thus reducing the amount of damages recoverable. The Supreme Court did not adopt the attorney's argument. It held that a client's right to rely upon an attorney's competence extends even to clients who have knowledge of the law.

There is no obligation on the part of the client to supervise the attorney's work. Only in the case of an obvious mistake by the attorney which was actually recognised by the client would an obligation arise to inform the attorney of his error.[70]

Time bars

An action based on a malpractice claim has to be brought within three years from the time the client discovers or could have discovered that he suffered a loss and that the loss was caused by the attorney. Therefore, if the client after 10 years finds out that he lost a proceeding due only to an attorney's failure to act properly, he may file suit against the attorney within the three years of that date. There is also an absolute time bar in Austria; after 30 years from the day of the harming event, no action can be instituted.[71]

LIABILITY

As long as an attorney practices alone, there is no question as to who is liable. In the case of a partnership, all the partners who were contractually bound by a certain mandate are jointly and severally liable if the contract with the client was breached. It suffices that the client can satisfy his burden of proof as outlined above as to one of the partners. Under Section 21 (d) of the RAO, all partners of an *Erwerbsgesellschaft* (professional corporations) are personally liable if they violate their professional obligations. This liability cannot be limited by the corporate charter. Therefore, like in a partnership all the partners are jointly and severally liable for losses caused by one of the partners.

It is not clear whether attorneys can limit their liability by means of risk limitation clauses in their contracts with their clients. The bar organisation is presently preparing a regulation which would allow attorneys to exclude liability for losses caused by slight negligence. However, the

70. See JBl 1989, 727, 11 April 1989, 5 Ob. 530/89.
71. ABGB, Section 1489.

bar organisation is not authorised to issue norms binding persons other than attorneys. It remains to be seen whether civil courts will be willing to enforce such risk limitation clauses.

INSURANCE

Under Section 21 (a) (3) of the RAO, every Austrian attorney is required to have a minimum insurance coverage in the amount of 500,000 Austrian Shillings. The statute, however, does not specify which risks have to be covered by this insurance. The standard form contracts of the insurance companies, which are not mandatory but widely used, exclude several risks. The form contract will not cover claims that are brought in foreign courts, even if they can be enforced within Austria; losses caused by Austrian attorney's failure to observe foreign laws; or losses caused while the attorney acted outside Austria. To achieve sufficient insurance coverage, law firms would have to negotiate the coverage with their insurance companies.

CHAPTER 2

BELGIUM

SIMON REICH
Antwerp, Belgium

INTRODUCTION

Before elaborating on this topic, it is important to set out some important legal concepts of Belgian law relevant to this discussion. Belgian law recognises various obligations and liabilities with respect to professional negligence. In civil law (i.e. non-criminal, non-administrative, non-deontological) the relevant statute is the *Code Napoleon* (1804), which establishes four sources of civil liability: contracts, quasi-contracts, crimes and statutory duties.

This classification has been criticised, and it is now preferable to classify duties as follows:

(1) Obligations by unilateral expression of one's will (e.g. offers);
(2) Contracts;
(3) Tort; and
(4) Quasi-contracts (e.g. obligations between neighbours).

For the purposes of this chapter, contracts concerning the liability of the lawyer towards the client and torts concerning liability towards third parties are of particular interest.

Professional liability can be defined as the liability that a professional (here, the lawyer) incurs when, in the exercise of his profession, he fails to meet his contractual obligations or when he commits a tort in the course of his professional activities.

Moreover, but outside the field of civil law, the chapter will deal with the deontological obligation. Criminal liability will not be discussed. In the following pages on civil liability, reference is made to both contractual and extra-contractual liability but not to deontological liability.

Formal sources of these obligations are to be found in Articles 1382 to 1386 bis of the *Burgerlijk Wetboek* (BWCC), the Civil Code, regarding liability for tort, in Articles 1142, 1146, 1148 and 1165 of the BWCC for contractual liability, and in conduct rules of the various bar associations and the National Order of Lawyers. As there are only a relatively small number of law provisions in the two first instances, one should not be surprised that not only the "law of torts", but also the law of contractual liability has been formed to a high degree by case law and doctrine. This applies to a lesser degree to deontology, where customary law is an important source.

PROFESSIONAL STRUCTURES

Legal professions and the bar

This chapter's treatment of lawyers' liability will be restricted to the professional liability of lawyers *sensu stricto*. It is therefore important to describe the profession of the lawyer in Belgium and to distinguish it from all other legal professions.

The lawyer faces the same tasks as members of other legal professions such as legal advisers, company jurists or notaries. For different reasons, their roles should not be confused with and must be distinguished from that of a lawyer.

First, the lawyer's profession is regulated by statute as to conditions regarding admission, use of a title and exercise of the profession.[1] This makes it "a protected profession".

The way in which the law then regulates the profession touches the essence of the lawyers' profession and emphasises its uniqueness. Article 444 of the GerW CJ reads: "Lawyers exercise their function freely to protect the law and the truth".

The lawyer's independence in his work is essential. This independence is valid against the authorities and permits him to defend the interest of his client and only this interest in a free and independent manner. It is also valid against the client himself. The lawyer may not be bound to his client.

Furthermore, under Belgian law, the lawyer has an almost complete monopoly on pleading,[2] and he enjoys a number of privileges which, broadly speaking, other legal professions do not enjoy. The preceding is sufficient to establish that the lawyers' profession is unique, and one whose important characteristics cannot be shared by other legal professions. Notaries are public servants and, as such, they are not independent from the authorities. A legal adviser is independent but cannot plead in court. The company jurist, on the other hand, is connected to the company for which he works.

1. Book III of the *Gerechtelijk Wetboek* (GerW), *Code Judiciaire* (CJ) Judicial Code (GerW CJ), Articles 428 *et seq.*
2. GerW CJ, Article 440.

CHARACTERISTICS OF THE LEGAL PROFESSION

As was mentioned above, the lawyers' profession is protected and regulated by the GerW CJ, and this regulation reveals the salient characteristics of the profession.[3] These characteristics have been strikingly summarised:

"1. The Belgian lawyer's profession has been organised by statute. The professional organs have been delegated much power in order to establish rules and customs concerning the relationship between lawyers, between lawyers and clients and between lawyers and judges.

2. The Belgian legal profession is independent, this having been guaranteed by its governing bodies, such having been elected, by its own disciplinary law and rulings by its legal recognition of the binding character of its customs and standing orders. Its decisions have the force of law for lawyers.

3. The working of the Belgian lawyer's profession is part of the judicial apparatus. It implies an independence towards the executive. The lawyer's profession is not however subordinate to the judicial power."[4]

PROFESSIONAL BODIES AND THEIR AUTHORITY

Organisation

The formal organisation of the legal profession (the Bar) in Belgium is made through the establishment of the National Order of Advocates. The National Order of Advocates is comprised of all Belgian lawyers and Belgian apprentices who have been registered as apprentices for at least two years. The National Order of Advocates has been incorporated.[5]

In each judicial district, there is a local bar, i.e. a local Order of Advocates,[6] except for the judicial district of Brussels where there are two: French and Dutch.[7] There is also a bar at the *Hof van Cassatie*, the *Cour de Cassation*, which is the Belgium High Court.

The local Orders are also incorporated. The Orders of Advocates have a Council of the Order which consists of the "staff-holder", the *batonnier* (President of the Bar) and a certain number of members, which varies

3. See, generally, Mathieu and Baudrez, *de Belgische Advocatuur*, Kuurne Leieland, 1980 and Stevens, *Regels en gebruiken van de advocatuur te Antwerpen,* Orde van Advocaten (ed.) Antwerpen, Kluwer, 1990.

4. Stevens, *Regels en gebruiken van de advocatuur te Antwerpen,* Orde van Advocaten (ed.), Antwerpen, Kluwer, 1990.

5. GerW CJ, Article 431.

6. GerW CJ, Article 430,1.

7. GerW CJ, Article 430,2.

according to the number of lawyers at the Bar.[8] Members of the Council are directly elected by the lawyers of the Bar the same is true for the President;[9] the Council has a Secretary, who fulfills the same function for the Order.[10] There is also the General Assembly of the Order.[11]

Authority

The batonnier

Article 447 of the GerW CJ stipulates that the President is the head of the Order. He has the internal charge of the Order and is its outside representative. He also has an advisory power in the judicial organisation.[12] and is the head of the administrative services of the Bar.

Another important task is the giving of advice and directives to the lawyers of his Bar and mediating conflicts which arise between lawyers. He is the executive organ for the decisions of the Council of the Order. He also has jurisdiction to hear disciplinary complaints against lawyers. He can act in disciplinary matters or bring the matter before the Council of the Order.[13]

The Council of the Order

The Council has decision-taking powers in matters of discipline at the Bar, and it is charged with upholding these.[14] It also has important tasks concerning the composition of the lists of lawyers at the various Bars (the *tableau* and the list of apprentices) the organisation and control of the apprenticeship and professional training[15] and *inter alia* legal aid to the poor.[16]

8. GerW CJ, Article 449.
9. GerW CJ, Article 450.
10. GerW CJ, Article 452.
11. GerW CJ, Article 447.
12. GerW CJ, Article 66,88.
13. GerW CJ, Article 457.
14. GerW CJ, Article. 456.
15. GerW CJ, Articles 435 and 456.
16. GerW CJ, Articles 446, 455,1 and 455 bis.

PRACTICE STRUCTURES AND FORMS OF PARTNERSHIP

An important element in establishing the professional liability of the lawyer is to know whether he practices alone, as a collaborator or as a partner in whatever capacity.[17] It should be remarked that technically, according to Belgian law, only the sole legal practitioner is recognised.

The bars enjoy a large degree discretion, which comes into play in this context. As the Belgian legislature did not elaborate a regulation concerning partnerships, the local bars have regulated this more or less by themselves.

The evolution from the single practitioner to more far-reaching forms of partnership is a very recent trend. Such expansion has occurred in the last few years. The starting point of this evolution was the deontological opposition and the prohibition of partnerships. Reality, however, soon caught up with this position because of the internationalisation of the profession and the expansion of legal specialisation. For example, at the Antwerp Bar a regulation of 30 January 1989 was issued concerning the collaboration of lawyers. Other bars have established and issued similar regulations.

TASKS OF THE LAWYER

Relation to the client

The exact nature of the relationship which the lawyer has with his client has given rise to many controversies in the past. It has been said that it was unthinkable for the lawyer to sign a contract with his client and that his obligations were "not of a contractual nature".[18] Now a broad consensus has been achieved, and both doctrine and case law recognise the existence of a contractual relationship between lawyer and client. To date, there is no agreement as to how the contract must be qualified.

This confusion has been caused by the variety of tasks that a lawyer takes upon himself when dealing with a case. It is assumed that the lawyer treats all aspects of his client's case, for example, studying documents, advising, negotiating to reach a compromise, initiating and pleading a case before the court and executing judicial decisions, distinctly equally, but how should this entire lawyer/client relationship be qualified?

17. See Stevens, *Regels en gebruiken van de advocatuur te Antwerpen,* Orde van Advocaten te Antwerpen ed., Antwerpen, Kluwer 1990, p. 824.

18. See Watelet, "*La responsabilité des avocats*" in Storrer (ed.) *Responsabilité professionelle et assurances des Risques professionelles*, Brussel, Larcier 1975, p. 127; *RPDB* v. *Avocat*, Brussel, Bruylant, p. 80.

For some, it is a contract *sui generis* or an unspecified contract with its own liability rules. For others, it is an enterprise of intellectual work, which in certain circumstances is coupled with a mandate when, for example, the lawyer takes it upon himself to make a specific legal act. The enterprise of work[19] approach is specifically characterised by its lack of an element of subordination, which represents better the real relationship between the lawyer and his client. According to another point of view, it is a mixed contract with elements of enterprise, mandate and deposit. The liability for a certain professional fault would then be fixed according to the rules which are in force for the element of the contract which has been violated.

To conclude, it should be noted that the lawyer is subject to the civil law of contractual liability regardless of how his legal relationship to his client is qualified. Accordingly, the conflict between these points of view is largely theoretical. Another aspect should also be considered. If the liability of the lawyer is to be established according to the rules of a particular type of contract, where fault has been committed (theory of the unnamed contract), then the liability for loss of documents (deposit) would be limited. The same is true for the mandate. This limited liability only applies when it is a cost-free deposit or mandate.

In case law, it is not always clear whether the liability of the lawyer is contractual or extra-contractual.

Tasks

Consideration of the different tasks of the lawyer can provide a better understanding of the nature and scope of his potential liability.

Advice

One of the most important tasks of the lawyer is to provide advice. Here he is "competing" with the various other legal professions, but the conduct rules of the profession give the client special guarantees. A further benefit is the perspective from which the lawyer operates as an expert. He can and will, when advising, take into account the consequences of his advice for the position of his client at a later trial. Based on his experience with trial reality he is extremely competent for this. Traditionally, it is accepted that the lawyer in this function is related to his client with an enterprise contract according to Article 1787 of the BWCC.[20]

19. BWCC, Article 1787.
20. *RPDB* v. *Avocat*, Brussel, Bruylant, p. 80 in fine.

Negotiations

As counsel for a party, but as one who is not directly identified with the party or his interest, the lawyer is placed in a better position to achieve an acceptable compromise than the party whom he is representing. He can also represent the party (mandate) and give assistance (enterprise). In addition, he is also able to draft agreements.

Mandate ad litem

In Belgium, lawyers are particularly distinguished for their skills in advocacy and in the preparation of pleadings. The lawyer, as opposed to the client, is *dominus litis*. This means that the lawyer, after having been instructed by the client, independently decides which steps must be taken in the interest of the case.

The lawyer acts as a representative (mandatary) for his client in all trial actions. Here we must clarify that in order to act in court as a representative of his client, he need not have an express mandate.[21] The lawyer can *inter alia* initiate proceedings in the name and for the account of his client, take conclusions (written arguments) and deposit documents.

The mandate *ad litem* covers all trial actions which are necessary in order to bring the trial to a successful conclusion, including the phase of forced execution. This mandate is considered to exist by operation of law. The lawyer's appearance in this role proves the mandate *ad litem*. If a party (the client or other persons) contests the mandate, then they must prove its non-existence.

It is important to note that Belgium has a procedure of negation of a trial action by which each party can state that the lawyer was not instructed or authorised to pursue such an action. This can arise for actions which are covered by the mandate *ad litem* and for actions which need a special mandate. Obviously, there remains a potential claim of professional liability against the lawyer in question.

For some trial actions, a special mandate is necessary. If, in such cases, the special mandate is contested, then the burden of proof of the existence or the extent of the mandate is upon the representing lawyer. The proof can be brought by all means known to the law.

The court proceedings which the lawyer takes as a representative of his client, both in the framework of the putative mandate or the proven mandate, are for the account of the client. This also applies to faults which the lawyer mandatary makes in executing his mandate. These faults do not operate as *force majeure* (act of God) for the client.

21. GerW CJ, Article 440,2.

Other mandates and judicial mandates

The mandate is also relevant outside of the mandate *ad litem*. This means that not only the proceedings which are covered by the mandate *ad litem* but also, for example, the dissolution of a lease contract on the signing of an agreement in the name and for the account of the client fall within its ambit. Obviously, the mandate must be proven as in civil law. If the lawyer takes actions as an administrator of bankruptcies or as commissioner or liquidator, he has a judicial mandate.

Deposit of documents

The lawyer often receives documents either from his client or from the opposing party. He may also receive funds or property which he must hold in trust.

Replacement of judges

In some cases, the lawyer will be called upon to replace judges. Article 442 of the GerW CJ stipulates: "In cases determined by statute, they are called upon to replace judges or prosecutors. They cannot refuse unless they have a valid excuse".

In this context, the liability of the lawyer is defined by the responsibility of the office he fills.

OBLIGATIONS OF THE LAWYER, GROUNDS OF LIABILITY

Contractual liability

In earlier doctrine and case law, one finds that the lawyer is only liable in cases of deceit, gross negligence or grave error. These concepts have now been entirely abandoned.

As discussed, the lack of agreement among legal scholars on the nature of the agreement between lawyer and client is highly theoretical. This is the more so since there is an important distinction between an obligation to use every effort and the obligation to achieve a result.

This last sort of obligation is the one in which the obligee takes upon himself to achieve a given result. His responsibility will be considered as existing if the obligor proves that this obligation validly existed and that the obligee did not perform it. The obligor thus has a lighter burden of proof and there is no debate about the means of meeting it. The obligee can be freed of his liability if he can show that his failure to achieve the result derives of a "strange cause" or *force majeure.*

The person relying on "external cause" must show that the execution of the obligation is absolutely impossible, such impossibility not having arisen by a fault of the person claiming the same. The above is to be applied in the situation of a lawyer who in some cases takes upon himself an obligation to achieve a given result, for example, when he has to make an appeal against a decision within a given time limit. His professional liability is established as soon as this time limit has expired, without an appeal having been made. He cannot rely upon the concept of "strange cause".

Some examples from case law can illustrate this type of duty: to attend a hearing, to adhere to the time limit for filing an appeal, bringing an action or making an answer, and to introduce an action before the competent court. In some cases, the obligation to inform the client can be an obligation to achieve a given result.

It has been held that the delicate nature of a matter, the special research it demands or a temporary deterioration of health are not sufficient enough to invoke the principle of *force majeure*.

The obligation of the lawyer to use his best endeavour is one in which the obligee takes it upon himself to make certain efforts to achieve a result. Which efforts an obligee must make is established by the criterion of the normal diligent and prudent obligee, who is placed in the same external circumstances (*bonus pater familias in abstracto*).

When establishing liability, it must be asked if a normal diligent and prudent obligee in the same situation would have acted in the same way as the obligee has actually done in this case. Liability is established when a *culpa levis in abstracto* is proven, this meaning a fault which a *bonus pater familias* would not have committed in these circumstances.

Applied to the lawyer, this means that the lawyer will be liable if it can be shown that he did not act in a way in which a normal diligent and prudent lawyer placed in the same circumstances would have acted. As already mentioned, the external circumstances of the case must be taken into account (complexity of the matter, urgency). However, the lawyer's personal frailties are not considered, for example, age, specialisation or health. The lawyer undertakes to use his best endeavours when he gives advice or pleads before a court.

Torts

In the performance of his duties, the lawyer is subject to the general rule of diligence, on the basis of which he has to act in a manner expected of a normal diligent and prudent lawyer in order not to cause damage to third parties. The BWCC stipulates as follows:

"Article 1382. Each act of a person which causes damage to another person obligates the one who caused such damage to remedy the loss caused."

"Article1383. Every person is liable, not only for damage caused by his acts but also any damage caused by his negligence."

The criterion is the same as that used in establishing contractual obligation, where the lawyer is expected to use his best endeavours. The burden of proof for the one who has suffered damage is, therefore, rather heavy. The claimant must prove that the lawyer committed a (professional) fault, that he suffered damage, and that there is a casual link. As far as the damage is concerned, he must also prove that it was foreseeable for the lawyer that damage would arise. Only the principle must have been foreseeable, not the extent of the damage.

PROFESSIONAL LIABILITIES

Civil professional liability: general aspects

Basis

Besides those elements outlined above, the lawyer is bound by the duty of professional confidentiality, the violation of which may lead to a civil liability claim or criminal action being brought against him.

With respect to the Code of Conduct, it must be borne in mind that a violation of the Code does not necessarily mean that a professional fault has been committed that will lead to the civil liability of the lawyer. A distinction has been made depending on whether the Code of Conduct rule is or is not a law in the material sense of the word. A law in the material sense of the word is a rule of law which, as far as the general scope is concerned, is lasting and derives its binding force from a unilateral order by the authorities.

As far as the conduct of lawyers is concerned, the authorities have delegated their competence to regulate to the bodies of the Order, which in these instances have an autonomous regulating power. Furthermore, the conduct rules issued by the Order of Lawyers do not need enforcement by the authorities to be binding, as is the case for the rules of most other professional organisations such as those for doctors.

It may be concluded that the conduct rules of a general nature as promulgated by the Order of Lawyers are laws in the material sense of the word.

The question of whether a third party, with respect to the conduct rules, somebody who is not a lawyer, can invoke the content of conduct rules to have force of law must be answered in the affirmative since conduct rules are generally binding, even if they impose a certain conduct only on a limited group of people. Doctrine also reaches the following conclusion:

"The violation of conduct rules of behaviour, which are a law in the material sense, are considered an extra-contractual fault, when the conduct rule imposes a certain behaviour and any subject of law can invoke this fault to determine that a liability exists on the condition that he also proves the damage and the causal link."[22]

If one deals with a conduct rule which is not a law in the material sense and this is possible when it is not generally binding or contains an individual decision, one must return to the general law of extra-contractual liability. There is liability only to the extent a normal reasonable and prudent lawyer faced with the same circumstances would not have violated the rule and in so far as the damage is foreseeable as a consequence of this violation. Here, the judge enjoys his full independent powers of appreciation.

Finally, a violation of a conduct rule can amount to a contractual fault to be invoked by the client in that the rules may be explicitly or implicitly incorporated into the contract of representation. This can give rise to contractual liability under the conditions which have been set out earlier concerning contractual liability.

Claimants

From what has been said earlier, one can consider classes of claimant. First, there is the client who must base his claim on the contractual relationship which exists between him and the lawyer. The liability will be contractual. Second, there is the third party who suffers damage due to the behaviour of the lawyer. This third party must base his claim on extra-contractual liability.

Professor Dalcq gives an example from 1914 where the Order of Lawyers of the Court of Appeal of Brussels claimed and received damages on the grounds that the name of a business agent was published in a certain publication together with the names of lawyers of this Bar whose dignity was therefore violated.

Procedures

CIVIL COURTS

Article 556, GerW CJ, stipulates that the courts and tribunals receive all claims, except those which statute withdraws from their jurisdiction. The

22. Cornelis, *Beginselen van belgisch buitencontractueel aansprakeligkheidsrecht*, Antwerp, Maklu, 1989, p. 267.

latter mainly concerns claims which can be brought before administrative jurisdictions. A procedure concerning liability, be it contractual or extra-contractual, is conducted before the civil courts and tribunals (unless as a civil party before criminal jurisdictions which are left out here).

Before introducing a claim before the court, the President of the Bar must first give his permission. He will aim to reach an agreement in order to avoid the need for litigation before the court.

Administrative jurisdictions have no competence because professional liability claims clearly concern litigation of a civil nature.[23] In the first instance, the competent tribunal is fixed for claims in liability taking into account the value of the litigation.[24] This value is the sum which is claimed in the writ (originating summons) plus interest. The interest begins to accumulate as soon as the debtor defaults on payment. Up to a value of BEF75,000, the Justice of the Peace is competent. Up to BEF50,000, the judgement of the Justice of the Peace is not appealable. For more than BEF75,000, the Tribunal of First Instance is competent.

The respective burdens of proof for the plaintiff and defendant have already been referred to.

DISCIPLINARY COURTS

Disciplinary courts which are competent for lawyers in disciplinary matters are not competent for claims based on liability, but they can adjudge violations of the Code of Conduct rules, which are also treated before the civil courts and tribunals. As was said before, a disciplinary violation of a lawyer is in many cases also a violation of the general norm of prudence or a breach of his contractual obligations, which can result in contractual or extra-contractual liability. It can be added that the reverse is also possible, such having to be adjudged by the disciplinary courts.

The option of a criminal prosecution is not open for the citizen since this is in essence a public prosecution. In the same way, the citizen has no access to the disciplinary complaints procedure. He can only ask for damages before the civil courts.

In addition, the intervention of the citizen who suffered harm in the disciplinary procedure is not provided for by the GerW CJ, which regulates this procedure in its Articles 456 and 477.

The regulation in the GerW CJ is rudimentary, so that the local bars have had to make their own regulations. As a consequence of a recommendation by the National Order of Lawyers on 18 June 1987 to unify the procedure in disciplinary matters, the Antwerp Bar has regulated this matter in a provision on Disciplinary Procedure of the Council of the

23. Constitution, Article 92.
24. GerW CJ, Article 557.

Order of 29 January 1990. Since the disciplinary courts (the Council of the Order, the Disciplinary Council of Appeal and the *Cour de Cassation*) have no jurisdiction in civil matters, it is of no interest to go into more details.

It must, however, be remarked that a disciplinary decision has no *res judicata* effect and is not enforceable upon another court in any further litigation (unlike the criminal decision valid *erga omnes*). Thus, the disciplinary decision does not bind the civil court. The court remains free to decide if the behaviour which has been sanctioned is or is not a fault by the lawyer on the civil level. Finally, disciplinary misdemeanours cannot be prescribed. The GerW CJ does not envision any prescription period.

Damage which can be claimed

Should the civil court establish a professional fault on the part of the lawyer, then the issue of damages will arise. Both with respect to a contractual shortcoming and a violation of the general norm of diligence, the principle is that the damage must be fully repaired, such being the loss suffered including any lost benefit. He who has suffered loss must be indemnified to the full extent of his loss. Damage and liability are not established where the lawyer repairs the fault, if possible, at his own cost. Furthermore, if there is no substantial damage and, therefore, no right to indemnification in case the trial action is annulled by way of the procedure of negation of trial action (see above), the costs of the court action are borne by the lawyer. Where a possible harm is alleged, its existence must be proven as a certainty. For example, in the context of a mandate *ad litem,* the possible damage exists in the loss of a chance when the lawyer by committing a professional fault brings the client in a situation where he loses the possibility of an appeal or where he causes the annulment of a procedure action or lets a time limit go by. If this possible damage is certain, it must be repaired. In other words, is it sufficiently probable that the damage would not have occurred without the fault of the lawyer?

This probability has been examined in two ways, both by doctrine and case law, especially concerning the loss of an instance of appeal. In the first approach, the judge assesses the likelihood of the case succeeding in court. He takes the place of a hypothetical appeal judge and examines the chance that the judgement would have been changed had there been an appeal or a motion for the High Court. The second approach is that the judge must examine the value of the chance. The damage is then the loss of the chance as such, i.e. the loss of the right to appeal or to put a motion before the High Court. In all fairness, it must be noted that both approaches lead to the same result.

Civil liabilities: special cases

Preliminary remark

The lawyer who has been contractually bound to represent his client can as a result of this, commit a professional fault if he knew or should have reasonably known that the case was outside the scope of his knowledge and competence. The lawyer must know his own limits and can commit a professional fault by ignoring this and not referring the client, as he should do, to another, more competent colleague.

Such a fault is an extra-contractual fault, but more specifically also amounts to a pre-contractual fault. The damage may arise as a consequence of an incorrect treatment of the case, e.g. the above described loss of a chance by letting a time limit which he did not know of expire.

The client who suffers the damage will *de facto* have the choice of claiming compensation on a contractual basis or on an extra-contractual basis. An incorrect assessment of the case can amount to such a contractual shortcoming.

Advice and assistance

It is generally accepted that a lawyer who gives assistance to a client takes upon himself an obligation to use his best endeavours. The case law has abandoned the point of view that in his function as legal adviser the lawyer is only liable in cases of deceit or grave intentional mistake. On the contrary, it is now accepted that the lawyer who gives advice is also liable for his normal mistake (*culpa levis in abstracto*), namely for errors in his advice that a normal, reasonable and prudent lawyer would not have committed in the same external situation.

The concept "same external situation" means the position of the doctrine and the ruling case law concerning the legal point for which the advice has been given. Lawyers often give advice in a contested matter. They cannot be blamed for giving a point of view which is not shared by the court, at least if the advice was not *a priori* wrong. What amounts to a fault, however, is the circumstance where the lawyer has failed to tell his client that there is some dissension in doctrine and case law and that his point of view is contested. There, he fails in his duty to inform. The lawyer cannot, therefore, be exonerated on the grounds that his fault was an error in the interpretation of the contested statute or law.

A lawyer will also be held liable where he, without carrying out the required examination, provides his client with incorrect advice.

Mandatary ad litem or special mandatary

FAILURE OR INCORRECT EXECUTION OF A MANDATE

When the lawyer stays within the limits of his mandate, he represents the client in the sense that he will be held fully accountable to his client for any actions he takes in court. It has already been noted that the same holds true for faults incurred where the lawyer executes his mandate and the client is bound. It has been said that the negligence of the lawyer to register a divorce judgement in the town hall is a circumstance independent of the will of his client and, therefore, not accountable. However, the lawyer is still contractually responsible to his client.

The question of whether extra-contractual liability of the lawyer towards third parties results as a consequence of a contractual shortcoming does not lend itself to consensus. It has already been mentioned that the client is bound by any mistakes incurred by his mandate, but does the third party have a claim based on extra-contractual liability against the lawyer? It has been established that the relativity of the agreement does not conflict with the notion that the lawyer is responsible when he acts incorrectly as a contracting party and harms a third party.

An example of a positive answer to this question is that of reckless and provocative court action. The introduction of a court case is regarded as reckless and provocative if no reasonable and diligent lawyer would have introduced it. In such circumstances, the lawyer commits a tort entailing his liability towards the third party who suffered harm and his contractual liability towards his client.

EXCEEDING THE LIMITS OF THE MANDATE

If one recalls the situation of the lawyer who exceeds his mandate *ad litem,* the general provision of Article 1998 of the BWCC is that the client is not bound unless he has ratified the excess by, for example, enforcing the court action. Such ratification can be express or implied.

A lawyer cannot enter into an agreement for his client unless he has been expressly authorised to do so. Payments made as a consequence of an agreement and accepted by the lawyer although he was not authorised to do so are not extinctive of the obligation for the party that pays in so far as the client has not derived any advantage of it. No agreement is formed where the lawyer does not have the proper mandate. The third party that pays also bears this risk.

THEORY OF THE APPARENT MANDATE

Generally, the third party must verify the existence and the extent of the mandate of the other party and he must bear the consequences if he fails to do so. Nevertheless, the lawyer's client can make it appear to the third party that the lawyer is entitled to take the contested action in his client's name and for his account. It is also possible that the mandate was given in such circumstances that, in the eyes of the third party acting in good faith, it was unclear what extent it had.

In some instances, the consequences of the non-existing mandate can be reduced for the third party. Indeed, the client may have made a mistake or was not diligent by reason of giving the impression that he had given a mandate. Conforming to the principle of indemnification, the client may be held liable against the third party who becomes his counterpart.

It is also possible that the authority of the lawyer mandatary was verified by the third party, but that the lawyer misled him concerning the extent of his authority. Should this be the case and the third party can prove this with all means of law, then the lawyer will be held liable for the consequences of the legal actions he took in excess of his mandate.[25]

NEGATION OF COURT ACTIONS

The theory of the apparent mandate, as stated above, is in essence a protection of the opposing party to the client. It does not function where there is no opposing party, namely, where there is no unilateral court action. This is the case with court actions such as the introduction of a petition. Such court actions will normally lead to a judicial executor decision and as sufficient grounds of nullity, the absence of competence of the mandate cannot be invoked against it. To deal with such situations, the procedure of negation exists, which has been described above.

Deposit of documents

The lawyer receives documents from his clients, which he may need in order to prove his point in law. To the client, the lawyer is the depository and, as such, he is obliged to return the documents according to Article 1993 of the BWCC. He is also liable for these documents and he must look after them in the same manner as he would his own documents,[26] at least if it is an unpaid deposit (*culpa levis in concreto*). If it is a paid deposit, then

25. BWCC, Article 1997.
26. BWCC, Article 1927.

the standard applied is stricter under Article 1928 of the BWCC, which means that the normal criterion of *culpa levis in abstracto* is applied, as was mentioned above.

It is possible that lesser liability would be imposed when it is a *pro deo* case, although professional conduct rules would probably oppose this. An old privilege of the lawyer also must be noted, providing that his word should be believed if he declares that the documents given to him by his client or an adversary were returned.[27] This privilege operates in any case until the prescription period for keeping documents has ended.

Curator and other judicial mandates

This concerns cases where the lawyer has been appointed by the court as, *inter alia*, an administrator of a bankruptcy, liquidator, sequestrator, guardian of an incompetent, provisional trustee, judicial counsel, curator of an unclaimed estate or guardian *ad hoc* of a minor. The liability is that of the concerned legal construction, which goes beyond the scope of this chapter.

Abuse of procedural law

The classic example of abuse of procedural law is the reckless and provocative court action, with the result that the party who initiated the court proceedings provides indemnification to the party who has suffered damage. Here, it is assumed that introducing a court action using legal means and defending in law must be conducted in a way to achieve results. Abusing procedural law is an application of the general theory of abusing a right, which is based in Belgium on tort liability.

If the reckless and provocative court action is a fault of the lawyer, his contractual liability to his client is involved, as noted above. Furthermore, such action involves what was recently called "abuse of the services of the judicial system" where the emphasis is not so much on the reparation obligation as on the fact that abuse of the procedural law is an abuse of the public service. This point of view is for the moment not very widespread. Examples of abuse of procedural law are an abusive executory seizure, a defence which comes too late or an unauthorised motion of cassation.

27. RPDB, Articles 109, 111, 112 and 114.

Professional confidentiality

Professional confidentiality is sanctioned by the criminal law, but does not find its basis in criminal law. It is an essential right and duty of the lawyer.[28]

This is an essential guarantee for the rights of the defence and the good operation of the judicial system. A judgement by the High Court states that the professional confidentiality of the lawyer finds its basis in the necessity for the person who exercises the profession to give indispensable guarantees of his trustworthiness. This is in the general interest because all who work with lawyers may be reassured that they can entrust them with their secrets without there being a danger that the confidentiality will be broken.

The basis is to be found in the essence of the lawyers profession. This also means that professional confidentiality has no contractual basis; on the contrary, the duty and the right of professional confidentiality is an unwritten but nevertheless binding principle of law which touches approaches public order. This conclusion is supported by the fact that the breach of professional confidentiality is sanctioned by criminal law.

Only in very exceptional cases may the lawyer violate his professional confidentiality, namely, in those cases where his moral and human duty to reveal secrets would be stronger than his duty to keep the secret. Such a case may be where a client tells his lawyer of his intention to commit a criminal act against the lives of third parties. However, some judgements have imposed less strict conditions.

Except for the case where he is summoned to testify in law, where the lawyer has the right but not the obligation to speak, he will have to keep his confidentiality.[29] Professional confidentiality covers only those items of information which, when revealed, could cause moral or material harm and which the lawyer received in his capacity as lawyer.

As mentioned above, the professional secret is criminally sanctioned (although not expressly for lawyers) by Article 458 of the Penal Code which stipulates:

"Doctors, medical officers, health officers, pharmacists, midwives and all other persons who by virtue of their status or profession have knowledge of secrets which have been entrusted to them and reveal them except in the case where they are called to testify or where the law obliges them to reveal secrets are to be punished with a prison sentence from eight days to six months and a fine of BEF100 to 500 (multiplied by 90)."

Violation of professional confidentiality is therefore a misdemeanour. This means that its violation can give rise to civil liability of the lawyer

28. Code of Conduct by the CCBE of 28 October 1988, Article 231.
29. Penal Code, Article 458.

against the client who entrusted him with the secret. This should probably be considered a contractual fault. Indeed, by the enforcement of Article 1135 of the BWCC contracts bind also to all consequences which arise by equity costume or law according to the nature of the contract. It is therefore concurrence of contractual and penal liability. The duty to professional secrecy has the character of an obligation to achieve a result. The lawyer must guarantee the absolute secrecy of the entrusted information. As a misdemeanour (in the sense of the criminal law) is also a tort (in the sense of the civil law), its violation can also give rise to liability of the lawyer against third parties on the condition that they can prove the damage the fault and the causal link between the two.

Pleading

The lawyer could also, when pleading, violate the good name and reputation of third parties which can give rise to his extra-contractual liability. Here, the lawyer benefits from the so-called immunity of the pleadings established by Article 452 of the Penal Code, on the conditions that his words and writings produced before court are relevant to the case or the parties. If those conditions are not fulfilled, the lawyer can be criminally prosecuted in addition to being held liable to those who suffered harm in the civil courts.

Article 444,2 of the GerWCJ, stipulates that immunity of pleadings is valid for "everything that is absolutely essential for the case".

Article 445 of the GerWCJ, stipulates that attacks in pleadings or in writings on the monarchy, the constitution, the laws of the Belgian people or the authorities may not necessarily amount to malicious intent. As far as writings are concerned, the immunity ceases to operate when they are made public.

Defence, exoneration and prescription

Burden of proof in obligations to achieve a given result

The lawyer can free himself of his contractual liability, when he can prove that the damage has been brought about by an external cause. The existence of an external cause is not accepted very often by the courts and tribunals. It is described as "an event which constitutes an absolute impediment to fulfilling the obligations of the debtor and which, as far as its origin is concerned, cannot be attributed to a fault of the debtor". If the lawyer can prove this, then the fault cannot be attributed to him, and his liability will not be involved.

The following are considered external causes: *force majeure*, coincidental acts of a third party or the creditor of the obligations (the counter party), acts of the Government or loss of the object without fault of the debtor of the obligation.

Burden of proof in obligations to use best efforts

If the lawyer took upon himself an obligation to use his best efforts, then the burden of proof is very heavy for the plaintiff. He will have to prove that the lawyer did not act as a normal reasonable and diligent lawyer would have done in the same circumstances. Judging this is a matter of fact to be decided by the judge.

Tort

The burden of proof in tort actions is, apart from the condition of foreseeability of the damage, the same as that for contractual obligations to use best efforts referred to above.

Exoneration

In principle, every person, including lawyers, is free to stipulate anything in an agreement with others which is not contrary to public policy, good morals or mandatory law.

Thus, one is free to lessen or exclude his liability in a contract. Only clauses which exclude liability for intentional fault or which annul the entire object of the contract are considered unenforceable. Legally, the lawyer can exclude his liability if he fulfils these conditions.

The question has been raised whether it is in accordance with the dignity of the lawyers' profession to tell the client that he will not be 100 per cent liable for his actions, but one should consider that, in cases with a great financial value, a lawyer can be ruined by a small fault (*culpa levis in abstracto*).

Indeed, on the one hand, exoneration for a small mistake would be unjustified and on the other, as will be seen later, the insurance only covers liability up to a certain limit. In a certain sense, it is the same debate as the one which has been raised concerning the need of liability insurance for professional faults. The difference is that, with exoneration, the liability is put aside whereas with insurance, only the financially detrimental risks of liability are quantified and distributed. It is useful to consider whether, in high-value cases, one should take a supplementary insurance for professional liability, considering the financial consequences of even a small mistake. Such a supplementary insurance is more justifiable than an exoneration where the victim of the fault would have to suffer the consequences.

Prescription periods

Article 2276 bis of the BWCC stipulates:

"The lawyers are relieved of their liability and are not responsible for keeping documents 5 years after ending their task. This prescription does not apply when the lawyer has been expressly ordered to keep the documents."

Here, the second part only deals with liability as a depositor and not with all the aspects of professional liability. The prescription period begins when the task of the lawyer ends. What is meant by the end of the task is a factual question to be decided upon by the judge. There is no case law which treats this point, although the law which incorporated Article 2276 bis into the BWCC entered into force on 24 September 1985.

Circumstances suggested in the preparatory works in parliament for ending the prescription period are death of the lawyer, taking back of the file by the client, closure of the procedure by a definitive ruling and returning the file to the client.

It is clear that the prescription begins when the task is completed and not when the fault is committed, even if there is a difference between those dates of more than ten years.

Vicarious and joint liability

It is possible for two or more lawyers to work together or each of them independently on a case for one client. The just liability of each of the lawyers who work together will be based on the obligations of each of them separately and their respective shortcomings. Liability *in solidum* is possible, in as far as the concurrent faults of both lawyers necessarily led to the damage.

The lawyer as a representative can give the work or part thereof to a sub-representative who replaces him but who is according to Article 1994 of the BWCC himself liable for the faults of the latter if he was not empowered to delegate, or alternatively, even if he had this power, he chose a person who was manifestly incompetent or without means. The client has the choice in that he can hold both the lawyer and the sub-mandatary liable even if only the latter committed the fault.[30]

30. BWCC, Article 1998,2.

If the lawyer undertakes intellectual work and he works with somebody else, then the latter is to be considered as a sub-contractor for which the main contractor is liable. For actions of his partners or apprentices who plead or take decisions in his name, the lawyer is liable no matter how the collaboration is qualified. The same is true for faults or negligent acts of his secretary or his employees.[31]

Regarding the relationship between the lawyer and the bailiff, whose intervention is necessary for some court actions, the doctrine is not settled. It is said that the bailiff is a sub-representative of the lawyer in cases of issuing writs and forced executions. The client would not have a contractual relationship with the sub-representative bailiff. He, however, has a direct action against the bailiff according to Article 1994,2 of the BWCC. This point of view was defended in a judgement of the Court of Appeal of Ghent of 26 February 1981.[32] The argument against this view was that the bailiff has a legal monopoly and, therefore, cannot be considered a mandatary of the lawyer: How could a lawyer be replaced for a task he himself is not empowered to perform?

The solution to this problem has, as its starting point, the lawyer as a representative who is bound to introduce court actions, lead the procedure and take care of enforcement of the decision which intervened. This mandate *ad litem* means also that he agrees in the name and for the account of his client an agreement with the bailiff to take the action which only he is empowered to do (issue of the writ, forced execution). The bailiff acts in the name and on behalf of the client as his representative and not as representative of the lawyer who, when agreeing the second mandate contract, was only the representative of the client. Here, the client can proceed directly against the bailiff[33] for any loss caused as a result of the bailiff's fault. The basis is contractual; more specific under the mandate contract, he can also take proceedings against the lawyer on the basis of the mandate contract he had with him. If both made faults which together led to the damage, then they are liable *in solidum*.[34]

It is also possible that the person who has suffered harm or damage (client or third party) may himself have made a mistake and, therefore, could be partly responsible for such harm or damage caused. According to the"theory of equivalence of causes of a loss", the contributory fault of the sufferer must also be taken into account when establishing the liability of the defendant.

The fault of the client or the third party frees the lawyer. A classic example is that of a client who does not (in time) tell a lawyer that a

31. BWCC, Article 1384.

32. RW 1982–83, pp. 439–446.

33. BWCC, Article 1998,1.

34. Paulus and en Boes , "De deurwaarder is niet de plaatsvervanger van de advocaat", in *Liber Amicorum Jan Ronse*, Brussel, Story-Scientia, 1986, pp. 10–14.

judgement has been notified so that the delay for appeal passes without the lawyer making the appeal; the lawyer may not be at fault.

He has the obligation to inform his client of the importance of notifying him for the further development of the procedure. The client is not expected to know the dangers of the procedure, but the degree of (legal) knowledge of the client is taken into account.

INSURANCE OF PROFESSIONAL LIABILITY

As was established above, there are many risks involved with the profession of the lawyer. These risks obviously strike, in the first place, the client and the suffering third party, who bear the real damage. Often, however, this damage, at least in part, is borne by the lawyer when he is liable. Even a small mistake can ruin the lawyer, and for the sufferer of the harm there is uncertainty as to whether he will ever recuperate his loss.

It is not against professional dignity that lawyers take out insurance to cover such risks. Moreover, the insurance, at least as far as there is coverage, lessens the relative impecunious state of the liable lawyer for the third party. It is therefore not astonishing that, on a European level, the Council of the Bars and Law Societies of the European Community (EC) have made a recommendation which points out the necessity of insurance against professional liability. In some EC member states, lawyers have been obliged by their bars to take insurance for a minimum sum per loss. In Belgium, the local bars have issued autonomous regulations.

In order to protect the interests of the lawyer, the client and third parties in an optimal way, a number of Belgian bars have opted for an automatic collective policy (such as in Brussels, Antwerp and Ghent). This way, all lawyers of the bar, by registering on the tableau or on the list of apprentices are automatically insured against most of the pecuniary consequences of their professional liability.

Prejudicial financial consequences are not always excluded, since the policies contain exemptions. The policy in Antwerp contains an exemption of 25 per cent of the damage, with a minimum of BEF30,000 and a maximum of BEF100,000 for the first damage case; 50 per cent exemption, minimum BEF60,000 and maximum BEF200,000 for the second, and 50 per cent exemption, minimum BEF90,000 and maximum BEF400,000 for the third case. After five years from the first damage case, the lawyer again enjoys the smallest exemption. Such professional liability insurance covers in principle the civil liability of the Antwerp lawyer, both contractual and extra-contractual, arising during the exercise of his profession. The coverage is not only given for actions of the lawyer but also for his collaborators, apprentices and other persons for which the lawyer as *dominus litis* is responsible.

Included among actions that are insured are *inter alia* professional faults (as described above), loss or damage of documents and loss of funds. Material and physical damage caused by the lawyer or his collaborator or his employee to the client or a third party is usually covered by the professional liability insurance. Exclusion of coverage is possible on legal grounds or on conventional grounds. According to insurance law, intentional damage or damage caused by a grave fault is not covered by the insurance company.

By agreement, damage by actions which have nothing to do with the profession of lawyer or where he advises outside the legal sphere are excluded. Also, damage as a consequence of actions of the lawyer as an administrator or an agent are usually not covered by the insurance company. For these cases, there are separate policies.

Coverage for damage as a consequence of insured actions are subject to a maximum limit. In the Antwerp policy the coverage goes to BEF15-million. This amount can be increased to a maximum of BEF50-million or to BEF100-million with a supplementary inscription. By way of conclusion, it can be stated that insurance for professional liability is a necessity for the lawyer's profession, for the lawyer who can avoid financial disaster as well as for the client or the third party who is indirectly protected by it. Insurance also has the advantage that the lawyer can exercise his profession with greater independence, without the threat of financial ruin.

CHAPTER 3

CANADA

PETER KALICHMAN
McDougall Caron
Montreal, Quebec

INTRODUCTION

Canada is a confederation made up of ten provinces, each of which has jurisdiction over civil law. It is, therefore, the provinces, and not the federal government, that govern the relationship between individuals and lawyers. It follows, then, that to study lawyers' liability in Canada, one must examine the provinces individually.

Except for Quebec, all the provinces of Canada have a Common Law system in the English tradition. Quebec has a Civil Law system rooted in the French tradition. Despite the differences between the Common Law and Civil Law systems, the sources of lawyers' liability and the standard of care do not differ substantially from one province to the next. Consequently, it is possible to examine lawyers' liability in Canada as a whole rather than focusing on each province separately. One must keep in mind, however, that while the general standards and obligations are similar in all provinces, there exist important distinctions among the provinces regarding both lawyers' liability as well as principles of liability in general.

On 1 January 1994, the Province of Quebec enacted a sweeping reform of its Civil Code. While the effect of certain new or modified Articles of the Code will only be clarified once the courts have been called on to interpret them, these changes will undoubtedly impact on the practice of law and lawyers' liability in general in the province of Quebec.

Each of the ten provinces has its own bar association or law society, a statute in virtue of which the association or society is constituted and a code of conduct for its members. The following is a list of the different provinces, the name of its law society and enabling statute, and its code of conduct:

Alberta
- (1) The Law Society of Alberta
- (2) Legal Profession Act, RSA 1990, chapter L–9.1
- (3) Professional Conduct Handbook

British Columbia
(1) Law Society of British Columbia
(2) Legal Profession Act, SBC, 1987, chapter 25
(3) Professional Conduct Handbook

Manitoba
(1) Law Society of Manitoba
(2) The Law Society Act, RSM, 1987, chapter L 100
(3) Code of Professional Conduct

New Brunswick
(1) Law Society of New Brunswick
(2) Law Society Act, RSNB, 1986, chapter 96
(3) Professional Conduct Handbook

Newfoundland
(1) Law Society of Newfoundland
(2) Law Society Act, RSN, 1990, chapter L–9
(3) Code of Professional Conduct

Ontario
(1) Law Society of Upper Canada
(2) Law Society Act RSO, 1990, chapter L–8
(3) Professional Conduct Handbook

Prince Edward Island
(1) Law Society of Prince Edward Island
(2) Legal Profession Act, RSPEI, 1988, chapter L–6.1
(3) Professional Conduct Handbook

Saskatchewan
(1) Law Society of Saskatchewan
(2) Legal Profession Act, RSS, 1990, chapter L–10.1
(3) Code of Professional Conduct

Quebec
(1) Barreau du Quebec
(2) An Act Respecting the Barreau du Quebec, RSQ, chapter B–1
(3) Code of Ethics of Advocates, RRQ, 1981, chapter B–1, r–1

Every lawyer licensed to practise must be a member of the law society in the province in which he or she is practising. By virtue of their enabling statutes, these societies are administered by a body of elected members and have responsibility over such areas as admission to the practice of law, establishment of the conditions and requirements of practice, and discipline, including disciplinary sanctions. The legal profession can thus be said to be "self-governing".[1]

The codes of ethics or conduct, which set out the guidelines for lawyers in the exercise of their professions, vary only slightly from one province to the next. This is due, in part, to the fact that several law societies, rather than drafting their own codes of conduct, have simply adopted the Canadian Bar Association's Professional Code of Conduct (Alberta, Saskatchewan, and Nova Scotia) or have based their codes on that of the Canadian Bar Association (British Columbia, Manitoba, and Ontario). The principal areas of conduct dealt with in the various codes are the following:

(1) Competence and quality of service;
(2) Advising clients;
(3) Treatment of confidential information;
(4) Conflict of interest;
(5) Outside interests;
(6) Fees;
(7) Withdrawal;
(8) Advertising; and
(9) Practice by unauthorised persons.

In addition to providing lawyers with guidelines of practice, the codes of conduct form the basis of the law societies' disciplinary systems. However, except for Quebec, none of the provincial codes of conduct have the force of law.[2]

PRACTICE STRUCTURES

Most private practice lawyers in Canada practise in partnerships or as sole practitioners. However, in recent years, certain provinces have enacted legislation enabling lawyers to practise in a corporate structure.

Organisation under the partnership form is the most common legal structure for the practice of law in Canada. The partnership enables lawyers to pool their resources and knowledge to carry on the activities of the firm. The partners share in the profits and the losses of the firm and assume personal liability for debts incurred during the ordinary course of business of the partnership.

1. *Pearlman* v. *Manitoba Law Society Judicial Committee* [1991] 2 SCR 869, at p. 887.
2. Code of Ethics of Advocates, RRQ, 1981, chapter B–1, r–l is a regulation adopted under the Act respecting the Barreau du Quebec, RSQ, chapter B–1.

Each province has its own legislation governing partnerships. However, in general, partners are jointly liable for the debts incurred. Therefore, each partner is liable to creditors of the firm in equal shares, though their share in the partnership may be unequal.

Under the new Civil Code of Quebec the liability of the partners in a partnership will depend on the nature of the debt incurred. Thus, if the obligation has been contracted for the service or operation of an enterprise of the partnership, the partners are solidarily liable for the debt. In every other case, the partners are jointly liable for debts incurred.[3]

At present, Alberta and British Columbia are the only Canadian provinces with legislation in force permitting the incorporation of law firms.[4] The principal purpose for using the corporate structure for the practice of law is to benefit from the tax advantages available to corporate entities. Canadian lawyers carrying on the practice of law in a corporation do not benefit from the limited liability feature normally associated with corporate entities. In fact, lawyers who hold shares in a law corporation are liable for the debts incurred to the same extent and in the same manner as if they were carrying on the business of the corporation as a partnership or, if there is a sole shareholder, to the same extent as a sole practitioner.[5]

Both Alberta and British Columbia require that all issued voting shares of the law corporation be vested in one or more barristers or solicitors who are active members of the respective law societies. Non-lawyers generally cannot hold equity in the corporation unless they fall within the classes of individuals related to a voting shareholder, such as the spouse, common-law spouse or child, who are specifically listed in Section 127 (3)(f)(ii) and (iii) of Alberta's Legal Profession Act and Section 82(1)(c) of British Columbia's Legal Profession Act, SBC, 1987, chapter 25. Most provincial law societies have set up committees to study the issue of legal corporations, and many are actively lobbying for the adoption of such legislation. In fact, the province of Ontario has tabled an act enabling law firms to incorporate, which has yet to be brought into force.

CAPACITIES OF A LAWYER

There no longer exists any distinction between the terms "barrister", "solicitor" and "attorney" in Canada. These terms are now essentially synonymous with the term "lawyer".

3. Civil Code of Quebec, Article 2221.

4. See Alberta's Legal Profession Act 1990, chapter L–9.1, Sections 125 *et seq.*; British Columbia's Legal Profession Act SBC 1987, chapter 25, Sections 80 *et seq.*

5. Alberta's Legal Profession Act, Section 129(1); British Columbia's Legal Profession Act, Section 85(1).

Several provinces have enacted legislation to define those activities that are the exclusive domain of a lawyer. These activities or functions include the following: appearing as counsel or advocate representing clients and pleading cases in court, drafting judicial proceedings, petitions, legal memoranda, wills, settlement deeds, trust deeds and other legal documents, providing legal advice and negotiating an offer for the settlement of a claim.

There are also certain activities or professions that are or under certain circumstances may be, incompatible with the practice of law. Without enumerating those activities or professions that are incompatible, the Canadian Bar Association's Code of Professional Conduct contains the following general guideline:

"The lawyer who engages in another profession, business or occupation concurrently with the practice of law must not allow such outside interest to jeopardise the lawyer's professional integrity, independence or competence."

Unlike the Canadian Bar Association code, Quebec's Code of Ethics of Advocates[6] provides a list, albeit unexhaustive, of professions that it deems to be incompatible with the legal profession. These include legal stenographer, bailiff, police officer, collection agent, and full-time judicial officer.

It is also prohibited in the province of Quebec for a lawyer to act as a notary. The distinction between the legal and notarial professions is unique to the province of Quebec. The principal functions of a notary, which is not to be confused with the notary public of the Common Law provinces, are to draft and execute deeds and to maintain a registry of these documents. The notary, like the lawyer, can offer legal advice and draft agreements. However, unlike lawyers, notaries are prohibited from appearing or pleading before the courts in contested matters.

DUTIES

In general, the duties of a lawyer stem from the lawyer-client relationship and are governed by the civil law of each province. The lawyer-client relationship is governed by the rules of mandate in the province of Quebec and the retainer in the Common Law provinces.

The courts across Canada have also referred to the various codes of conduct adopted by provincial bar associations to determine the duties of a lawyer. As was stated above, these codes do not have force of law, except in the province of Quebec, but the rules set out therein nonetheless provide guidelines for conduct and assist the courts in setting the requisite standard of care.

6. RRQ, chapter B–1, r–1.

Yet another source of lawyers' duties is the case law of the courts. Several recent cases have extended the duties and responsibilities of a lawyer beyond the strict letter of the law.[7] In the case of *Location Panorama Inc.* v. *Gaucher*,[8] a lawyer was held liable in damages for having proceeded with the sale of a seized item despite her knowledge that it did not belong to her client's debtor. While the Court recognised that the lawyer had conformed to the letter of the law in carrying out the seizure and sale, it nonetheless concluded that she committed a fault not in the execution of her mandate but in the more general context of her role as an officer of the Court.

The case law has also been the source of lawyers' duties and obligations with respect to third persons. It is now well established in Canada that a lawyer may incur liability to third persons who rely on his or her special skills or knowledge,[9] to whom she or he owes fiduciary obligations,[10] or who are in a position of sufficiently close proximity that in the reasonable contemplation of the lawyer, the lawyer's carelessness could result in damage to the third party.[11]

STANDARD OF CARE

The standard of care to which a lawyer is held was one of the principal issues dealt with by the Supreme Court in the case of *Central Trust Co.* v. *Rafuse.*[12] LeDain, J writing for the Court in Rafuse, described the standard in the following terms:

"A solicitor is required to bring reasonable care, skill, and knowledge to the professional service that he has undertaken. The requisite standard of care has been variously referred to as that of the reasonably competent solicitor, the ordinary competent solicitor, and the prudent solicitor."[13]

What constitutes reasonable care, skill and knowledge will depend on the particular professional competence at issue. In order to determine the standard of reasonableness against which a lawyer's error is to be measured, the courts have traditionally referred to expert testimony and other objective indications as to the state of the practice of law at the time the error was committed.[14]

7. *Bellavance* v. *2838206 Canada Inc.* (1994) LPJ–94–4287 (Que.Sup.Ct.); *Desfosses* v. *Caisse populaire de Macamic*, 18 June 1992; Rouyn-Noranda, 600–02–00242–910 (Court of Quebec) JE92–1194.

8. [1991] RJQ 1237 (Que. CA).

9. *Hedley Byrne & Co. Ltd.* v. *Heller & Partners Ltd.* [1964] AC 465 (HL).

10. *Tracy et al* v. *Atkins* (1977) 83 DLR (3d) 46 (BCSC).

11. *Peake* v. *Vernon & Thompson* (1990) 49 BCLR (2d) 245.

12. [1986] 2 SCR 147.

13. [1986] 2 SCR 147, at p. 208.

14. *Gauthier* v. *Leclerc* (1 November 1985) Quebec 200-09-000751-831 (Que. CA).

In 1991, the Supreme Court, in the case of *Dorion* v. *Roberge*,[15] extended the notion of "reasonable competence" beyond common professional practice. To avoid liability, the common practice itself must be seen by the court to be demonstrably reasonable. While the error at issue in the *Dorion* decision was that of a notary and not a lawyer, there is little justification for not extending the principal to lawyers as well as to other professionals. In fact, the *Dorion* decision has been cited in cases involving lawyers' liability both in Quebec as well as in the Common Law provinces.[16]

In general, therefore, it can be said that the standard of care expected of a lawyer in any given situation is relative to the state of common practice, as long as that practice can be demonstrated to be reasonable. Generally, the obligation is one of means and not of result. However, it is to be noted that, in certain situations, the lawyer may have an obligation of result as opposed to means.[17]

CIVIL LIABILITY

Bases

Contract

As stated above, the duties of a lawyer stem principally from the contract with the client — the mandate in Civil Law or the retainer at Common Law. This contract imposes on a lawyer the obligation to exercise reasonable diligence and care. It is the breach of this obligation that is most often the basis on which a lawyer's liability will be incurred.

Tort or delict

Following the decision of the House of Lords in *Anns* v. *Merton London Borough Council*,[18] it is now a well-established principle of Canadian Law that a duty of care exists by virtue of a sufficient relationship of proximity that is independent of contract.[19] Torts have traditionally been the basis of liability for damage caused to third parties. However, in

15. [1991]1 SCR 374.

16. See *Marcotte* v. *Simard* [1992] RRA 226 (Que.Sup.Ct.) and *Gauvreau* v. *Paci* [1993] O.J. Number 1429 (Ont.CJ).

17. *Wilson* v. *Rowswell* [1970] SCR 865; Civil Code of Quebec, Article 2100.

18. [1978] AC 728 (HL).

19. *Whittingham* v. *Crease & Co.* (1978) 88 DLR (3d) 353 (BCSC) and *Heath* v. *Ivens McGuire Souch & Ottho* [1991] 6 WWR 201 (BCSC).

Rafuse, the Supreme Court established that there exists concurrent liability in contract and tort for acts committed in the context of the lawyer-client relationship. In *Rafuse*, the plaintiff engaged the defendant attorneys to give an opinion as to the validity of a mortgage. The plaintiff advanced funds based on the opinion of the attorneys that the mortgage was valid. The mortgage was found to be void and the plaintiff's security was worthless. The plaintiffs' claim in damages was prescribed, or time-barred, if based on the contract, but timely if based in tort.

The Court held that the duty of care created by sufficient proximity is not restricted to relationships arising in the absence of a contract. This duty of care exists independently of the obligations or duties set out in the contract. The Court cautioned, however, that concurrent liability in tort cannot be relied on to circumvent the operation of a contractual clause limiting or excluding the attorney's liability.[20]

It should be noted that while the rules contained in the various ethical codes applicable to lawyers are used as an indication or point of reference for determining the standard of care in a given situation,[21] they are not a separate or distinct basis on which civil liability can be based.

Fiduciary duty

A lawyer's fiduciary duties, which can form the basis of liability to clients, former clients and third parties, exist independently of his or her duties in tort and in contract. McLachlin, J, in *Canson Enterprises Ltd.* v. *Boughton & Co.*,[22] examines the fiduciary relationship as a basis for liability, with contract and tort:

> "In negligence and contract the parties are taken as independent and equal actors, concerned primarily with their own self-interest. Consequently the law seeks a balance between enforcing obligations by awarding compensation and preserving optimum freedom for those involved in the relationship in question, communal or otherwise. The essence of a fiduciary relationship, by contrast, is that one party pledges herself to act in the best interest of the other. The fiduciary relationship has trust, not self-interest, at its core, and when breach occurs, the balance favours the person wronged".

A lawyer may incur liability based on a breach of his or her fiduciary duties in many different ways, for example: representing clients with

20. *Rafuse* [1986] 2 SCR 147, at p. 206.

21. See, for example, *Marcotte* v. *Simard* [1992] RRA 226 (Que.Sup.Ct.); *McKay* v. *Cowan*, 39 BCLR (2d) 192 (BCSC).

22. [1992]1 WWR 245 (SCC), at p. 272.

opposing interests;[23] failing to disclose material facts to clients;[24] failing to disclose a conflict of interest;[25] misappropriating funds;[26] and breaching the duty of client confidentiality.[27]

Damages recoverable

Generally, the damages for which a lawyer is held liable in professional negligence suits are compensatory in nature. They can be either pecuniary or non-pecuniary. The principle behind compensatory damages, whether in Civil or Common Law, is that the injured party should be placed in the position he or she would have been in had the injurious act not been committed. While there are certain distinctions between the factors that are taken into consideration in determining damages in tort as opposed to contract, these distinctions are gradually disappearing[28] and have little practical effect on damage awards.

Apart from being ordered to pay compensatory damages in a civil suit, the negligent or abusive conduct of a lawyer can also be sanctioned by an order to pay court costs[29] or exemplary damages.[30]

Third party liability

It is well established in the Common Law provinces that a lawyer owes a duty of care toward persons with whom he or she may have neither a contractual nor a fiduciary relationship.

Following the decision of the House of Lords in *Hedley Byrne & Co. Ltd.* v. *Heller & Partners Ltd.*, the courts in the Common Law provinces have consistently held that where a third party reasonably relies on a lawyer's special skill and knowledge, the lawyer is liable to that person for the loss that may result from his or her carelessness or negligence.[31]

23. *Nadeau* v. *Rice* (1990) 109 NBR (2d) 243.

24. *Canson Enterprises Ltd.* v. *Boughton & Co.* [1992]1 WWR 245 (SCC); *Korz* v. *St. Pierre* (1987) 43 DLR (4th) 528 (Ont.CA).

25. *MacCulloch* v. *Corbett* (1982) 133 DLR (3d) 43 (NSCA).

26. *McKay* v. *Cowan*, 39 BCLR (2d) 192 (BCSC).

27. *Ott* v. *Fleishman* [1983] 5 WWR 721 (BCSC).

28. Grant and Rothstein, *Lawyers' Professional Liability* (Toronto, 1989) at p. 83.

29. *L* v. *G* [1982]CS578, Droit de la Famille -1777 [1993] RJQ 1176 (Que.Sup.Ct.) on appeal; *Pacific Mobile Corp.* v. *Hunter Douglas Canada Ltd.* [1979]1 SCR 842; *Evans* v. *Savarin Ltd.* (1980) 109 DLR (3d) 510 (Ont.HC); *O'Neil* v. *Pacific Great Eastern Railway* (1971) 24 DLR (3d) 628 (BCCA).

30. *Guay* v. *La Société franco-manitobaine* (1985) 37 Man.R (2d) 16 (Man.QB).

31. *Tracy et al.* v. *Atkins* (1977) 83 DLR (3d) 46 (BCSC); *Dorndorf* v. *Hoeter* (1981) 122 DLR (3d) 758 (BCSC) *392980 Ont. Ltd.* v. *Welland* (1984) 6 DLR (4th) 151 (Ont.HC).

Several decisions have held that the third party need not necessarily rely on the lawyer in order for liability to be incurred.[32]

In the province of Quebec, it is unclear whether the principles set out in *Hedley Byrne* apply.[33] However, in the recent case of *Kovalik* v. *Laidley*,[34] which concerned the liability of an accountant and is presently on appeal, the Superior Court concluded as follows:

"According to the law of Quebec, as elsewhere in Canada, a person whether a stockbroker, chartered accountant or other professional who accepts to give advice to a client or customer concerning the purchase of an investment, owes to the latter the duty of doing so carefully, completely, honestly and in good faith. If he fails to conform to that standard, he may be held to reimburse to the person who relied on that advice any losses that were incurred as a result of the purchase of the investment."[35]

It would seem, therefore, that even if the principles set out in *Hedley Byrne* do not apply as they would in a Common Law province, the applicable rules of civil liability in Quebec would lead to the same basic conclusions.

The test set out in *Anns* broadens the principle established in *Hedley Byrne* and treats it as an application of a general principle of liability in tort for negligence based on the breach of a duty of care arising from a relationship of sufficient proximity. The *Anns* test was approved by the Supreme Court in the case of *Barratt* v. *North Vancouver*,[36] and has been applied to decisions regarding lawyers' liability.[37]

SPECIFIC CIVIL LIABILITIES

A number of specific areas of conduct in which lawyers are most often held liable can be identified. They include litigation conduct (from institution through to settlement) conflicts of interest and, broadly, "commercial transactions".

Litigation conduct

The litigation process is inherently risky and offers little in the way of guarantees. It is an area of practice in which lawyers must routinely make

32. *Whittingham* v. *Crease & Co.* (1978) 88 DLR (3d) 353 (BCSC); *Heath* v. *Ivens McGuire Souch & Ottho* [1991] 6 WWR 201 (BCSC).

33. *Caisse Populaire de Charlesbourg* v. *Michaud* [1990] RRA 531 (Que. CA).

34. [1992] RRA 501 (Que. SC).

35. *Kovalik* v. *Laidley* [1992] RRA 501 (Que. SC), at p. 506.

36. [1980] 2 SCR 418.

37. *Tracy et al.* v. *Atkins* (1977) 83 DLR (3d) 46 (BCSC); *Peake* v. *Vernon & Thompson* (1990) 49 BCLR (2d) 245.

decisions regarding, among other things, chances of success, choice of recourse, choice of defendant, evaluation of quantum, and the limitation period or period of prescription.

Instituting proceedings

One of the most common examples of negligent litigation conduct involves the failure to institute legal proceedings within the time limitation or prescription period.[38] The case of *St-Onge* v. *Pelletier*[39] is a rather remarkable example of this situation in that it involves two attorneys neglecting the prescription period for the same client in two separate actions.

In the *St-Onge* case, the plaintiff initially consulted his lawyer to pursue a claim against the driver of an automobile who caused injuries to his wife and children. His lawyer told him to come back to see him after his wife's operation. Following these instructions, the plaintiff again consulted his lawyer after the operation, only to discover that his claim was now time-barred. The plaintiff then retained the defendant to sue the first lawyer. The defendant neglected to institute the claim against the first lawyer within the required delay with the result that it, too, was time-barred. The Court held that both lawyers were negligent in failing to commence their respective actions within the proper delays. The defendant, the second lawyer, was held solely liable for the loss that could have been recovered had the initial suit been properly instituted.

Nevertheless, the failure to institute proceedings within the legal delays does not necessarily give rise to damages. In the case of *Band R Farms* v. *Ulmer*,[40] the defendant lawyer was found to be negligent in failing to institute plaintiff's claim under an insurance policy within the limitation period. However, the action was dismissed because the damages sought by plaintiff were not covered by his insurance policy. Similarly, in the case of *Pound* v. *Nakonechn y Busch & Heinrich*,[41] despite finding that the defendant attorneys were negligent in failing to institute plaintiff's claim in tort within the limitation period, the Court nonetheless dismissed the action in damages against the lawyers since the plaintiff still had a contractual recourse against the author of his damages.

Thus, in order to award damages against a lawyer for failing to institute proceedings within the proper delays, the Court must be satisfied

38. See *Temple du Réveil Miraculeux du St-Esprit Inc.* v. *Pion* [1991] RRA 230 (Court of Quebec); *Fyk* v. *Millar* (1973) 41 DLR (3d) 684 (Ont.HC); *Collins* v. *Weninger* [1983] 6 WWR 742 (Sask.QB).

39. (1986) 67 NBR (2d) 399 (NBQB).

40. (1987) 55 Sask. R 309 (Sask.QB).

41. (1983) 5 DLR (4th) 427 (Sask.CA).

that there exists a probability that the forfeited claim would have succeeded. It is not necessary for the plaintiff client to show that the action would in fact have succeeded, as this would impose a greater burden than would otherwise exist in a civil action.[42]

Settlement of actions

A lawyer may incur liability in recommending or failing to recommend a particular settlement. Generally, however, where a lawyer exercises reasonable diligence in reviewing the evidence as well as the state of the law in arriving at a recommendation, no negligence will be found. In the case of *Maillet and Palmer* v. *Haliburton and Comeau*,[43] the plaintiff had been awarded Can. $75,000 as damages for personal injuries in first instance. The judgement was appealed and the defendant lawyer advised his client to accept to settle her claim for the sum of Can. $40,000, which she did. The court examined the defendant lawyer's conduct prior to recommending the settlement and determined that he had adequately researched awards in similar cases and had properly instructed his client regarding the risks, costs and delay on appeal. The court dismissed the malpractice suit, concluding that the lawyer was not negligent in recommending acceptance of the settlement by his client. In reaching its decision, the Court referred to *Karpenko* v. *Paroian Courey Cohen & Houston*,[44] which sets a seemingly less rigorous standard of care in regard to settlements than in other areas of practice.[45]

On the other hand, where the preparation and review conducted by a lawyer prior to recommending a settlement is not adequate, the courts will not hesitate to find negligence. In the case of *Workers' Compensation Board* v. *Riggins*,[46] a badly injured worker retained a lawyer to represent him in his injury claim. The worker accepted to settle his claim for Can. $70,000.00 on the advice of his lawyer. However, the lawyer failed to review the current cases on damages, to consider all proper heads of damage and to assess the value of the claim including past lost income, the cost of future care and pre-judgement interest. The lawyer's conduct was held to be negligent both under the implied terms of the contract and in tort. The measure of damages awarded was the difference between the settlement arrived at and the court's assessment of damages. A similar

42. *Fyk* v. *Millar* (1973) 41 DLR (3d) 684 (Ont.HC); *Marcotte* v. *Simard* [1992] RRA 226 (Que.Sup.Ct.); and *Temple du Réveil Miraculeux du St-Esprit Inc.* v. *Pion* [1991] RRA 230 (Court of Quebec).

43. (1983) 55 NSR (2d) (NSSC).

44. (1980) 30 OR (2d) 776 (Ont.HC).

45. See Grant and Rothstein, *Lawyers' Professional Liability* (Toronto, 1989) at p. 67.

46. (1990) 75 Alta. LR 13 (Alta.QB).

decision was reached in the case of *Fawell* v. *Atkins*,[47] on the basis of the lawyer's failure to interview an important witness before recommending settlement.

Trial preparation and presentation

Unlike the traditional "barrister immunity rule" in England and Wales,[48] attorneys in Canada do not benefit from immunity for negligent preparation or presentation of a court case.[49] However, just as in the assessment of the reasonableness of a proposed settlement agreement, the courts are reluctant to substitute their judgement for that of a lawyer who has conducted himself reasonably in the preparation and presentation of his case.[50]

There are, of course, numerous decisions in which the lawyer's conduct in preparing or presenting his client's case has been found to be negligent. One such case is that of *World Wide Treasure Adventures Inc.* v. *Trivia Games Inc.*[51] In that case, a lawyer prepared an application for injunction which was dismissed because the affidavit in support of the application "was so hopelessly deficient".[52] The lawyer was found liable because he completely ignored the clear position of the Supreme Court in applications such as the one at issue, which, the Court held, ought to be part of the working knowledge of competent counsel.

A number of recent decisions suggest that a lawyer can be condemned to pay damages even if his or her conduct is not in violation of the mandate or the strict letter of the law. In the case of *Location Panorama Inc.* v. *Gaucher*,[53] a lawyer seized a truck in the exercise of her client's rights as creditor. Despite her knowledge that the truck had been leased and that it, therefore, did not belong to her client's debtor, the lawyer, who had received no opposition from the truck's true owner, proceeded to have the truck sold. The Quebec Court of Appeal held that the lawyer had committed a civil fault, not in the exercise of her mandate, but in the wider context of her role in the administration of justice. The Court

47. (1981) 28 BCLR, 32 (BCSC).

48. Grant and Rothstein, *Lawyers' Professional Liability* (Toronto, 1989), at p. 8; See also *Rondel* v. *Worsley* [1969] 1 AC 191, where the limited immunity rule was established.

49. *Demarco* v. *Ungaro* (1979) 95 DLR (3d) 385 (Ont.HC); *Karpenko* v. *Paroian Courey Cohen & Houston* (1980) 30 OR (2d) 776 (Ont.HC).

50. *Wechsel* v. *Stutz* (1980) 15 CCLT 132 (Ont.Co.Ct.).

51. (1987) 16 BCLR (2d) 135 (BCSC).

52. *World Wide Treasure Adventures Inc.* v. *Trivia Games Inc.* (1987) 16 BCLR (2d) 135 (BCSC), at p. 138.

53. [1991] RJQ 1237 (Que.CA).

further held that the strict observance of the rules of procedure did not exonerate the lawyer from her responsibility for the consequences of her improper conduct. The lawyer was condemned to pay damages.

The Courts have demonstrated on numerous occasions that a client cannot hold his lawyer responsible for actions that were either guided by the client or based on information provided by the client. A lawyer who relies on his or her client to provide information in the preparation of the case is not necessarily negligent if the client loses his right of action due to errors in the information he himself provided, even though the lawyer could have detected the error.[54] Similarly, in the case of *Girardet* v. *Crease & Co.*,[55] it was held that even though the defendant lawyer did not conduct himself as a "first-rate solicitor" in explaining his advice repeatedly in order to ensure that his client understood, he was nonetheless not liable for damages. However, where the lawyer leaves important decisions to the client or where he or she fails to properly advise the client, it is unlikely that the lawyer could avoid liability for the resulting error.[56]

Conflicts of interest

In the case of *MacDonald Estate* v. *Martin*,[57] the Supreme Court analysed the notion of conflict of interest with respect to lawyers. In this case, the appellant was represented by an attorney who was assisted by a graduate articled student. Two years later, the student became a junior lawyer at the firm representing the respondent, and the appellant brought a motion for a declaration that the respondent's law firm was ineligible to continue to act for the respondent, because of the junior's conflict of interest.

The Court held that in order to determine whether there exists a conflict of interest in a particular case, three competing values must be weighed, namely: maintaining the high standards of the legal profession and the integrity of the justice system; the concern that a litigant ought not to be deprived of his or her counsel of choice without good cause; and the desirability of permitting reasonable mobility in the legal profession. The test set out by the Court to determine whether or not a conflict of interest exists is that a reasonably informed person must be satisfied that no use of confidential information would result.

54. *Duncan* v. *Cuelenaere Beaubier Walters Kendal & Fisher* [1987] 2 WWR 379 (Sask.QB).

55. (1987) 11 BCLR (2d) 361 (BCSC).

56. Grant and Rothstein, *Lawyers' Professional Liability* (Toronto, 1989), at p. 68.

57. [1990] 3 SCR 1235.

To apply this test, the Court asks the following two questions:

(1) Did the lawyer receive confidential information attributable to a solicitor-and-client relationship relevant to the matter at hand?
(2) Is there a risk that it will be used to the prejudice of the client?[58]

In the *MacDonald Estate* case, the Court answered the first question in the affirmative. On the second question, the Court concluded that there was insufficient evidence that measures, specifically "independently verifiable" measures, were taken to rebut the strong inference of disclosure. The test set out in the *MacDonald Estate* decision has been applied numerous times across Canada.[59]

Apart from being forced to withdraw from the file in which he or she is in conflict, a lawyer can also incur his or her liability as a result of a conflict of interest. This was the case in *Nadeau* v. *Rice*,[60] where the New Brunswick Court of Appeal equated representing two clients with opposing interests with a breach of fiduciary duty. The offending lawyer in *Nadeau* was held liable to one of his clients for the value of a claim that had been time-barred as a direct result of his conflict of interest.

Commercial transactions

The term "commercial transaction" covers an extremely wide range of services that a lawyer may be called on to provide, including real estate law, drafting of commercial contracts and other agreements, incorporation of companies, registration of documents and the drafting of opinions.

Apart from the standard obligations and duties of all lawyers, real estate lawyers have a particular duty to advise and inform their clients on relevant aspects of title. Where a lawyer fails to advise a client that the property he is purchasing is subject to a registered right of way, this will constitute a breach of duty and expose the lawyer to damages.[61] The same is true where the lawyer fails to advise his client that the land he is purchasing does not include all the parcels described in the deed of sale[62] or

58. *MacDonald Estate* v. *Martin* [1990] 3 SCR 1235, at p. 1267

59. See *APV Pavailler Inc.* v. *Bonischot* (21 Februayr 1992 Montreal 500–09–000999–912, JE92–717 (Que.CA); *Everingham* v. *Ontario* (1992) 88 DLR (4th) 755 (Ont.Ct.Gen.Div.); *Calgas Investments Ltd* v. *784688 Ontario Ltd.* (1991) 81 DLR (4th) 518 (Ont.Ct.Gen.Div.).

60. (1990) 109 NBR (2d) 243 (NBCA).

61. *Moorcraft* v. *Doraty & Kebe* (1990) 71 OR (2d) 470 (Ont.HC).

62. *Spencer* v. *King and Mockler Allen & Dixon* (1991)119 NBR (2d) 358 (NBCA).

where the description of the land to be purchased is improper.[63] A lawyer will also be responsible for failing to ascertain that a mortgage is invalid, as was the case in *Rafuse*.[64]

The basis of many commercial transactions is the contract or agreement between the parties, which, more often than not, will be drafted by a lawyer. Where a lawyer fails to translate the wishes of a client into the document he drafts, he may be held responsible for the damages his client suffers as a result of this failure.

In *Elcano Acceptance Ltd.* v. *Richmond et al.*[65] a lawyer failed to include in the promissory notes he was mandated to prepare, an express statement of the applicable yearly rate or percentage of interest. As a result, the client was unable to recover from his debtor a portion of the interest that would otherwise have been owing. The Ontario Court of Appeal held that even though the error at issue was isolated in the context of the lawyer's overall practice, this fact could not exclude him from liability.

A similar conclusion was reached in the case of *Davies and Davies* v. *Fiddes*[66] where a lawyer failed to include a "best efforts" clause in an agreement of sale despite his client's clear instructions to that effect. The Court held that the lawyer had breached his obligation to exercise reasonable care but dismissed the action on the basis that the breach did not cause the loss at issue. Finally, in the case of *Jacobson Ford-Mercury Sales Ltd.* v. *Sivertz*, a lawyer who had undertaken to prepare a lease with purchase option was held liable in damages to the client because the option was found unenforceable.[67]

Certain tasks that a lawyer involved in commercial transactions may be called on to perform require only minimal skill, but can be of great significance to the transaction. Where a lawyer undertakes to register mortgage documents before a certain date and fails to do so, he is potentially liable in damages not only to his client but to any party to the transaction who, in the reasonable contemplation of the lawyer, could likely suffer damage as a result of his carelessness.[68] Similarly, where a lawyer fails to incorporate a company in accordance with the instructions of his client, he is liable for the resulting inconvenience and aggravation as well as the costs of remedying the deficiencies.[69]

63. *Knox* v. *Veinote* (1982) 54 NSR (2d) 666 (NSSC); *Bank of Montreal* v. *Chedore* (1985) 63 NBR (2d) 361 (NBQB).

64. [1986] 2 SCR 147.

65. (1985) 47 CPC 256, 31 CCLT 201 (Ont.HC) rev'd 55 OR (2d) 56, 9 CPC (2d) 260 (CA).

66. (1989) 34 BCLR (2d) 137 (BCCA).

67. [1980] 1 WWR 141 (BCSC).

68. *Peake* v. *Vernon & Thompson* (1990) 49 BCLR (2d) 245.

69. *PA Wournell Contracting* v. *Allen* (1979) 100 DLR (3d) 62 (NSSC).

A legal opinion is often requested in the context of a commercial transaction. It is well established that a lawyer is not liable for an opinion that turns out to be wrong as long as he or she was not negligent in its preparation.[70]

It has long been established that a solicitor does not warrant the correctness of his opinion on a question of law where the opinion is honestly founded and given. A solicitor does not undertake to his client not to make mistakes, but only not to make negligent mistakes.[71]

In drafting a legal opinion, the lawyer is not expected to know or to research all the law dealing with the subject at issue. However, the courts have determined that there is an obligation to research all points of law that are relevant to the opinion to be rendered. In *Rafuse*, Le Dain J stated as follows:

"The requirement of professional competence that was particularly involved in this case was reasonable knowledge of the applicable or relevant law. A solicitor is not required to know all the law applicable to the performance of a particular legal service, in the sense that he must carry it around with him as part of his 'working knowledge', without the need of further research, but he must have sufficient knowledge of the fundamental issues or principles of law applicable to the particular work he has undertaken to enable him to perceive the need to ascertain the law on relevant points."[72]

Limitation period (prescription)

The length of the legal delay in which to institute proceedings is governed by Provincial law. In establishing limitation periods, each province distinguishes between actions arising in tort from those based on a contract. The principal distinctions are in the length of the limitation period and the moment at which it begins to run.

In every province except Quebec, the limitation period for a contractual action is six years and begins to run from the time the negligent act was committed. In Quebec, the limitation period is three years and, where the damage does not immediately manifest itself, will commence running from the time the damage first appears.[73] For an action based in tort, the limitation period in every province except Quebec is two years and will

70. Estey, *Legal Opinions in Commercial Transactions* (Toronto, 1990) at p. 279.

71. Sopinka, *Professional Responsibility in Civil and Common Law* (Toronto, 1985), p. 247, at p. 253.

72. *Rafuse* [1986] 2 SCR 147, at p. 147.

73. Civil Code of Quebec, Articles 2925, 2926.

commence from the time the damage was discovered or ought to have been discovered.[74] In Quebec, the limitation period for an action in tort, or delict, is three years and commences from the time the damage first appears.

It should be noted, however, that the distinction between the limitation period in contract and in tort is much less relevant since the *Rafuse* decision: Since it is now established that there is concurrent liability in contract and tort for an action against a lawyer for professional negligence, lawyers cannot invoke a defence of prescription where the contractual action is time-barred but the delictual action is not.

ADMINISTRATIVE LIABILITY

The breach of an ethical rule set out in the various Provincial codes of conduct can result in disciplinary measures being brought against the offending lawyer by the law society. The autonomy and authority of the various law societies to enforce their respective codes of conduct have been strongly confirmed by the courts.[75]

The disciplinary process differs slightly from one province to the next. In general, however, the process commences with an investigation of the allegations, which will generally be brought by a client, a former client or other members of the profession. The investigation will be carried out by a disciplinary committee composed of lawyers who are members of the law society, which will determine whether or not to bring a complaint or charge against the lawyer. If the charge or complaint is authorised, a hearing will take place before a judicial committee, which is also composed of lawyers who are members of the law society, which will decide whether the charge is merited and, if it is, determine the sanction. Sanctions will range from reprimands to disbarment.

As was stated above, only the province of Quebec has given its code of conduct force of law by adopting it as a regulation.[76] In the other provinces the power of the law societies to discipline their members is drawn from their enabling statutes.[77] The language employed in these various statutes is vague and somewhat similar. Essentially, the law societies are given the power to discipline their members for "professional misconduct" and "conduct unbecoming a barrister and solicitor".

74. *Rafuse* [1986] 2 SCR 147 at p. 224; *City of Kamloops* v. *Nielsen* [1984] 2 SCR 2.

75. *Pearlman* v. *Manitoba Law Society Judicial Committee* [1991] 2 SCR 869; *Shaw* v. *Law Society of Prince Edward Island* (1992) 97 DLR (4th) 504 (PEISC).

76. Code of Ethics of Advocates, RRQ, 1981, chapter B–1, r–1.

77. These are listed at the beginning of this chapter.

The following is a list of certain acts that have been found to constitute "professional misconduct":

(1) Misappropriation or misapplication of funds held in trust;
(2) Creating false documents;
(3) Forgery;
(4) Assisting clients in attempting to defraud creditors;
(5) Continuing to act while in a conflict of interest without disclosure or to the detriment of the client;
(6) Attempting to mislead clients or other lawyers;
(7) Making false representations in court;
(8) Practising law while under suspension; and
(9) Failing to maintain books and records as required.[78]

"Conduct unbecoming a barrister or solicitor" is generally used to describe conduct that would, and often does, constitute the basis for criminal charges. Examples include income tax evasion, manslaughter and possession of narcotics for the purposes of trafficking.[79]

INSURANCE

Each province has its own legislation dealing with lawyers' liability insurance. In all provinces, it is compulsory for practising lawyers to hold professional liability insurance. Every province has a group insurance plan that covers the members in good standing of the provincial law societies who practise in that province.

Scope of coverage and obligations

Although there are inevitable differences among the various policies in force in Canada as to scope of coverage, exclusions, premiums, and other issues, certain general principles apply. Typically, all policies foresee the obligation of the insurer to defend all claims for damages made against the lawyer resulting from the rendering of or omission to render professional services. The policies also provide that the insurer must pay all sums that the lawyer is legally obligated to pay pursuant to such claims, up to the policy limit, which varies according to each policy. In Quebec, for instance, the policy limit is currently at Can. $600,000 per claim,

78. Examples drawn from MacKenzie, "Law Society Discipline Proceedings", *The Advocates Society Journal*, July 1992, Vol. 11, Number 2, pp. 3–30 at p. 9.
79. MacKenzie, "Law Society Discipline Proceedings", *The Advocates Society Journal*, July 1992, vol. 11, Number 2, pp. 3–30 at p. 11.

including a CAN. $5,000 deductible, and premiums are set at CAN. $1,200 for all lawyers with more than three years' experience. Supplemental insurance may be obtained privately for coverage over the policy limit of the compulsory insurance plan.

All claims made against the insured during the period where the policy is in force are generally covered by the liability insurance, even if such claims relate to services rendered by the lawyer before the policy came into force. This characteristic sets professional liability insurance apart from other types of damage insurance that operate on an occurrence basis.

To be covered, the lawyer must give notice to the insurer not only of claims made against him, but of any act that may give rise to such a claim. As well, the lawyer must co-operate fully with the insurer in conducting the defence.

Exclusions and limits

The term "professional services" is generally defined in the policies to exclude acts committed by a lawyer acting in his or her capacity as director or officer of a corporation, real-estate broker, or business person, as well as any other activity unrelated to the practise of law. The true nature of the term "professional services" remains, nonetheless, a question of fact to be determined on a claim by claim basis. Policies also have exclusions for fraudulent, dishonest, criminal, and malicious acts and do not cover punitive or exemplary damages.

CONCLUSIONS

The area of lawyers' liability in Canada has seen a number of significant developments in recent years. Most notable are the recent decisions regarding standard of care, liability to third parties, the role of law societies in disciplining their members, conflict of interest, and concurrent liability. Overall, the effect of these numerous recent developments has clearly been to expand the scope of lawyers' liability in Canada.

With the ever-increasing level of dissatisfaction with the quality and cost efficiency of legal services and the growing number of new attorneys across Canada, it is likely that the trend toward expanding the scope of lawyers' administrative and civil liability will continue.

Note: The author would like to express his appreciation for the valuable assistance of his colleagues Dimitra Diplarakos, Pierre-André Hamel, Morrie Hotter, and Martin Latulippe in preparing this chapter.

CHAPTER 4

ENGLAND AND WALES

John Lapraik
Mills & Reeve
Cambridge, England

INTRODUCTION

Types of legal advisers

The legal profession in England and Wales is principally divided between legal advisers who are solicitors and those who are barristers. In broad terms, solicitors will normally deal with clients in the first instance and give general advice. The solicitor will tend to instruct a barrister to advise or act on behalf of a client if either the area of law is specialised or complicated or if the client will require representation in court. There is no geographical limit as to where a solicitor or a barrister may practise within England and Wales.

The historical division between the roles played by the solicitor and the barrister is being eroded. The development and size of some substantial solicitors' practices have allowed those firms to specialise to a much greater degree than in the past to a point where the quality of the advice matches that traditionally available from a specialist barrister. In addition, the barristers' exclusive rights of audience in the higher courts are currently being removed, opening up the possibility of solicitors performing a role as advocates, which was historically limited to the lower, County Courts.

At the same time, barristers, who are all individually self-employed, are moving towards a more "corporate" structure. Chambers, where they practise together, are increasingly seeking to develop a "firm" approach in handling work referred and are also developing the support side, with an increased investment in meeting rooms, secretarial services, etc.

Barristers are now able to accept referrals direct from foreign lawyers and other professional people, such as accountants.

The changing roles of both barristers and solicitors are gradual and, at the time of writing this, the majority of legal work still starts in a solicitor's office and is referred to a barrister for expert advice, the drafting of pleadings, or to provide representation in court.

Professional bodies and regulatory framework

In the case of solicitors' entry into and the conduct of the profession is regulated by the Law Society of England and Wales pursuant to powers conferred by the Solicitors Act 1974.

Section 1 of the Solicitors Act 1974 provides that no person is qualified to act as a solicitor unless:

(1) He has been admitted as a solicitor, which generally involves obtaining a certificate from the Law Society confirming its satisfaction as to the applicant's character and suitability, and the fact that he has complied with the training regulations;
(2) His name is on the roll (a list of all the solicitors of the Supreme Court); and
(3) He holds a current practising certificate issued by the Law Society.

On the grant of a practising certificate, a solicitor will be indemnified by the Solicitors Indemnity Fund Limited in respect of claims made arising out of his practice as a solicitor. The current limit of indemnity is £1-million

The conduct of the profession is further regulated by the issue of rules by the Law Society made under the authority of The Solicitors Act 1974. The rules relate to matters such as a solicitor's financial dealings, professional practice, conduct and discipline of solicitors. Additionally the Council of the Law Society has the power, under Section 35 of the Solicitors Act 1974 to intervene in a solicitor's practice in certain circumstances — for example, a failure to comply with the Solicitors Accounts Rules.

The conduct of barristers is regulated by the General Council of the Bar of England and Wales. This has primarily been through codes of conduct intended to provide the standards of conduct on the part of barristers that are appropriate in the interests of justice and in relation to barristers in independent practice to provide common and enforceable requirements and prohibitions.

The introduction of the Courts and Legal Services Act 1990 has, however, introduced a degree of statutory control on aspects of the barristers' practice. Rule 301 of The Code of Conduct of the Bar of England and Wales 1990 requires that a barrister who wishes to practise independently as such must hold the requisite qualifications, have completed the appropriate periods of training, and be indemnified by the Bar Mutual Indemnity Fund Limited in respect of claims made against him and have paid his subscription to the Bar Council.

Disciplinary control

Solicitors

In the case of solicitors this is exercised through the Solicitors Disciplinary Tribunal. It is made up of solicitors and lay members. Its function is to determine complaints relating to alleged breaches of the Solicitors Act 1974 or general professional misconduct. Complaints may be made by anyone, although most are made on behalf of the Law Society, which acts as the monitor of the profession.

Section 47 of the Solicitors Act 1974 entitles the Tribunal to make such Orders as it thinks fit, which can range from the striking off of solicitors to, in less serious cases, a fine and orders for payment of costs.

Barristers

In the case of barristers, the Code of Conduct of the Bar sets out the duties which a barrister in independent practice must observe. It also sets out the obligations laid down in statutes, regulations and codes that must be complied with and the fact that failure to comply will constitute professional misconduct rendering him liable to disciplinary proceedings.

Any complaints whether by the Bar Council or otherwise are investigated by the Professional Conduct Committee. It has powers to deal summarily with charges of professional misconduct by means of a summary hearing panel. In more serious cases, it will refer matters to a Disciplinary Tribunal, which has wider powers including the ability to disbar a barrister from practising.

The courts

The courts also exercise disciplinary control over the solicitors' profession. Generally, Solicitors' Disciplinary Tribunal Orders may be appealed to the Courts.[1] The option of issuing proceedings in the Courts, rather than referring a matter to the Solicitors' Disciplinary Tribunal, is also conferred by the Act, in certain circumstances, as under Section 41 (where a solicitor employs someone who has been struck off or suspended).

The courts' inherent jurisdiction to make orders in respect of solicitors' misconduct is also preserved by the Act although, generally, the courts have not shown any desire to intervene.

1. Solicitors Act 1974, Section 49(1).

PRACTICE STRUCTURES

Solicitors

Private practice

Solicitors may practise as sole practitioners or in partnership with other solicitors. A sole practitioner or a minimum of one partner must have been admitted for at least three years to satisfy rule 13 of the Solicitors Practice Rules 1990. The Courts and Legal Services Act 1990 removed the prohibition on solicitors practising with non-solicitors. This is, however, subject to the rules of the Law Society and rule 7 of the Solicitors Practice Rules 1990 (which deal with fee sharing) prohibit solicitors entering into partnership, in England and Wales, with a non-solicitor. This originally prevented foreign lawyers from practising in partnership, in England and Wales, with solicitors. It is now possible, by virtue of the Multi-National Practice Rules 1991, to practise in partnership in England and Wales with a practising foreign lawyer where the foreign lawyer has registered with the Law Society as a registered foreign lawyer.

The Solicitors Overseas Practice Rules 1990 entitle solicitors practising outside England and Wales to enter into partnership with lawyers from other jurisdictions or members of the Bar of England and Wales, subject to compliance with those rules, any relevant overseas laws or rules of conduct and to the extent permitted by the Bar.

Professional corporations

The Solicitors Incorporated Practice Rules 1988 will allow solicitors to incorporate all or part of a practice (in accordance with the rules). The date the rules will come into operation has yet to be specified. The rules will apply to the overseas office of an incorporated firm having its registered office and place of business in England and Wales as much as to that part of the firm practising within the jurisdiction.

The rules do not apply to practices operating solely outside England and Wales. Solicitors practising solely outside England and Wales may incorporate provided they comply with the Solicitors Overseas Practice Rules 1990 and local law. Rule 9 of the Solicitors Overseas Practice Rules prohibits solicitors from practising in corporate form unless:

(1) All directors and shareholders are solicitors, members of the Bar of England and Wales (acting in accordance with the Overseas Practice Rules) or practising lawyers of another jurisdiction; or
(2) Permitted by rule 7 (which deals with solicitors employed by non-lawyers).

Miscellaneous

Solicitors may also be employed by lay employers, including non-commercial organisations. Subject to a few exceptions, a solicitor employed by a lay employer shall not, as part of his employment, do for anyone (save that employer) work that is or could be done by a solicitor acting as such.[2]

Barristers

Rule 207 of the Code of Conduct of the Bar of England and Wales 1990 prohibits a practising barrister from entering into a professional partnership with another barrister and prohibits a professional partnership or association with non-barristers.

Rule 301(d) of the Code prevents a barrister (unless he has obtained a waiver from the Bar Council) who has practised for less than three years in independent practice since the conclusion of 12 months pupillage from practising other than from a library designated by the Bar Council or from chambers, at least one member of which has had no less than five years' experience in independent practice since the conclusion of 12 months' pupillage.

Barristers may also be employed (so long as they comply with specified requirements). Employment can range from contracts with companies, to public authorities, to the holding of an office under the Crown, or in the institutions of the European Community.

Barristers may also provide certain legal services at, or be employed by, Law Centres or Legal Advice Centres (as defined in the Code of Conduct of the Bar of England and Wales) subject to the compliance with the Law Centres and Legal Advice Centres Rules and the Code (unless the rules otherwise provide). These rules allow barristers to supply some legal services on behalf of clients without the instructions of a solicitor.

The Overseas Practice Rules also entitle practising barristers to employ outside the United Kingdom any person who is not a solicitor practising in England and Wales and to enter into any association (including partnership) with any lawyer other than with a solicitor practising in the United Kingdom for the purpose of sharing offices or services outside the United Kingdom or any fees relating to work permitted by those rules. The Foreign Lawyers (Chambers) Rules permit foreign lawyers practising as such outside the United Kingdom to use chambers for professional purposes subject to compliance with those rules.

2. Solicitors Practice Rules 1990, Rule 4.

GENERAL CAPACITIES

Solicitors

Subject to limited exceptions (which include barristers) only solicitors may perform the functions specified in Sections 22 and 23 of the Solicitors Act 1974 "in expectation of a fee, gain or reward". These functions include the preparation of documents relating to land, and papers for probate.

Registration of foreign lawyers with the law society does not authorise that lawyer to perform such functions.

Barristers

The Code of Conduct of the Bar of England and Wales refers primarily to the supply by barristers of legal services. These are defined (in Rule 901) to include "legal advice, representation and drafting or settling of any originating process, pleading, affidavit, witness statement or other document".

The Written Standards for the Code of Professional work — General Standards refers to "advocacy, drafting pleadings and other legal documents and advising on questions of law" as work within the ordinary scope of a barrister's practice.

Barristers once had almost exclusive rights of audience before the higher courts: the House of Lords, Court of Appeal, High Court and Crown Court. The Courts & Legal Services Act 1990 is eroding these rights.

A major difference between the professions is that barristers in independent practice may only accept instructions from a professional client. This is usually a solicitor but does now extend to other professionals including foreign lawyers.[3]

DUTIES

Statute and statutory rules

The Solicitors Act 1974 is the principal statute affecting solicitors. Various rules have been made, pursuant to that Act, which are also relevant. These include the Solicitors' Practice Rules 1990 and their related codes, for example, the Solicitors' Publicity Code 1990, the Solicitors' Introduction and Referral Code 1990 and the Employed Solicitors' Code 1990. There are also the Solicitors' Overseas Practice Rules 1990 regulating solicitors practising overseas. Finally, there are rules that regulate solicitors'

3. Code of Conduct of the Bar of England and Wales, Rule 210.

financial dealings including the Solicitors' Accounts Rules 1991 and the Accountant's Report Rules 1991. Other relevant statutes include the Financial Services Act 1986. This Act places controls on those who provide financial services in the course of a business. The effect is that virtually every private solicitor now requires authorisation under the Act. The Law Society is able to issue such authorisation to the majority of solicitors.

In the case of barristers, there is no equivalent statute to the Solicitors Act. The Code of Conduct of the Bar of England and Wales 1990 requires that barristers comply with the Legal Aid Act of 1988 and any regulations to give effect to or prevent abuses of that Act, plus the Courts and Legal Services Act 1990, and any orders or regulations made pursuant to that Act or powers conferred by it. In addition to requiring compliance with certain statutes Rule 802.1 of the Code of Conduct of the Bar of England and Wales 1990 states that barristers must comply with a variety of codes and rules (including the Code of Conduct for Lawyers in the European Community).

Principles of professional conduct

There are principles of professional conduct that have developed with time, which, for example, bind a solicitor to carry out his client's instructions, once accepted, with diligence and to exercise reasonable skill and care and to keep his client's affairs confidential. A solicitor's personal liability for barristers' fees is a matter of professional conduct.

The Council of the Law Society has issued non-statutory guidance in the form, for example, of council statements, commentaries and written professional standards. Written professional standards require, for example, that a client should be given the best information that can be given regarding costs, and whether the likely outcome will justify the expense.

In the case of barristers, Part II of the Code of Conduct of the Bar of England & Wales lays down fundamental principles with which barristers must comply. Thus, for example, Rule 203 requires a practising barrister to promote and protect his lay client's best interests and to act towards his client at all times in good faith. Part VI sets out general requirements of conduct with which barristers must comply, for example, they must act promptly and with reasonable competence and take all reasonable and practical steps to avoid unnecessary expense or waste of the courts time.[4] In addition they must have regard to the written standards for the Conduct of Professional Work which give guidance as to the way work should be carried out.

4. Rule 601(a).

Rule 202 also stresses that the practising barrister has an overriding duty to the Court. Rule 610(c) requires that a practising barrister when conducting proceedings at court informs the court of all relevant legislation and decisions of which he is aware, whether or not favourable to his case and brings any procedural irregularity to the court's attention.

Jurisdiction of the courts

The court exercises an inherent jurisdiction over its officers. Section 50(1) of the Solicitors Act 1974 confirms that solicitors are officers of the Supreme Court and therefore owe duties to it. These duties also operate in proceedings before a tribunal or inquiry. The orders that can be made if a duty is breached may arise under the Court's inherent jurisdiction and the statutory extension of that jurisdiction by the Solicitors Act 1974.

The courts may also have jurisdiction by virtue of Court Rules that enable the court to make orders relating to deeds, documents and monies in the custody or control of a solicitor. The courts can also make a solicitor personally liable for costs incurred in litigation that the Court believes resulted from improper, unreasonable or negligent acts or omissions on the part of the solicitor.

The courts have also developed a broader jurisdiction, which rests principally on the special relationship between the solicitor and the client, which gives rise to certain fiduciary duties, for example, there is a duty to make no gain from a fiduciary position. The courts will use this jurisdiction to protect the interests of the client.

STANDARDS OF CARE

At Common Law — based on previous court decisions — the standard required of the professional is one of "reasonable skill and care".[5]

Failure to attain the required standard may expose a professional to liability in tort or contract. This is because an obligation to meet this standard is implied into the contract between the solicitor and his client, even if no express term to this effect was agreed.[6] A tortious claim may succeed even if there is a parallel contractual liability.[7] There are many reported cases that illustrate the approach adopted by the courts in assessing the appropriate standards of care.

5. Statutory confirmation of this standard can be found in the Supply of Goods and Services Act 1982, Section 13.

6. *Midland Bank Trust Co. Ltd* v. *Hett Stubbs & Kemp* [1978] 3 All ER 571.

7. *Menderson* v. *Merred Syndicates Ltd* [1994] 3 All ER 506.

Whether the required standard is met is to be considered in the light of the circumstances at the time of the negligent action, not with the benefit of hindsight.

What is required to meet this standard may be affected by the nature of the plaintiff. If the claim is contractual, the standard will be judged in the light of the contract and the client's need for advice. A solicitor whose client was experienced in business matters was not negligent in *Carradine Properties Ltd* v. *D J Freeman & Co.* (a firm),[8] for failing to ask whether a client had a particular insurance cover.

The test to be applied to solicitors, in deciding whether they meet the "reasonable skill and care" standard, was specified by Oliver J in *Midland Bank Trust Co. Ltd* v. *Hett Stubbs & Kemp* (a firm)[9] as that of the reasonably competent practitioner having regard to the standards normally adopted in his profession.

Generally, if a solicitor holds himself out as an expert in a particular field, the standard by which he will be judged is likely to be more stringent than a solicitor engaged in general practice. It is open to doubt whether the standard would vary depending on the experience of the solicitor but, in any event, an inexperienced solicitor might be found negligent because he has acted beyond his competence, or his firm found negligent for giving him such work or inadequately supervising him.

Pressures of time, whether or not imposed by the client, are unlikely to impact on the standard required. A solicitor must ensure that he is able to do properly the work he takes on and must warn the client of the risks if pressures are imposed. Given the requirements of the Code of Conduct of the Bar of England and Wales (which requires barristers to warn solicitors if there is an appreciable risk that a brief will not be attended to in time and to return it, if required, in time to enable another barrister to be instructed), the same is likely to apply to barristers.

There are fairly rare circumstances where liability will arise even though reasonable skill and care have been exercised. The most obvious examples are the breach by the solicitor of an actual contractual obligation or a breach of client confidentiality.

The test to be applied to barristers, in deciding whether they meet the requisite standard, is specified in *Mathew* v. *Maughold Life Assurance Co. Ltd*[10] namely whether he has exercised the skill and care "of the ordinary skilled man exercising and professing to have a specialist skill".

Rule 501 of the Code of Conduct of the Bar of England and Wales states that a barrister must not accept a brief that would cause him to be "professionally embarrassed". The Rule then goes on to list circumstances

8. *The Times* 19 February 1982 CA.
9. [1978] 3 All ER 571.
10. *The Times* 19 February 1987 CA.

when such "embarrassment" might arise. These include the lack of sufficient experience or competence, the lack of adequate time and where to act would risk a breach of confidence.

The written standards for the Conduct of Professional Work — General Standard 5.4 requires a barrister to:

". . . act promptly conscientiously and diligently and with reasonable competence and [to] take all reasonable and practicable steps to ensure that professional engagements are fulfilled".

CIVIL LIABILITIES

Contractual liability

Contracts between solicitors and clients may be formally created and, as there is no requirement for contracts to be in writing, they may be inferred by conduct where the parties act as if the solicitor-client relationship exists. The terms are those expressly agreed and those which in the absence of agreement the law implies.

Contractual liability may arise because a solicitor deviates from the terms of the contract or because he breaches the duties it imposes. The scope of the duties can be difficult to define. Claims for breach are normally made on the basis that the solicitor has breached a duty implied by the law to exercise reasonable care and skill, rather than for breach of an express term agreed between the solicitor and his client.

Until recently, a barrister escaped contractual liability as he could make no contract with the client or the client's solicitors. The barrister's relationship with a solicitor was, historically, governed solely by rules of professional conduct. As a result of foreign lawyers and other specified professional people being granted rights of direct access to the Bar, the Courts and Legal Services Act 1990 allows barristers to enter into contracts. The scope of the Act is presently limited by paragraphs 25, 26 and 27 of Annex D of the Code of Conduct of the Bar 1990, which provide that no contractual relationship arises when a solicitor instructs counsel, unless the contrary is agreed in writing.

Tortious liability

For a plaintiff to succeed in a claim in tort, it is necessary to be able to prove that:

(1) A duty of care was owed;
(2) There was a breach of that duty; and
(3) Damage resulted.

The case of *Crossnan* v. *Ward Bracewell & Co.*[11] illustrates that a duty of care can arise even though no contractual relationship exists. After the plaintiff was charged with reckless driving, he consulted solicitors. They advised that he could defend himself or instruct them, in which case they would require money on account of their costs. No advice was given as to the possibility of the costs being met by the plaintiff's insurers. The plaintiff decided to represent himself and did not notify his insurers of what was happening, with the result that they withdrew his insurance cover.

The plaintiff subsequently made a claim against the solicitors who were held liable in tort, despite the fact that the plaintiff and the solicitors had never entered into a contract. The court considered that they owed the plaintiff a duty of care, by holding themselves out as qualified to assist as to the sources of funds for litigation without advising him of the possibility of legal aid or the fact that his motor insurers would pay.

The fact that a duty of care can arise independent of a contract means this is a liability to which barristers, as well as solicitors, are exposed. Tortious claims are regularly made against barristers, but in only one reported decision — that of *Mathew* v. *Maughold Life Assurance Co. Ltd*[12] — has a claim succeeded at trial and that decision was reversed on appeal. Various reasons have been given for this, including the nature of the barrister's work, his duty to the court and the desire, in the interests of public policy, to avoid matters being re-litigated. With developing rights of direct access to barristers, it seems likely that, to the extent that there is currently a difference in the standard of care expected, a common standard will develop.

Liability as an Officer of the Court

A solicitor can, in certain circumstances, be liable as an Officer of the Court. In broad terms, the circumstances include matters such as a solicitor being in contempt of Court or in breach of an undertaking that is given to the court or to a third party.

Liability as an agent

A solicitor contracting as his client's agent may incur liability in the same way that any agent can potentially be liable — for example, if he acts without authority.

11. (1989) 5 PN 103.
12. (1985) 1 PN 142.

Liability as a trustee

A solicitor will not incur liability as a trustee simply because he is instructed by or acts as agent for trustees. The court will be prepared to deal with a solicitor as if he were a trustee to the extent that he uses his fiduciary position improperly — for example, to obtain a private gain, even if that gain is not at the expense of his client.

General advice

A solicitor may be in breach of contract if he conducts business other than that for which he is retained. A solicitor's duty to exercise reasonable skill and care is generally related to the confines of the contract. Circumstances can, however, arise when a solicitor will have a duty to make enquiries and give advice, even though not expressly called on to do so. *Hall* v. *Meyrick*[13] indicates that a solicitor who knows that a testator intends to marry ought to advise that the marriage will revoke the will unless the will is expressed to be made in contemplation of it. Likewise, in *Raintree Limited* v. *Holmes & Hills*,[14] a solicitor who knew his client intended to buy land for development purposes was negligent in failing to ascertain when the planning permission was due to expire. A duty also exists to advise of obvious risks, to the client, of which the client may not be aware even if outside the terms of the contract.[15]

Case law indicates that the client's expertise might be relevant in determining the degree of advice required as in the previously mentioned *Carradine Properties Ltd* v. *D J Freeman & Co.* (a firm).[16]

There are no English authorities dealing with barristers, but similar principles are likely to apply. In the Canadian case of *Smith* v. *McInnis*,[17] the Supreme Court held that experienced counsel called upon to advise on the preparation of proofs of loss by a solicitor was not negligent in failing to advise about periods of limitation. The view is, however, put forward in *Jackson & Powell on Professional Negligence* (Third Edition) that a finding of negligence might be made in circumstances where it is obvious that instructing solicitors are acting under a misunderstanding, even though the barrister has not been requested to advise on that point.

13. [1957] 2 QB 455.
14. (1984) 134 New LJ 522.
15. *Boyce* v. *Rendells* [1983] 268 EG 268.
16. *The Times* 19 February 1982.
17. (1978) 91 DLR (3d) 190.

A barrister is required to ensure that advice which he gives is practical, appropriate to the needs and circumstances of that particular client and clearly and comprehensively expressed. The Barristers' Code of Conduct states that:

"A barrister acts only on the instructions of a professional client and does not carry out any work by way of the management, administration or general conduct of a lay client's affairs nor the management, administration or general conduct of litigation."

Despite the above, it should be noted that the preamble to the Code of Conduct for Lawyers in the European Community defines a lawyer's functions as being not simply to "plead his client's cause" but to "be his adviser" and states that his duties "do not begin and end with the faithful performance of what he is instructed to do".

Specialist advice

As has been stated previously, a solicitor who holds himself out as a specialist in a particular area may be required to exercise a higher standard of skill and care than that of the general practitioner.[18]

Generally, a solicitor will not be liable where advice is given in reliance on the specialist advice of others.

This principle applied when the specialist was a barrister who had been properly instructed. There seems to be a tendency to move away from this approach — possibly as solicitors specialise more and are better able to exercise their own judgement. In *Davy-Chiesman* v. *Davy-Chiesman*,[19] May LJ confirmed the principle but said that a solicitor:

". . . is under a duty at all times to exercise that degree of care, to both client and the court that can be expected of a reasonably prudent solicitor. He is not entitled to rely blindly and with no mind of his own on counsel's views."

Commercial transactions

Normally a solicitor has no duty to advise the client on matters of business, that is whether a sale is prudent or a good bargain. In *Yager* v. *Fishman & Co.*,[20] a solicitor was not asked to advise and did not advise a client as to whether it would be better business to determine rather than keep on a lease. The court did not consider this negligent. Goddard LJ said:

18. *Duchess of Argyll* v. *Beuselinck* [1972] 2 Lloyd's Rep. 172.
19. [1984] 1 All ER 321.
20. [1944] 1 All ER 552 CA.

"To impose on a solicitor the legal responsibility of answering such a business question would require both unequivocal instructions and unqualified acceptance, for it is no part of a solicitor's normal duty to profess the skill and experience for giving such advice."

In the *Yager* case, Goddard LJ considered that the advice a solicitor ought to give will vary with the client. A solicitor will be expected to give more extensive advice to a person wholly unacquainted with business than to an experienced businessperson. A similar view was expressed by Danckwerts LJ in *Neushul* v. *Mellish and Harkavy*.[21] He held that, on the particular facts of that case, (in which the solicitor had been giving the client business advice and had placed himself in a position in which there was a conflict of interest) the solicitor was not justified in expressing no view when it was plain the client was rushing into an unwise adventure.

Although the cases concern solicitors, such decisions are likely to be relevant to cases concerning barristers.

Agreements

It is the solicitor's duty to explain the nature and consequences, or at least ensure that the client understands the material points, of any document prepared by the solicitor or which he asks the client to execute-sign. Unusual provisions relevant to the client's activities, as known to the solicitor, ought to be explained.[22]

Regulatory compliance

There are specific duties created by the Financial Services Act 1986 that must be observed in connection with the conduct of investment business such as sponsoring companies when investment is sought.

Litigation conduct

This is another area where, whilst the cases involve solicitors, the decisions are also likely to be relevant to the liability of barristers. In contentious business the solicitor is obliged to consider and advise the client on the merits of his case.[23] Lord Justice Donaldson MR, however, said it is

21. [1967] 111 SJ 399.
22. *Sykes* v. *Midland Bank Executor and Trustee Co.* [1970] 2 All ER 471.
23. *Homes* v. *National Benzole Co.* [1965] 109 SJ 971.

". . . not for solicitors or Counsel to impose a pre-trial screen through which a litigant must pass before he can put his complaint or defence before the courts."[24]

A solicitor's duty, in contentious business, was described in *Godefroy* v. *Dalton*.[25] A solicitor is liable for the consequences of ignorance or non observance of the rules of practice of the court, for want of care in the preparation of the case for trial, or of attendance thereon, and for mismanagement of so much of the conduct of the case as is easily and ordinarily allotted to his department of the profession. He is not answerable for errors of judgement on points of new occurrence or of advice on doubtful construction.

Some 19th century authorities suggest that a solicitor has the authority to enter into a reasonable compromise on his client's behalf, unless specifically forbidden. These authorities now conflict with the solicitor's duty to keep the client informed. Certainly a solicitor must exercise reasonable care in giving such advice and conducting settlement negotiations. A solicitor who gave advice, having failed to make proper enquiries, was held liable in *McNamara* v. *Martin Mears & Co.*[26]

Administration

There is no special obligation owed by a solicitor acting on behalf of a company or trust.

Conflicts of interest, disclosure, withdrawal

It is a general principle of professional conduct that a solicitor may not accept instructions to act for two or more clients where there is a conflict of interest between those clients; in the event that a conflict develops, then the solicitor must cease to act.

In addition, Rule 6 of the Solicitors' Practice Rules 1990 expressly prohibits a solicitor, his partners or associates, from acting for both buyer and seller on the transfer of land, a lease or a mortgage. The Rule sets out limited exceptions.

Conflicts of interest do not invalidate the solicitor-client contract. Written Standards for the Conduct of Professional Work requires that barristers are always alert to the possibility of conflict whether between the lay and professional client, the lay client and the legal aid fund or more than one client.

24. *Orchard* v. *South Eastern Electricity Board* [1987] 1 QB 565.
25. (1830) 6 Bing 460.
26. (1983) 127 SJ 69.

Even if there is no conflict of interest, General Standard 3.5 prohibits the barrister from accepting a brief or instructions for a client in respect of any further stage in proceedings without obtaining the instructions of the client for whom he acted in any earlier part of the proceedings.

The Code of Conduct for Lawyers in the European Community stresses the need for lawyers to maintain independence and to avoid any impairment of that independence by response to outside pressure or personal interests. The Code provides that lawyers should not act on behalf of two or more clients in the same matter if there is a conflict or a significant risk of conflict and must cease to act if a conflict of interest arises.

Confidentiality

The Code of Conduct for Lawyers in the European Community describes confidentiality as a "primary and fundamental right and duty of the lawyer" which is "not limited in time".

The Code of Conduct for Lawyers in the European Community[27] also requires a lawyer to cease to act if there is a risk of breach of confidence and to refrain from acting for a new client where the knowledge possessed by him of the former client's affairs would breach a confidence entrusted to him or give an undue advantage to the new client.

CLAIMANTS

The client, the former client and successors

Claims against solicitors can be made by either current or former clients. Rights of action pass to a client's personal representatives on the client's death or his trustee in the event of being declared bankrupt.

Clients may make claims against barristers in tort. The Courts and Legal Services Act 1990 permitted barristers to enter into contracts for the provision of legal services for the first time. Whether a contractual claim should be made by the solicitor or his client has yet to be judicially decided. No reported cases determine whether former clients or successors in title may claim, but there seems no reason to expect that the classes of claimants against solicitors will be substantially wider than those against barristers.

27. Rule 3.2.

Third parties

Liability as agent

A solicitor may be personally sued on a contract he enters into when acting as agent for a client unbeknown to a claimant in the same way that any agent can potentially be liable.

Generally a claimant who knows a solicitor is acting on behalf of a client, will only be able to sue the client in accordance with the general rules that an agent should not be liable where he is acting for a disclosed principal.

Liability in tort

The principle of liability to third parties for negligent misstatements on which they rely was established in 1964 by the case of *Hedley Byrne & Co. Ltd* v. *Heller & Partners Ltd*.[28]

This area of the law is evolving almost on a weekly basis and decisions from earlier cases are constantly being rejected, upheld or refined. It can be dangerous to place too much reliance on older authorities to determine precisely how the courts will approach claims in tort. The concept of liability to third parties in tort was approved in *Mathew* v. *Maughold Life Assurance Co. Ltd*[29] where the court held that a barrister instructed on behalf of a company owed a duty of care to the family which was to be benefited by a scheme that the company marketed. This specific point was not discussed further on the reversal of the decision on appeal. In a House of Lords decision, *Caparo Industries plc* v. *Dickman*,[30] the court tried to tackle the question as to what was required to establish liability. The decision is less favourable to potential claimants than some previous decisions. It was stated that the relevant criteria were neither intended to be all inclusive nor conclusive. What is required is that, to be capable of being liable, the adviser must know (actually or by inference) that:

(1) When giving the advice it is for a purpose known to the advisor;
(2) The advice will be communicated to a known advisee, as an individual or member of a class, for use by the advisee for that purpose;
(3) The advisee subsequently acts on the advice; and
(4) The advisee acts to his detriment.

28. [1964] AC 465.
29. (1985) 1 PN 142.
30. [1990] 2 AC 605.

A particular problem arises in cases where a solicitor has been negligent in the preparation or execution of a will for a client who dies (as will normally happen) before the mistake is discovered. The former client or his estate has suffered no financial loss but, at the same time, one or more beneficiaries have suffered a loss if the solicitor is negligent. It can hardly be said that the disappointed beneficiaries acted in reliance on the solicitor's advice to the deceased. In *Ross* v. *Caunters*[31] a solicitor was held liable to a beneficiary who lost a gift in a will, made by the solicitor's client because her husband had witnessed the will.[32] The reason given by the court for its decision was that a solicitor, instructed to carry out a transaction that will confer a benefit on an identified third party, owes a duty of care to that party if he is within his direct contemplation as someone likely to be so closely and directly affected by his acts or omissions that he can reasonably foresee that he is likely to be injured by them.

There is some doubt as to whether the decision reached in *Ross* v. *Caunters* is correct, and a current case — *White* v. *Jones* — is being taken to the House of Lords with a view to getting a definitive decision on the issue. Even if *Ross* v. *Caunters* is upheld, it is likely that cases involving wills will be treated as a special category — by not allowing beneficiaries to claim, it will be possible for lawyers negligently to prepare wills without any prospect of there being a means of redress, provided the mistake was not identified prior to the death of the client.

A solicitor or barrister will not owe a duty of care to their client's opponent.[33] Any such duty would generally be inconsistent with their duty to do the best for their client. It has, however, been recognised that a duty might arise in special circumstances, such as where one solicitor gave a certificate on which the other party was expected to act.

An order to meet both parties' costs was, however, made against solicitors in *Davy-Chiesman* v. *Davy-Chiesman*.[34] This decision has been explained on the basis that the liability arises from the duty of care to the court, and the exercise of the court's jurisdiction to compensate for such breach, rather than from any duty to the opponent.

A solicitor was also made liable for an opposing party's physical and mental injuries in *Al Kandari* v. *Brown (J R) & Co*.[35] The solicitor acted for a client involved in a custody dispute. He voluntarily agreed to hold his client's passport to the order of the Court as there was a risk that his

31. [1979] 3 All ER 580.

32. To minimise the risk of fraud, all witnesses and spouses of witnesses are not able to receive any benefit under a will and the solicitor was, or should have been, aware that the witness was married to a beneficiary.

33. *Gran Gelato* v. *Richcliff (Group) Ltd & Another*, *The Times* 19 December 1991.

34. 1 All ER 321: A solicitor failed to inform the Legal Aid Committee of a change in the circumstances of the litigation.

35. [1988] 1 All ER 833.

client might abduct the children who were being cared for by his client's opponent. The client obtained the passport and abducted the children. The court held that the solicitor had breached his duty to inform his client's opponent of the fact that the passport had left his possession. It explained this decision on the basis that the solicitor had stepped outside the normal solicitor-client role by voluntarily agreeing to hold the passport to the court's order. In normal commercial transactions, the case of *Gran Gelato* v. *Richcliff Group* is authority for the fact that one party to a transaction does not owe a duty of care to the other party.

Liability as a trustee

Where a solicitor acts as a trustee or a court holds that the solicitor — by virtue of the nature of the solicitor-client relationship — is in a position of trust, then a solicitor may be liable.

Liability under statute

One example of liability under statute arises in the field of insolvency where there are strict rules designed to ensure that one creditor is not given preference over others in an unfair way. Section 340 of the Insolvency Act 1986 entitles a trustee in bankruptcy to demand, from the solicitor of a petitioning creditor, repayment of all monies that constitute a preference received by the solicitor from the bankrupt. This applies even though the solicitor has paid out the monies to his client.

PROCEDURE

For reasons of space, it is not possible to give more than an outline. A claimant will pursue a claim through the civil courts and such a claim will generally take a minimum of 18 months, and often substantially longer, to get to trial. The procedure consists, in broad terms, of:

(1) Service of written pleadings;
(2) A preliminary hearing at the court to fix a timetable for the conduct of the action through to trial;
(3) Discovery — disclosure by list by all parties to the action of all relevant documents, both helpful and unhelpful;
(4) Exchange of witness statements containing factual evidence of the parties;
(5) Exchange of expert reports (if appropriate);
(6) Application to court for a trial date; and
(7) Trial.

The winning party is potentially entitled to recover his costs from the losing party although, in practice, the winning party is unlikely to recover more than approximately 75 per cent of the costs actually incurred when his claim for costs is taxed by the court.

DAMAGES

The aim of an award of damages is to put the plaintiff, so far as money can, in the position in which he would have been had there been no breach. Damages may only be claimed if the solicitor's breach of duty caused the damage. In *Clark* v. *Kirby-Smith*,[36] the plaintiffs were unable to renew a lease because of their solicitor's negligence. The court refused to allow them to recover monies paid to the landlords, for dilapidations. That loss was not caused by the solicitor's negligence — it was the result of the plaintiffs' own breach of covenant.

The burden of proving causation falls on the plaintiff. This view was confirmed in a case (not involving a solicitor) namely *Wilsher* v. *Essex Area Health Authority*.[37]

If the damage was, in fact, caused by the breach then it is potentially recoverable, subject to the damage having been foreseeable by the parties. If the damage was not foreseeable, it will be held to be too remote to be recovered. As a general principle, foreseeability is judged, in the case of claims in contract, as at the time the contract is made and, in tort claims, it is judged as at the time the breach occurs. The rule is not rigid and is subject to an overriding aim of the Courts to ensure that the damages awarded do compensate the plaintiff for his losses.

Generally, if a client acquires property as a result of negligent advice, the client will be entitled to claim damages representing the diminution in value of the property resulting from the error of the solicitor as of the date of breach. However, in a case where the client had acquired a lease of premises which had a rent review clause which was so badly drafted as to result in the client having to pay to surrender the lease and bring its liability to an end, the Courts held that the cost of negotiating the surrender would be recoverable provided the sum paid was reasonable *County Personnel Ltd* v. *Pulver and Co*.[38] The Court felt this to be the most appropriate way of calculating damages given the overriding aim to put the plaintiff in the position it would have been in had it not suffered a wrong.

36. [1964] 2 All ER 835.
37. [1988] 1 All ER 871.
38. [1987) 1 All ER 289.

In *Hayes* v. *Dodd (James & Charles)* (a firm),[39] premises were bought for business purposes. Title was defective due to the defendant solicitor's breach. The business failed. The property took about six years to sell. The court held that all expenses incurred during those years, including rates, insurance, redundancy payments and conveyancing costs, were recoverable.

So long as the plaintiff acts reasonably costs incurred in correcting the error are recoverable. In the Canadian case of *MacCulloch* v. *Corbett*,[40] such costs were allowed even though the attempt at correction was unsuccessful.

Damages have been awarded for physical inconvenience and discomfort caused by the breach as in *Bailey* v. *Bullock*[41] and for distress affecting health in *Malyon* v. *Lawrance Messer & Co.*[42] The court's attitude, however, has been more cautious where claims are made for mental distress which has not affected health. In the case of *Hayes* v. *Dodd* (*James & Charles*) (a firm).[43] The court said that such damages in contract ought to be limited to contracts the purpose of which was to provide peace of mind or freedom from distress.

Anyone who seeks to pursue a claim to recover losses is required by law to take reasonable steps to reduce or avoid the losses. The courts will not require a plaintiff to commence speculative litigation to try and reduce the losses it suffers, but will expect the plaintiff to take reasonable steps. In *Dickinson* v. *James Alexander & Co.*,[44] a wife who had divorced her husband on unfavourable financial terms was found to have failed to mitigate her loss in delaying for six years in making an application to the court to alter these terms.

Conseqently, in the case of *Pilkington* v. *Wood*, the court rejected a suggestion that the plaintiff should be required to commence difficult litigation even with an indemnity.

The assessment of loss is not without problems. These can be seen particularly when the loss constitutes loss of the opportunity to bring or defend proceedings. In these circumstances the test to be applied was set out by Lord Evershed MR in *Kitchen* v. *Royal Air Force Association*.[45] He said it was not the function of the court to decide whether, on the balance of probabilities, the action or defence would have succeeded. The court had to determine whether what was lost was of value.

39. [1990] 2 All ER 815.
40. (1982) 133 DLR (3d) 43.
41. [1950] 2 All ER 1167.
42. [1968] 2 Lloyd's Rep. 539.
43. [1990] 2 All ER 815.
44. [1990] 6 PN 208.
45. [1958] 2 All ER 241.

In deciding value, other factors may also be relevant. In *Islington Investments Ltd* v. *Day Ault & White*,[46] the fact that the defendant had not the means to satisfy a judgment was relevant. The possibility that court proceedings might be compromised at a lower figure may also be relevant, although in *Dickinson* v. *James Alexander & Co.*,[47] the judge refused to reduce the award to take account of this possibility because he considered, on the facts, such a compromise would have been unlikely.

Exclusions

Section 60(5) of the Solicitors Act 1974 renders void any attempt, in a contentious business agreement, by a solicitor to avoid liability for negligence. There is no corresponding provision covering non-contentious business agreements. The Law Society, while taking the view that it is unacceptable for solicitors to attempt to exclude all liability to their clients in contract, has no objection to solicitors seeking to limit liability to clients provided the limitation is not below the minimum cover required by the Solicitors Indemnity Rules.[48] It also recognises that it may be reasonable for solicitors to seek to limit or exclude liability to persons other than the client.

Attempts to exclude or limit liability are also subject to the Unfair Contract Terms Act 1977. This requires that clauses seeking to exclude liability for loss or damage resulting from breach of contract are subject to a "reasonableness" test. The terms must be fair and reasonable having regard to the circumstances that were or ought reasonably to have been known or in the contemplation of the parties when the contract was made. Such clauses must also be clearly brought to the client's attention and understood and accepted by him.

Defences

Immunity

When solicitors or barristers act as advocates they are immune from "negligence" actions in contract and tort in and about the conduct of the client's case in court. The immunity can cover pre-trial work if it can be said to be a preliminary decision affecting the way that case is conducted when it comes to the hearing.

46. (1978) 7 CCLT 46.

47. (1990) 6 PN 205.

48. The Law Society Council Statement on Liability of Liability by Contract, 27 May 1987 (Revised 1990).

Client's funds or papers

Certain defences are applicable to actions concerning dealings with or the retention of client's monies or papers. Applications for orders in respect of the above (whether deriving from the court's inherent jurisdiction, its statutory extension, or court rules) are subject to defences contained in case law, e.g. that the solicitor-client relationship never existed or that the solicitor received money in a capacity other than that of a solicitor.

Time Bars

The general rule is that the limitation period for commencing proceedings in both contract and tort is six years from the date the cause of action accrued.

In contract, the cause of action accrues at the date of the actual breach of the contract of retainer by the solicitor. In tort, the cause of action only accrues when damage is suffered as a result of the breach of duty. Only then is the breach acknowledged. This can produce unexpected consequences. In a situation where a solicitor fails to register a restriction against a property that is intended to stop the landowner disposing of the property, time will start to run in contract from the date of the breach of contract when the registration should have been made. In tort, time will only start to run against him once the property has been disposed of in breach of the restriction that should have been registered on the basis that, until that date, no damage flowed from his negligent omission.

It was also relatively common for a solicitor to make a mistake on a file and for the problem not to come to light until more than six years after the matter had been finished. By the time the client knew that he had a cause for action, he was already out of time.

The Latent Damage Act 1980 was supposed to try and stop what was perceived as being an unfair situation insofar as a claimant was concerned. The Act provides an alternative limitation period, which runs for three years from the date that the claimant knew or ought to have known that he had a cause of action. This alternative limitation period is subject to a qualification that there is a "long stop" of 15 years. If the claimant has not discovered that he has a cause for action by that date then, as before, he will be time barred.

More generally, it should also be mentioned that there are special rules relating to children (in broad terms, time does not start to run until they have reached their 18th birthday) and, also, in cases of fraud or deliberate concealment.

A solicitor's liability for co-partners

Section 5 of the Partnership Act 1890 makes co-partners liable on a contract made by one if it is a contract for carrying on in the usual way business of the kind carried on by the firm of which he is a member. Co-partners will not be liable to third parties who did not know or believe the contracting party to be a partner, nor to third parties who actually knew of the limited authority of the contracting partner.[49]

Section 10 of the Partnership Act makes co-partners liable for the wrong doings or omissions of one, acting in the ordinary course of the business of the practice or with his co-partners' authority.

Section 11 of the Partnership Act 1890 makes co-partners liable to make good loss arising as a result of the misappropriation of money or property received by a partner acting within the scope of his apparent authority or by the firm in the course of its business.

Section 17 of the Partnership Act 1890 provides that a partner is not liable to creditors for anything done by his co-partners before he becomes a partner, nor for debts and obligations incurred after his retirement, unless caught by Section 14. This Section renders a partner who has represented, or allowed himself to be represented, as a partner, liable to third parties who give credit on the basis of that representation.

After dissolution the obligations of the partners and their authority to bind the firm continues, but only so far as is necessary to wind it up and complete transactions begun, but not finished, at the time of dissolution.[50] A co-partner will not be liable under this Section for the acts of a bankrupt partner unless he represents, or knowingly suffers himself to be represented, as a partner of the bankrupt after the date of the bankruptcy.

The estate of a deceased or bankrupt partner is not liable for debts incurred after the date of death or bankruptcy.[51] A solicitor's representatives will, however, be liable for the solicitor's negligence.[52]

As a matter of conduct, no liability for breach of undertaking will normally pass to a solicitor who becomes a partner after it is given. A solicitor who leaves a partnership, or who was a partner in a dissolved partnership, will remain liable for undertakings given whilst he was a partner.

Every partner is responsible for compliance with the Solicitors Investment Business Rules 1990. The same is also true in respect of the rules relating to solicitors' accounts and the delivery of the accountants' report. All will therefore be liable to disciplinary action in the event of

49. Partnership Act 1890, Section 8.
50. Partnership Act 1890, Section 38.
51. Partnership Act 1890, Section 36(3).
52. Law Reform (Miscellaneous Provisions) Act 1934, Section 1.

breach. The institution of disciplinary action is, however, likely to depend upon the degree of personal involvement of the partners concerned.

Liability for agents

A solicitor is liable for the negligence of both legal and non-legal agents who act within the scope of his authority under the general principles of agency law.

Liability for employees

A partner, as a matter of conduct, is *prima facie* responsible for the acts, undertakings and omissions of his staff, whether qualified or not.

Barristers

Rule 206 of the Code of Conduct of the Bar of England and Wales prohibits a barrister from delegating responsibility for his conduct and work and from agreeing to assume responsibility for the work of another. Every practising barrister is required to be individually responsible.

INSURANCE

A solicitor, practising as such in England and Wales, must comply with the Solicitors Indemnity Rules. These require the compulsory insurance of all solicitors who are principals in private practice against the risks of claims arising out of professional negligence. Solicitors can effect more extensive cover if they regard the compulsory cover of £1-million provided by the Solicitors Indemnity Fund Limited as insufficient.

Rule 17 of the Solicitors Overseas Practice Rules 1990 contains similar provisions in respect of solicitors practising, as such, as principals in private practice, outside England and Wales.

Rule 302 of the Code of Conduct of the Bar of England and Wales requires that every barrister in or intending to engage in independent practice shall apply to be entered as a member with the Bar Mutual Indemnity Fund Limited and shall pay the requisite premium so as to be insured against professional negligence claims.

The Law Society also maintains a Compensation Fund. It aims to make grants to those who have or are likely to suffer loss by virtue of the dishonesty of a solicitor or his employee in connection with the solicitors' practice or any trust of which the solicitor was a trustee, or which is likely to be suffered due to a solicitor's failure to account for monies. This is intended to be a fund of last resort. No grant will be made if the applicant can be indemnified or the loss made good by recourse elsewhere. In practice, payments by the Compensation Fund tend to be made in respect of dishonest acts of sole practitioners. If more than one solicitor is in partnership, the "innocent" partners will normally be able to look to their professional indemnity insurance to provide cover.

INTERNATIONAL AND PRIVATE LAW ASPECTS

European community

Articles 52 and 59 of the Treaty of Rome, respectively, provide for the gradual abolition of restrictions on the freedom of establishment of nationals of a member state in the territory of another and on the freedom to provide services within the Community.

On 28 October 1988, the national delegations representing the Bars and Law Societies of the Community adopted a Code of Conduct. This states the common rules applicable to all lawyers from the Community. Rule 4 of the Solicitors Overseas Practice Rules 1990 requires solicitors to observe the rules of the Code. The Law Society has expressed the view that, with very few exceptions, Rule 4 will be met by observing the rules, principles and requirements of conduct otherwise applicable to solicitors.

Legislation on establishment (as opposed to the provision of services)[53] has not yet been adopted. This is largely due to differences over the extent to which the rules and controls of the State in which lawyers propose to establish are to apply.

The Law Society and the Bar Council have agreed that solicitors and barristers will have the same rights to establish and provide services in other Member States. Lawyers from other Member States, wishing to establish or provide services in England and Wales, must choose the branch of the profession in which they propose to practise.

Foreign lawyers subject to domestic standards

Sections 20 and 21 of the Solicitors Act 1974 prohibit anyone, who is not qualified to practise as a solicitor[54] from acting as or pretending to be one. Sections 22 and 23 also prohibit anyone, other than a solicitor, from performing certain functions in expectation of a "fee gain or reward".

53. The subject of EEC Council Directive 77/249 of 22 March 1977 and implemented in the United Kingdom by the European Communities (Services of Lawyers) Order 1978 (SI 1978/1910).

54. In accordance with the Solicitors Act 1974, Section 1.

Any foreign lawyer who wishes to carry out these functions for "fee gain or reward" must, therefore, qualify as a solicitor.

Those foreign lawyers who establish themselves, or provide legal services, in England or Wales must comply with the standards of conduct applicable to the legal profession of England and Wales. This obligation applies whether or not they also remain subject to the standards of their own jurisdiction. If financial advice is to be given, compliance with the Financial Services Act 1986 is necessary. The Law Society may only register English and Welsh solicitors. Foreign lawyers who give financial advice, have to register with the Securities Investment Board.

It is possible for foreign lawyers to have or be a member of chambers subject to compliance with the Foreign Lawyers (Chambers) Rules. This provides that the foreign lawyer will be subject to the same rules of practice as govern a barrister in independent practice in England and Wales except in so far as they conflict with the ordinary and usual way that the foreign lawyer properly conducts himself or with the rules of his own profession.

In relation to the foreign lawyers practising in the United Kingdom there are specified paragraphs of the Code that must be observed, otherwise the rules apply.

Domestic lawyers subject to foreign standards and liability

Solicitors practising outside England and Wales must observe:

(1) The Solicitors Overseas Practice Rules 1990 and rules referred to;
(2) All relevant requirements of local law or rules applicable to them as solicitors practising, as such, outside England and Wales;
(3) Subject to some exceptions, rules made under the Solicitors Act 1974. This includes the Solicitors Compensation Fund Rules 1975; and
(4) The principles of professional conduct which apply in England and Wales, even when no specific reference to a principle is covered by any of the above rules.

A barrister in independent practice who appears in a court or provides legal services as such outside England and Wales must comply with the Overseas Practice Rules and save as otherwise provided by those rules will also remain subject to the Code of Conduct of the Bar of England and Wales, as well as to the local law and rules of professional conduct of the place where the services are provided.[55] The Overseas Practice Rules allow instructions to be accepted from lay clients as well as foreign

55. Rules 103 and 306.

lawyers, in the circumstances set out in those rules. A practising barrister qualified both in England and Wales and in some other system who practises concurrently within the jurisdiction and abroad must comply with the Dual Qualification Rules. It is possible for barristers to be called to the Bar for temporary and defined purposes only.[56]

CONCLUSION

Liability and trends

The law relating to claims for professional negligence is relatively well developed. There are areas that are changing — the extent to which a lawyer can be held liable in tort to people other than his client is an obvious example — but, generally, the legal framework is clear. The major change is the increasing consumer awareness and ease with which claims can be pursued. Decisions which 30 years ago would have been regarded as an error of judgement of a professional person are now capable of being held to be negligent decisions.

Risk reduction methods

There has been a consequential change in the attitudes of lawyers. In part this is reflected in an acceptance that a negligence claim is not out of the ordinary. More positively, there is also a growing awareness of the need to take specific steps to avoid and minimise the risk of being sued. There is an increased emphasis on diary and reminder systems to avoid the simple error of missing time limits. Precedents and check lists are being adopted to reduce matters — so far as possible — to a routine where error will, hopefully, be avoided. There is also recognition that notes of all contact with the client and third parties are essential, both to have an accurate record as to what is happening and, also, as a defensive measure to assist in dealing with any allegation of negligence or misconduct that may be made.

By specialising to a greater degree and not taking on work outside that field of expertise, the technical ability of the average lawyer to do the work is increased.

There is also an increased emphasis on the need to ensure that practising solicitors are kept up to date with developments in the law. In this

56. Code of Conduct of the Bar of England and Wales, Rule 704, and the Inns of Court Consolidated Regulation 40.

connection, the Law Society is in the process of extending a scheme (which already requires solicitors who qualified after November 1982 to undergo 16 hours per annum continuing education) with the intention that by 1998 it will cover all solicitors who are practising.

All of the sort of steps mentioned are seen not simply as "best practice" but, also, as an increasing commercial necessity. The increase in the size of professional indemnity premiums and excesses mean large firms, unless they take out additional (expensive) insurance, can now pay up to £150,000 towards a claim.

CHAPTER 5

FRANCE

LOUIS B. BUCHMAN
Caubet Buchman Spalter
Paris, France

INTRODUCTION

The legal profession in France has traditionally been divided among various professionals, and it is only recently that the government has acted to reduce the number of professionals licensed or authorised to render legal services in France.

The professionals involved include *Notaries Public*, *Avocats*, *Avoués*, *Huissiers*, *Administrateurs Judiciaires*, *Commissaires-Priseurs* and *Conseils en Propriété Industrielle*.[1] Moreover, and to a limited extent, accountants and *juristes d'entreprise* are also authorised to practise law.

The *Avocats* are themselves a mixed breed. Before 1971, two types of *Avocats* co-existed, as well as two types of *Avoués*, each with specialised activities, plus the *Agréés*.

The *Agréés* were lawyers specialising in litigation before the commercial courts, for the most part limiting themselves to acting as solicitors for the *Avocats à la Cour*, that is, preparing court papers, lodging them with the commercial courts, and following-up the commercial procedures for them.

The *Avocats à la Cour*, also known as *Avocats au Barreau* (no meaningful difference there), for the most part would act as barristers still do in England, that is, litigating cases before courts of the first instance and courts of appeals, but also advising generally on all legal matters. However, unlike English barristers they had direct contacts with clients.

The *Avocats au Conseil d'Etat et à la Cour de Cassation* still exist today and specialise in advising on and conducting litigation before the French Supreme Court (*Cour de Cassation*) and before the French Superior Administrative Court (*Conseil d'Etat*).

The *Avoués près le Tribunal de Grande Instance* acted as solicitors preparing court papers for the *Avocats à la Cour* and lodging them with the civil courts of first instance. For the most part, they would only receive instructions from the *Avocats à la Cour*, who had the contacts with the clients.

1. These terms are defined below.

Lastly, the *Avoués près la Cour* were solicitors doing before the courts of appeals exactly what the *Avoués près le Tribunal de Grande Instance* were doing before the lower courts.

After a limited reform resulting from the law of 31 December 1971, the professions of *Avoués près le Tribunal de Grande Instance* and of *Agréés* were merged with that of *Avocats à la Cour,* i.e. the former *Avocats à la Cour* were now authorised to lodge their court papers themselves, and simultaneously, a new profession was created — that of *Conseils Juridiques*, who were legal advisers not having rights of advocacy, and who could, therefore, only appear before courts where rights of advocacy were not required (such as commercial courts).

The regulatory framework has again been modified by two laws each dated 31 December 1990, which unified the professions of *Avocats à la Cour* and *Conseils Juridiques* into a single profession, the practitioners of which are now uniformly known as *Avocats* (*à la Cour* or *au Barreau* indiscriminately).

What remains from the former framework is that the Avocats must be admitted to practice by a court of appeals and must have their legal domicile within the territorial reach of that court of appeals; they must be members of the bar organised within the territorial reach of that court of appeals; they may advise in all legal matters and may appear before any jurisdiction or administrative agency having quasi-jurisdictional authority without any restriction.

The professions of *Avoués près la Cour* and *Avocats au Conseil d'Etat et à la Cour de Cassation* have not been affected by the recent statutory change.

Law is also practised in France by *Notaries Public*, who enjoy two legal monopolies: that of intervening in all sales and purchases of real estate located in France, and that of granting authenticity to all papers filed by or with them. They are able to advise generally in all matters, but for the most part, they still limit themselves to real estate conveyancing, wills and estates, and advising private clients on their patrimonial interests, often doing private client tax planning.

The *Huissiers* are bailiffs, i.e. officers appointed by the Justice Department for the service of writs and for carrying out attachments, garnishments and other seizures. They may advise in all legal matters, but for the most part, they confine themselves to debt collections. Some of them are also court officers (*Huissiers-Audienciers*) and may be appointed as special masters.

The *Administrateurs Judiciaires* are court-appointed insolvency practitioners who act either strictly as *Administrateurs Judiciaires*, i.e. managing companies undergoing a reorganisation or a composition with creditors; as *Représentant des Créanciers* who gather creditors' claims; or as *Mandataires-Liquidateurs*, who are in charge of the winding-up of bankrupt companies under the supervision of a judge.

The *Commissaires-Priseurs* are officers in charge of all auctions, which they conduct, and they also intervene in insolvency proceedings as appraisers.

The *Conseils en Propriété Industrielle* are regulated by Law No. 90–1052 of 26 November 1990 and by Decree No. 92–360 of 1 April 1992. The members of this profession are patent and/or trademark attorneys specialising in the prosecution of patents, industrial designs, models and trademark applications. Some of them, doing mostly trademark law, were also *Conseils Juridiques* before 1990 and have elected to become *Avocats* when the law of 31 December 1990 came into force, thus losing their former title of *Conseils en Propriété Industrielle* (the *Avocats* are not prevented from prosecuting trademark, design or model applications and a few were already doing so before 1990). It is anticipated that this profession will realign itself, the engineers remaining *Conseils en Propriété Industrielle* and concerning themselves, for the most part, with patents, and the non-engineers migrating towards the *Avocats*' profession.

The accountants (*Experts-comptables*) have, since an ordinance dating back to 1945, the right to advise their existing clients, for whom they do accounting work, in related legal matters, such as preparing tax filings and acting as company secretary in the handling of corporate minute books. In actual fact, there have been numerous instances of encroachments by accountants going beyond what they are allowed, and there is a relentless pressure on the part of the accountants to see their restrictions waived or at least lessened.

The *juristes d'entreprise* are corporate or in-house lawyers who, apart from advising their corporations on the legal matters submitted to them, may also occasionally appear on behalf of their employers before bodies that do not require a right of advocacy, e.g. quite often before labour courts. The professional bodies regulating the above professions are:

(1) For the *Notaries Public*, the *Conseil Supérieur du Notariat*, which is a national body, in each region, a *Conseil Régional des Notaires*, and in each district (*département*) a *Chambre Départementale des Notaires*;
(2) For the *Huissiers*, the *Chambre Nationale des Huissiers de Justice* and in each region, a *Chambre Régionale des Huissiers de Justice*;
(3) For the *Commissaires-Priseurs*, the *Chambre Nationale des Commissaires-Priseurs* and in each region, a *Chambre Régionale des Commissaires-Priseurs*;
(4) For the *Avoués*, the *Chambre Nationale des Avoués* and for each Court of Appeals, a *Chambre de Discipline des Avoués*;
(5) For the *Conseils en Propriété Industrielle*, the *Compagnie Nationale des Conseils en Propriété Industrielle*;

(6) For the *Avocats au Conseil d'Etat et à la Cour de Cassation*, the *Ordre des Avocats au Conseil d'Etat et à la Cour de Cassation*; and

(7) For the *Avocats*, on a national level, the *Conseil National des Barreaux* (National Council of the Bars), and locally, the bars or *Ordres des Avocats*.

(8) The *juristes d'entreprise* are not self-regulated.

The above introduction indicates the complexity of the different forms of the practice of law in France. This indication has been too successful if the reader is under the impression that the legal profession is totally fragmented. In actual fact, the *Avocats* are by far the largest segment of this spectrum, and now number about 22,000 professionals, about half of whom practice in Paris and the balance in the provinces (which shows to what extent France still is an overly centralised country). Given the numerical superiority of the *Avocats* as compared to the other professionals, further discussion shall be limited to them.

PRACTICE STRUCTURES

Since the coming into force of the two laws of 31 December 1990, the *Avocats* have had a wide choice of practice structures, ranging from sole practitioner to partnerships. These include:

(1) Sole practitioner: Most *Avocats* in France still practise in that way. It should be noted that being a sole practitioner does not imply that one cannot use the services of one or several assistants (*Avocats collaborateurs*);

(2) Office sharing — *cabinets groupés* and *société civile de moyens* (SCM): The *Avocats* having adopted any of the two above structures merely share expenses relating to office space and possibly law library, receptionist, switchboard operator, telephone, fax, photocopying equipment, word-processing equipment, and the like. They do not share profits nor do they intermingle their clients. The difference between a *cabinet groupé* and a SCM is their tax status and the fact that in a *cabinet groupé*, one of the *Avocats* is the tenant (or the owner) of the premises and the others his sub-tenants or lessees, as the case may be, whereas a SCM is often itself the tenant or owner;

(3) Associations are unincorporated partnerships, purely based on contractual arrangements, whereby the members of the Association agree to share profits according to a percentage scale; and

(4) Professional corporations come in many guises: *Sociétés Civiles*, *Sociétés Civiles Professionnelles* (SCP), *Sociétés Anonymes*, *Sociétés à Responsabilité Limitée*, *Sociétés en Participation*,

Sociétés d'Exercice Libéral à Forme Anonyme (SELAFA), *Sociétés d'Exercice Libéral à Responsabilité Limitée* (SELARL), *Sociétés d'Exercice Libéral à Commandite par Actions* (SELCA), and even partnerships constituted under laws other than French law (which are called *groupements*). All these forms of professional corporations offer different variations of tax status and control of decision-making. Some of them, such as the SCP, offer the possibility of creating equity partners and non-equity partners.

These practice structures may combine with some of the other structures, not necessarily of the same kind, to create either one of the two following groupings:

(1) The *Groupement d'Intérêt Economique* (GIE), which is an economic interest grouping not able to practise law in its own name, but capable of rendering services to its members and facilitating their respective practices; or
(2) The *Groupement Européen d'Intérêt Economique* (GEIE), which is a European economic interest grouping, identical to a GIE except that it must have members in more than one member State of the European Community.

CAPACITIES

The *Avocat* is an adviser and an advocate and may be an intermediary, a custodian, an arbitrator, a trustee, and much more. He cannot be the chairman or chief executive officer of any company or corporation.

As an adviser, the *Avocat* may issue opinions, may draft any contractual documents, and may participate in their negotiation.

As an advocate, the *Avocat* may represent a party in litigation as agent for service, and may present written and oral arguments to the court or to the arbitration tribunal, as the case may be, on behalf of that party.

As an intermediary, the *Avocat* acts as the agent of his client, but the scope of the agency must be limited, and the *Avocat* cannot agree to become a *de facto* principal or manager of his client's business or finances.

As a custodian, the *Avocat* may receive funds, which must be deposited on a client's account, and he must be able to account for them at all times. Moreover, he may be appointed custodian of documents that have to be kept in escrow.

As an arbitrator, the *Avocat* acts as a judge. This means that he must remain totally independent from the parties and will ultimately be rendering an award enforceable under French law or, as the case may be, under any applicable international convention.

As a trustee, the *Avocat* must act in accordance with the laws that govern the trust, but he must ascertain for himself that the trust has a legitimate purpose.

As a lobbyist, the *Avocat* acts as the representative of his client *vis-à-vis* national or international authorities, in which case he must disclose to such authorities in which capacity he is acting and the identity of his clients.

It has been mentioned that an *Avocat* cannot be the chief executive officer of any company or corporation, but he may be a director (*administrateur*) or a member (and even the chairman) of the supervisory board (*Conseil de Surveillance*) of a *Société Anonyme*.

There are also several restrictions on the *Avocat* who holds a public position (e.g. an *Avocat* who is a Member of Parliament cannot act against the French State, any administrative authority thereof, or against State-owned corporations).

DUTIES

The duties of an *Avocat* have evolved from custom to statute, most recently as a consequence of the provisions of Law No. 90–1259 of 31 December 1990, amending Law No. 71–1130 of 31 December 1971, and of its implementing Decree No. 91–1197 of 27 November 1991.

However, codes of practice and case law still play a large part in shaping the duties of the Avocat, and in this respect, the *Conseil National des Barreaux* (hereinafter referred to as the CNB), which is the national body instituted by Law No. 90–1259 of 31 December 1990 to oversee the local bars, will be instrumental in ironing out the discrepancies among the various local codes of practice (*Réglements Intérieurs*) enacted by the local bars. In due course, and thanks to the CNB, it is likely that the codes of practice shall be harmonised and ultimately unified into one single code of practice.

It should be noted that several local bars, including the largest by far, i.e. the Paris Bar, have incorporated into their code the European code of practice adopted in Strasbourg by the Consultative Council of the Bars of Europe (CCBE). No doubt that the provisions of the European code of practice shall also influence the contents of the local codes of practice and have on them a harmonising effect.

In short, the duties of an *Avocat* are to abide by the canons of the profession, i.e. to act with dignity, conscientiously, independently, and with humanity. More practically, his duties are to maintain and preserve the integrity of the confidentiality obligation that he has undertaken in his relationship with his client, to educate himself in the law, to keep informed of the developments of his sphere of interest in the law, and to refrain from accepting briefs or instructions from clients that are beyond the scope of his expertise, which cannot be diligently carried out, or which are conflicting with some interests of which he is already in charge.

Standards

Although the profession of *Avocat* strives to maintain the highest ethics, its standards as interpreted by case law are more relative than absolute.

In other words, there is no question of a guaranteed result; the *Avocat* is only under an obligation to use his or her best efforts to achieve the result best suited to the overall interests of his client. The efforts should not merely be reasonable, but should be the best a competent lawyer is able to provide in like circumstances.

Civil and administrative liabilities

Civil liabilities

The basis for the civil liability of the *Avocat* lies in tort and is statutory insofar as it derives from the provisions of Articles 1382 and 1383 of the French Civil Code, which read as follows:

"Article 1382. Any action whatsoever by someone, which causes to another any harm, obligates the person by the fault of whom it occured, to repair it."

"Article 1383. Everyone is liable not only for any harm caused by his actions, but also by his negligence or imprudence."

It can readily be seen from the above texts that in order to collect under a civil liability claim against an *Avocat*, a three-part test should be met:

(1) The *Avocat* must have committed a fault (or must have been negligent);
(2) A person with whom he is in a client-attorney relationship must have been harmed; and
(3) There must be a demonstrated causation link between the said fault and such harm.

The claimant in such an action may either be the client, a former client, the client's shareholders, the directors of the client company, but not the creditors of the client or its sub-contractors unless the *Avocat* has engaged in some fraudulent conduct.

As provided by Article 26 of Law No. 71–1130 of 31 December 1971, which states that "Civil liability actions against the *Avocats* shall follow ordinary procedural rules", the procedure in a civil liability action against an *Avocat* is initiated by the claimant in a law court,[2] and is independent of any disciplinary procedure that may be initiated by the bar against the *Avocat* after the claimant has notified the Bar of the conduct or misconduct of the *Avocat*.

The damages recoverable are estimated by the judges in their discretion.[3] The amount awarded must reflect the monetary value of the harm suffered, irrespective of the seriousness of the fault committed.[4]

In other words, no punitive damages may be awarded. Otherwise, all types of damages, that is, moral or material harm (the latter including not only actual harm but also the loss of an anticipated gain or profit), are recoverable as long as this harm is personal to the claimant, directly linked to the fault committed and certain to have occurred or to occur. Regarding the recovery of attorneys' fees, it should be noted that in France, the winning party may shift the costs of the action to the losing party only to a certain extent. This extent is at the discretion of the judges. Article 700 of the French Code of Civil Procedure provides that if so requested by one party, the judge may order the losing party to bear in whole or in part the costs which the winning party has incurred "when it appears inequitable to let the costs incurred by a party be borne by it". In practice, judges are reluctant to award much in this respect, and it is extremely rare that the full amount of the fees incurred by the winning party is assessed, in the judgement, against the losing party. As a result, each party has basically to bear its own lawyers' fees when litigating in a French court.

Specific civil liabilities

ON-GOING AND ONE-OFF REPRESENTATIONS

There are no significant differences in the analysis of the civil liability of an *Avocat* by a court depending on whether he is in an on-going relationship with a client or if it is a one-off representation. However, in an on-going relationship, the client and/or the *Avocat* will probably rely on past conduct in like circumstances to prove what is acceptable behaviour on the part of the *Avocat*.

2. The *Tribunal de Grande Instance*, which shall hear the case in chambers.

3. *Cour de Cassation*, Civil Chambers, Ruling of 23 May 1911, *Dalloz Périodique* 1912.1.421.

4. *Cour de Cassation*, 2nd Civil Chamber, Ruling of 8 May 1964, *Juris-Classeur Périodique* 1965.II 14140 and *Revue Trimestrielle de Droit Civil* 1965.137.

GENERAL ADVICE AND SPECIALIST ADVICE

Specialist advice is an old concept, but it is only very recently that it has officially been recognised by a Ministerial Decision of 8 June 1993.[5] True enough, the former *Conseils Juridiques* could claim specialised knowledge of tax law, labour and employment law, and corporate law, but this Ministerial Decision has opened to the *Avocats* a wider spectrum of legal areas in which to claim specialised knowledge. However, it is too early to look for any case law on point. Nevertheless, it is clear that claiming specialised knowledge may be at least as dangerous as claiming to be able to render general advice to a client. A glaring example is in the area of opinion letters, in which the *Avocat* is requested by his client to render an opinion on which a third party will be relying.

Should the contents of the opinion so rendered be inaccurate, the client may suffer huge damages, such as the termination of loans or the waiver of insurance guaranties, for which the lawyer could be held accountable.

COMMERCIAL TRANSACTIONS

The *Avocat* is absolutely prevented from being the general agent of his client. This means that any mission whereby he would act as an intermediary must have a limited scope and be defined beforehand. This is to protect the integrity of the profession and to ensure that no action by an *Avocat* will turn him into a trader or a businessperson, which would entail a number of consequences in France. On the one hand, it may generally be said that the status of *Avocat* is incompatible with that of trader or businessperson. On the other hand, this does not imply that the *Avocat* is prevented from advising on all legal aspects of the commercial transactions of his clients.

On the contrary, the *Avocat* must be able to advise in such matters, but not to a point where he would become the partner of his client in the contemplated commercial transaction, because he would then lose his independence. By retaining his independence, the *Avocat* is ensuring that the ultimate business judgement regarding the contemplated commercial transaction is exercised by his client, thus exonerating himself of any liability should the said transaction turn sour.

AGREEMENTS

Likewise with regard to agreements, the *Avocat* may advise on all legal aspects of any agreement contemplated by his client. He may sign it on

5. Published in the *Official Journal* of 12 June 1993, p. 8407.

behalf of his client if he is specially empowered to do so by a power of attorney. He may participate in the negotiation of the terms of the agreement on behalf of his client, provided that he has been careful in asking for and has received specific instructions from his client. The danger area lies in the circumstance where the *Avocat* is asked to draft the agreement. Most trades have their own technical jargon and specialised trade terms, and quite often particular clauses that are not to be found in another trade. This is obviously true of commodities trading, shipping, insurance and bank lending, among others, and an *Avocat* who has no experience in a particular trade would unnecessarily create for himself some contingent liability by accepting to draft an agreement in which, more likely than not, a few important clauses would be missing. This is even more so in the area of mergers and acquisitions, if the *Avocat* is entrusted, as is often the case, with the task of carrying out due diligence searches and verifications.

REGULATORY COMPLIANCE

In the context of regulatory compliance, the principle that "no one is deemed to ignore the law", as is said in France, applies, but there are so many laws and regulations being churned out by the legislators and the administration every day that it has become quite impossible for the average person or businessperson not to run afoul of the law.

Therefore, one sees a growing trend of asking the *Avocat* to conduct specialised audits, not necessarily linked with any mergers and acquisitions situation, to ascertain that, for instance, a company is in compliance with certain regulations (e.g. environmental audits, labour law audits, antitrust and competition law audits). Of course, the *Avocat* who undertakes such a mission must himself be quite sure of which relevant statutes are in force, or he may be held liable for any inaccurate and/or incomplete opinion he eventually rendered.

LITIGATION CONDUCT

Litigation is the area where case law on the responsibilities of the *Avocat* is the most developed, because the *Avocat* was traditionally perceived as a litigator rather than an adviser — which he also was. Most cases turn on the failure of an *Avocat* to have lodged pleadings with a court or to have taken some action before some deadline, after which his client was barred from filing pleadings or from taking that action, thus in effect depriving his client of a chance of improving his position in the proceedings.[6] It is, therefore, essential that the *Avocat* be very alert as to

6. See, for example, *Cour de Cassation*, First Civil Chamber, Ruling of 9 December 1992.

the developments in the case, making sure that he complies not only with the general requirements of the Codes of Civil Procedure, Tax Procedure or Criminal Procedure, as the case may be, but also with those of the particular court before which litigation is being conducted.

ADMINISTRATION

In the administration of companies and trusts, certain principles apply. As already mentioned, an *Avocat* should not manage a company, but he may administer a trust as trustee. He can also be a member of the board of directors of a *société anonyme* (a corporation), or a member of its supervisory board (*conseil de surveillance*), including the position of chairman of the supervisory board. However, special care must be exercised by the *Avocat* in carrying out such duties, and a separate insurance cover is required.

Exercising such special care, he would, for instance, be mindful not to accept a power of attorney from the chairman of the board by which the *Avocat* would become the *de facto* or acting chairperson of the company. An *Avocat* who is appointed director or member of a supervisory board of a company must inform his bar thereof, and must already have some relevant experience.[7]

At the Paris Bar, an *Avocat* cannot accept the duties of chair or of vice-chairman of the supervisory board of a company without the prior approval of the Bar. The above restrictions do not apply to an *Avocat* who is also running a family business or a company the sole purpose of which is to practise the legal profession.

CONFLICTS OF INTEREST, DISCLOSURE, WITHDRAWAL

The *Avocat* must be sensitive to any appearance of conflict of interest, be it actual or potential. As soon as there is a conflict between his clients in a given matter, he should cease representing at least one of them. This rule also applies when there is a serious risk of conflict, unless all the clients concerned have been informed by the *Avocat* that he is advising them, and all the clients concerned have consented to such a situation.

The *Avocat* must also ascertain, when instructing a corresponding lawyer in a given matter on behalf of his client that the corresponding lawyer has no conflict of interest of his own.

7. Article 6 of Law No. 71–1130 of 31 December 1971, as amended by Law No. 90–1259 of 31 December 1990 provides that, unless the local Bar decides to shorten that period, the *Avocat* must have been admitted for seven years.

In litigation, the *Avocat* may withdraw if he feels he has to, provided that the client is informed with reasonable notice, so that his interests are not jeopardised, and that the continuity of the representation of the client is ensured *vis-à-vis* the court.

Generally, non-compliance with any rule governing conflicts of interest will result in disciplinary sanctions against the infringing *Avocat*, but not in any civil liability, unless harm and a causation link are proven.

CONFIDENTIALITY

The statutory basis for the confidentiality obligation of the *Avocat* is to be found in Article 378 of the French Criminal Code.

However, this text is not expressly referring to lawyers and gave rise to numerous interpretations which resulted in conflicting court decisions, some courts holding that the confidentiality obligation of the *Avocat* and the attorney-client privilege applied only in the case of litigation and not in the case of advice given in non-litigious matters, and some courts holding that they applied in all situations. The controversy has now been resolved by two recent statutory changes: On the one hand the Law No. 92–583 of 22 July 1992 (not yet in force) has created a new Criminal Code, Article 226–13 of which states:

> "The divulging of secret information by a person to whom it has been confided . . . pursuant to his profession . . . shall be punished by one year in jail and a fine of FF 100,000."

On the other hand, Article 4 of Law No. 93–2 of 4 January 1993 has modified the provisions of Article 66–5 of Law No. 71–1130 of 31 December 1971, which now states:

> "In all matters, the advice sent by an *Avocat* to his client or intended for the latter, and any correspondence between the client and his *Avocat*, are covered by professional secrecy."

The combined effect of these statutory changes is that it is now clear that the *Avocat* may and should invoke the privilege in all circumstances to defend the interests of his client, and that were the *Avocat* to breach such secrecy obligation, criminal, and not only civil, sanctions could be imposed upon him.

The rationale behind the obligation and the privilege is that the general public should be trustful of *Avocats* insofar as secrets confided to an *Avocat* are kept in confidence.

Defences, exclusions, time-bars

The primary defence to a civil liability claim would be for an *Avocat* to prove that he committed no fault, or to prove that the client suffered no actual harm and will not suffer any harm, or to prove that if the client suffered actual or potential harm, it was not as a result of the *Avocat's* actions or omissions. If none of the above defences is available to the *Avocat*, he may rely on a partial defence of the client having contributed to the harm by his mistaken or ineffectual interpretation of the *Avocat's* advice. No exclusion or limitation of civil liability is possible, the *Avocat* being a professional fully liable *vis-à-vis* his clients for any harmful consequences of the way he practises his profession.

Until not long ago, the time-bar for a claim against an *Avocat* was the standard thirty years provided by Article 2262 of the Civil Code, but two statutory changes have drastically reduced this time-span: for a claim involving the inability of an *Avocat* to return to the client original documents given to him in connection with a court case, the time-bar is now down to five years.[8]

For other claims against an *Avocat* based on their professional liability, the time-bar is ten years, running from the end of his mission,[9] unless the former time-bar of thirty years would have been tolled earlier than ten years after the coming into force of the amending law.[10]

Liability for partners, associates, staff

The principle of vicarious liability applies to *Avocats*, and an *Avocat* liable for the harm possibly caused by his associates and/or staff.

Regarding partners in a law firm, in other words, all *Avocats* involved in practice structures described at the beginning of this chapter except those involving only office sharing, the principle is that of joint and several liability of all partners. For instance, Article 16 of Law No. 66–879 of 29 November 1966, as amended by Law No. 90–1258 of 31 December 1990, provides that in an SCP, the partners and the SCP itself are jointly and severally liable for any harmful consequences.

Regarding the exposure of new partners for the firm's prior acts and of former partners for the firm's acts subsequent to their departure, it is usually contractually regulated in the articles of association or partnership agreement of the law firm concerned, and generally in the sense of the new partners assuming no liability for the firm's prior acts and the former partners not being responsible for the firm's acts further to their departure.

8. Civil Code, Article 2276, as amended by Law No. 71–538 of 7 July 1971.

9. Civil Code, Article 2277–1, as introduced by Article 6 of Law No. 89–906 of 19 December 1989.

10. Law No. 89–906 of 19 December 1989.

INSURANCE

Insurance coverage is not only available, but it is compulsory for the *Avocat*, as a guarantee provided by operation of law to the general public.[11] The bars have negotiated group insurance policies for their respective members, since Decree No. 91–1197 of 27 November 1991, which implements the above Law, having set a minimum level of coverage, which is FF 2-million per year per *Avocat* insured. The Paris Bar, being by far the largest with about 11,000 members, has effected insurance coverage which guarantees to the clients that if the *Avocat* is unable to account for funds which have been remitted to him, the amount of such funds will be paid to the clients up to FF 30-million per claim.

If the *Avocat* has committed a fault or a professional neglect resulting in harm to the client, the insurers of the Paris Bar will pay up to an amount of FF 25-million per claim (the so-called "basic insurance").

However, additional coverage is available and is not yet outrageously expensive. It is not uncommon for large law firms to have subscribed additional coverage in an amount of FF 75-million or even FF 175-million, thus bringing total coverage per claim up to FF 100-million or FF 200-million, respectively.

The cost of basic insurance is usually included in the annual dues to be paid by all practising *Avocats* to the local bar to which they belong.[12] At the Paris Bar, for instance, this has been so since 1972, and the insurance premium represents on average one-third of the annual dues. The cost of additional, voluntary, insurance varies according to the level of coverage sought.[13] In a law firm, the total premium would be equal to the number of partners multiplied by any of the above premium figures.

The following are excluded from professional liability insurance coverage: any activity of the *Avocat* as company director or in a capacity which he is prevented by law from assuming (such as businessman); any wilful or intentional misconduct, any permanent activity of the *Avocat* in the United States or Canada, or if there is no such permanent activity, but a claim arises, punitive and exemplary damages, if any, awarded to the plaintiff.

As already mentioned, no punitive damages are, as a rule, awarded in a civil liability action. Therefore, there is no practical need to insure against such a liability (which is nevertheless most often expressly excluded by insurers).

11. See Law No. 71–1130 of 31 December 1971, Article 27, as amended.

12. Pursuant to the provisions of Article 15 of Law No. 71–1130 of 31 December 1971, an *Avocat* must be a member of a bar.

13. For example, for FF 75-million in additional coverage, the premium is currently FF 2,595 per year per insured *Avocat*, and for FF 175-million, the premium is FF 6,095 per year per insured *Avocat*.

INTERNATIONAL PRIVATE LAW ASPECTS

In terms of his civil liability, a foreign lawyer advising his clients in France is subject to domestic standards. The question of whether he should carry the same insurance coverage as French *Avocats* is moot since the coming into force of Law No. 90–1259 of 31 December 1990, insofar as a foreign lawyer must become a member of a local bar to continue practising in France. Not doing so entails severe sanctions.

Regarding the civil liability of a French *Avocat* practising abroad, it is in most cases covered by his basic insurance (with the exception, as was mentioned, of a permanent establishment of that *Avocat* in the United States or in Canada), and there is little doubt that he is subject to both French standards and to the applicable foreign standards and liability. This is the direction in which the CCBE has indicated to the European Commission it should go in its current drafting of a Directive on the establishment of lawyers throughout the European Community.

CONCLUSION

The French *Avocats* are professionals proud of being responsible for their acts. There is no perceivable trend towards a limitation of such professional liability, and this is not a subject of debate in the profession.

However, there is a clear trend towards more numerous claims against *Avocats*, which comes as no surprise when one thinks how shielded the French were and still are as compared to their North American colleagues. Of course, not all claims ripen into lawsuits, many being settled out of court.

In the short term, this will no doubt result in an increase of the insurance premiums to be paid in order to obtain a reasonable level of insurance protection.

An even more ominous danger looms from Brussels, and the legal profession has yet to comprehend its impact if it is not averted: Reference is made here to a draft proposal of a European Community Council Directive relating to the liability of professionals,[14] which the European Community Commission has been trying to move through the European Parliament for about two years. This draft reverses the onus of proof, rendering the professional whose liability is being claimed automatically liable, unless he can disprove the allegation put forward by the claimant. Many European professionals (not only lawyers) have expressed through the European Secretariat for the Liberal Professions their displeasure with the new version of the draft and their desire that these ideas be abandoned. The draft

14. Doc Com (90) 482 Final - Syn 308.

proposal was, for all practical purposes, withdrawn from examination by the European Parliament in December 1992, but indications are that a new version is presently being prepared in Brussels.

Lastly, the only risk reduction measure that is likely to become effective in the long term is slowly making its way into France: The introduction into law firms of quality control procedures, ultimately resulting in the law firm being certified under the International Standards Organization ISO 9000 certification process. This could generate a significant reduction in insurance premium levels for law firms having obtained such a certification.

Conversely, it could also have the negative effect of splitting the French Bar into the haves and the have-nots. The National Council of the Bars will certainly have to think deeply about the consequences of such an evolution.

CHAPTER 6

GERMANY

THOMAS LINDEMANN
Boesebeck, Barz & Partner
Berlin, Germany

INTRODUCTION

Professional liability may occur where a lawyer wilfully or negligently has violated his obligations under a contract with a client or during the phase in which a contract with a client was under negotiation.

VIOLATION OF DUTIES

Pre-contractual obligations

In principle, a lawyer is free in accepting or refusing a mandate. However, if he wishes to refuse a mandate, he must do so without undue delay[1] failing which he may be liable to the prospective client in respect of those damages that he suffered because of a delayed refusal to act on behalf of the client.

Particularly in cases in which, for instance, deadlines for filing an appeal are on the verge of expiring, the lawyer must indicate immediately whether or not he is prepared to take up the matter since otherwise the client may find himself in the difficult position where, on the one hand, the lawyer addressed by him refuses to act on his behalf and, on the other hand, he may not be able to find another lawyer who would be willing to meet a fast approaching deadline.

Under certain circumstances, a lawyer may be barred from accepting a mandate. Under Article 45 of the Act on Lawyers (BRAO), he must not accept a mandate if he has advised another party with opposing interests in the same matter. Similarly, he may not advise a client as to the construction of a deed that has been notarised by him or one of his partners in their capacity as notaries.

The Civil Code of Procedure (*Zivilprozessordnung* – ZPO) and the BRAO stipulate that in certain circumstances, a lawyer must accept a mandate and that he is only entitled to refuse it in the case of a serious justification. This applies, for instance, in cases where a lawyer has been

1. Act on Lawyers (*Bundesrechtsanwaltsordnung – BRAO*), Article 44.

appointed by the court in divorce matters or incapacitation proceedings. Similar provisions apply if a lawyer has been appointed as mandatory defence counsel in criminal cases.

Parties to the contract

Under German law, the liability of lawyers is mainly based on contract. It is therefore essential to identify the parties to the contract since this has an obvious impact on the range of obligations of the lawyer and the potential number of persons entitled to damages.

On the side of the client, the party to the contract will normally be the person contacting the lawyer unless such person is acting as a representative for a third party and this agency has been made clear to the lawyer. Sometimes, a number of persons or legal entities together may be the clients of the lawyer in the same matter provided that they have the same interest in the outcome of a certain matter. In case of deviating interests, as explained above, a lawyer must choose a certain client and he is barred from acting on behalf of the others.

If the lawyer has his own law firm in which he is the only lawyer, he is the only party to the contract. The situation changes when he — actually or apparently — is co-operating with other lawyers. Sometimes, a number of lawyers work in the same offices although they do not form a partnership of lawyers. In this case, each lawyer has his own stationery, his own firm plate, and may thereby be identified as a sole practitioner lawyer. Breaches of contract and tort actions of a certain lawyer will not be imputed to the others. Should a number of lawyers share the same office but fail to show that they do not form a partnership, all lawyers may become liable *vis-à-vis* one lawyer's client in the same way as the members of a partnership.

There is an increasing tendency of lawyers to form partnerships in the context of which they practise their profession by using a joint name, joint stationery and a joint firm plate. The main characteristic is that the intention of a partnership is to share clients, mandates and fees.

In case of a partnership, the contract is usually concluded not with a single lawyer only but with all partners of the partnership. However, there may be exceptions: In cases where a client wishes to rely on the specific expertise of a certain lawyer of the partnership, which expertise a client would not find with other lawyers of the same partnership, it might well be the case that the contract is concluded between this very lawyer and the client only. A mandate may also be limited to a particular partner in the partnership if the mandate has been given to him on the basis of a strong personal relationship to the client resulting in the mutual understanding that the mandate in any case must be dealt with by this lawyer alone.

In all cases in which the mandate has been given to the partnership as a whole, each member of the partnership is personally liable for damages unlawfully caused by one of the members of the partnership to the client. The client may request payment of the full amount of damages by any one or any group of the partners. A recent change of the BRAO allows the limitation of liability to a certain quantum by way of the standard business conditions (AGBG). This requires the client's explicit acceptance in writing.

Partners who have left the partnership are only liable for damages caused during the time of being partner in the partnership. Partners joining the partnership at a later stage are not liable for damages caused up to that date.

Obligations vis-à-vis the client

A lawyer or a partnership of lawyers may be liable for damages if he or one of the partners acted in breach of the obligations arising from the contractual relationship. The contract between the lawyer and the client is based on mutual trust and duties. The range and nature of the obligations to be fulfilled *vis-à-vis* the client vary with the contents of the very mandate given to a lawyer. The contract between the lawyer and the client may be characterised as a contract by which one party is obliged to render particular services to the other. A number of mutual obligations are laid down in Articles 675and 611 *et seq.* of the German Civil Code (BGB). For instance, the lawyer must adhere to the instructions of the client,[2] he must render full, comprehensive information and account to the client,[3] and he must deliver monies or other things he has obtained in the fulfilment of his contractual duties.[4] These provisions, which are not explicitly designed to characterise the obligations of a lawyer *vis-à-vis* his client cover only a few aspects of the variety of obligations to be fulfilled by the lawyer.

As a general guide-line, one may say that the lawyer is obliged to comprehensively protect the interests of his client in all respects. He must clarify the facts, evaluate the legal implications and take all necessary steps to preserve the rights of his client.

Verification of facts

The quality of the advice rendered is highly dependent on the correct ascertainment of the facts of the particular case. Both client and lawyer

2. BGB, Article 665.
3. BGB, Article 666.
4. BGB, Article 667.

have specific obligations with regard to the requirement to assemble all necessary pieces of information.

In the first instance, it is the obligation of the client to bring all facts and documents to the attention of the lawyer that, according to the client's view, are essential for the lawyer in order to handle the case. The client must inform his lawyer completely, correctly and as quickly as possible. Information obtained by the client subsequently which in his view might be of importance to his case must be submitted to the lawyer as early as possible.

Usually, the client is not legally trained. His selection of facts and documents to give to his lawyer usually has not been filtered according to the specific perspective of a lawyer. One of the key obligations of the lawyer consists in putting those questions to the client which from a legal perspective are necessary to round off the picture of the case. The range of questions to be put forward to the client depends completely on the individual case. If necessary, he must urge his client to complete missing pieces of information and to advise him as to potential disadvantages that may arise in a lawsuit if no detailed information can be given to the court.

Of course, there are limits to such obligations to extract information of the client: The more experienced the client is in his business and his legal surroundings, the more the lawyer may rely on an accurate description of the case by the client even if he fails to use particular legal terminology. Moreover, a lawyer may rely on the information given by his client although he must make sure that there are no obvious misconceptions or contradictions. However, as a general rule, he is not obliged to verify the correctness of the information submitted to him.

Evaluation of the legal situation

Upon clarification of the factual situation, the lawyer must evaluate what rights and obligations his client has in the current situation and to which measures he may have access.

One of the most important points when starting to evaluate the legal situation is to check whether there are any statutory deadlines or grace periods set by the law, the court or an administrative authority within which certain actions have to be taken. In most cases, it is indispensable to start from this point since time-consuming legal considerations may be too late to be put into practice if such a deadline has elapsed in the meantime.

As regards the legal implications of the case, a lawyer is expected to have at least a certain amount of knowledge in the core areas of the law. He is not expected to be familiar with all aspects of the law however remote they may be. The client may nevertheless expect that his lawyer will be able to determine the applicable laws and the pertinent precedents. Only in cases of extremely recent changes in the law, may a lawyer claim that he was not aware of a change in the legal situation without becoming subject to a charge of negligence. Once he has taken up a mandate, a lawyer cannot resort to the argument that he was not familiar with certain laws since he is expected to acquire the necessary knowledge applicable to the case.

Apart from the written laws, there are no guide-lines on to what extent a lawyer must be familiar with court decisions. There is a clear tendency in German court practice that a lawyer is required to follow closely the decisions of the German Supreme Courts (Civil Court, Administrative Court, Criminal Court) to the extent that he is active in that legal area. Although he is not required to read those publications that are specifically designed for specialists in a particular field, every lawyer is expected to follow at least the publications in the main legal newspapers. The Federal Supreme Civil Court (*Bundesgerichtshof* — BGH) has also ruled that a lawyer should take note of recent important decisions within an adequate period of time, namely one month to six weeks.

There is no similar obligation to follow the court practices of the Courts of Appeal of the District Courts. This may be different if for statutory reasons certain cases cannot be dealt with by the BGH but where the final instance lies with the Court of Appeal.

Moreover, there is no obligation to closely follow the legal literature. On the other hand, a lawyer will mostly utilise the standard legal commentaries in order to find the pertinent judgements dealing with similar cases. Hence, he might well be considered to have acted negligently when he has failed to conduct adequate research in the legal literature, especially in the commentaries, to evaluate what court decisions have been rendered in a certain area and what the legal arguments were.

Advice to the client

Upon clarifying the facts and evaluating the legal situation, the lawyer is in the position and obliged to advise his client as to the legal situation and as to the alternative steps that may be taken. He must put his client into a position where the client may decide whether to take any steps at all, what steps are to be taken, if any, and how they should be taken. The Federal Supreme Civil Court ruled that a client is entitled to comprehensive and exhaustive advice as to all implications of his case. All aspects that are related to the case have to be taken into account and it must be assured that any detrimental effects will be avoided to the extent that one could realise and avoid them.

These are rather broad guide-lines, which have to be applied to the specific circumstances of a given case. Of course, the advice of a lawyer is limited to the particular mandate; he is not obliged to secure his client against any and all risks that are not related to a particular case. On the other hand, it is clear that it is sometimes difficult to determine whether certain aspects still belong to the "case" or not.

Particularly, in pending litigation or when the client is contemplating the initiation of proceedings, his lawyer is required to advise as to the prospects of winning the case. Since the client is not aware that the risk of losing the case may be related to the uncertain outcome of the taking of evidence or an uncertainty arising from the construction of a certain provision of the law, a lawyer must call his client's attention to these issues. There is no obligation to indicate any theoretical risk that may arise in the course of litigation. It is rather expected that the specific risks of a particular case will be outlined to the client. This applies equally to the question of whether or not to file an application or an appeal, and with respect to how and to what extent to defend a case.

Usually, a lawyer need not advise his client as to the cost consequences of a potential lawsuit. Under German law, costs of litigation have to be borne by the parties in proportion to their respective loss. This means that a claimant awarded 20 per cent of the claim submitted to the court must bear 80 per cent of the overall costs of litigation, i.e. the court costs and the costs of his lawyer and the opponent's lawyer.

In light of the fact that this is a general rule, the lawyer is normally not required to advise his client accordingly. Only in very particular circumstances, for instance, if the client has an obvious misconception of how the costs will be dealt with, may a lawyer be required to clarify this point.

As an exception to this rule, the successful party in labour law matters cannot request reimbursement of costs at first instance. The labour courts have concluded therefrom that this exemptive rule puts the obligation on the lawyer to advise his client accordingly. Non-compliance with this requirement may result in losing the claim for fees against the client.

In addition, one of the principles to be observed by a lawyer is that he must choose the safest way of dealing with a client's case. If the client may choose among a series of measures, the lawyer must advise which one in his opinion is the least dangerous one.

Finally, a lawyer must advise his client as to potential claims for damages against the lawyer himself.

Deviation from instruction

The obligation to choose the safest way to protect the interests of the client may sometimes collide with deviating instructions of the client. In principle, a lawyer must adhere to such instructions even if their consequences may be detrimental to the client. Nevertheless, the lawyer must make sure that such an instruction had been given on the basis of a proper understanding of the legal situation.

Of course, a lawyer is barred from accepting instructions that would result in unlawful actions or actions against public policy. In such a case, even a definite instruction of the client would not oblige the lawyer to follow.[5]

Otherwise, there is little room for the lawyer to deviate from instructions of the client. Deviations from specific instructions are only permissible if it was not possible to obtain the client's approval beforehand and if the lawyer could rightly expect the client to agree on the intended deviation from his instructions. There will be only few cases in which these conditions will be fulfilled since mostly it will be possible to postpone court hearings and similar appearances in order to obtain the prior approval of the client.

ELEMENTS OF LIABILITY

Bases of liability

Under Articles 284 *et seq.* and Article 326 of the BGB, the lawyer is liable for damages arising from delayed performance of his obligations. Articles 280 *et seq.* and Article 325 of the BGB provide for claims for damages in cases where it has become impossible for the lawyer to discharge his obligations. In both cases, delay and impossibility, liability only exists provided that the lawyer acted at least negligently.

Mostly, damages to the client do not occur because of delayed or impossible discharge of obligations, but because of improper or incomplete discharge of contractual obligations. This applies both to principal and ancillary duties existing under the contract. In these cases, claims for damages are not covered by the above provisions. It is an interesting feature to note that the written German law does not provide for any claims for damages under these circumstances at all. The legal literature and the subsequent court practice developed a separate institute called "positive breach of contract" (*Positive Vertragsverletzung* — PVV). Under PVV the client has a claim for damages, if the lawyer's actions were in breach of his obligations under the contract, if such actions were performed at least negligently, and if there is a particular link between the lawyer's action and the damage suffered (causality).

As already outlined, liability may arise if a lawyer unduly postpones rejection of a certain mandate.[6] In addition, Article 627 of the BGB provides for claims for damages if the lawyer terminates the mandate at an improper point in time which, for instance, may be the case if termination takes place immediately before an important procedural step to

5. BRAO, Article 45 No. 1.
6. BRAO, Article 44.

the effect that the client may face considerable problems in finding another lawyer who could take this step within the remaining time frame.

As claims based on PVV usually cover most of the client's damages, claims under the laws of tort particularly relate to damage suffered by third parties. This may be the case if an application for the opening of criminal proceedings is filed with the public prosecutor despite his being aware or unaware through gross negligence that no criminal offence has been committed. Apart from such extraordinary cases, there is no liability of a lawyer for commencing civil or criminal legal proceedings if it proves later that the opposing party acted rightfully.

Another area where claims of third parties against a lawyer under the laws of tort may come into play is the enforcement of court judgements obtained on behalf of the client. In order to enforce the judgement, the successful plaintiff must instruct the bailiff to take the money from the debtor on the basis of the judgement. If no or insufficient funds are available, the bailiff may attach the assets of the debtor. The plaintiff may also instruct the bailiff as to which assets should be seized. Such an instruction may include assets not belonging to the debtor. The bailiff cannot and will not verify prior to seizing the assets whether they do belong to the debtor or not. It may well happen that assets are seized although the debtor is not the owner of these assets. Of course, the owner may appeal against such seizure and he may succeed in having his assets returned. If the owner suffers damages due to the delayed release of his assets, the lawyer may be liable for these damages provided that he was positively aware or should have been aware that the assets were not the debtor's property.

Unlawfulness

A lawyer is not expected to deliver a certain result but to render specific services on behalf of his client. Lawfulness or unlawfulness of his actions, therefore, cannot depend on whether or not particular results have been obtained. In addition, professional mistakes of a lawyer will stem from omissions (for instance, failure to meet a certain deadline) rather than from positive actions. It is therefore more appropriate to look at the lawfulness of his behaviour from the viewpoint of what he was expected to do rather than from the viewpoint of what result he has obtained.

In light of this, unlawfulness may be described as neglecting the proper care which a lawyer could be expected to apply according to the circumstances of the given case. Whether or not he failed to apply such standard of care must be answered by reverting to the range of obligations to be fulfilled by him. These duties and their range of priority vary from case to case. For instance, filing an appeal instantaneously may be a reasonable thing to do even though chances of a successful judgement may turn out to be bad if the deadline for filing the appeal elapses on the same day as when the mandate has been received. Filing the same appeal may be a blatant violation of the lawyer's duties to carefully consider the client's position if the deadline for filing the appeal does not elapse until a few weeks later.

It must be borne in mind that any behaviour would be considered unlawful if it does not meet the highest possible standard of care, seen from an objective point of view. Any behaviour of a lawyer that does not comply with this standard would be held unlawful. Whether or not a lawyer has applied the highest possible standard of care must be evaluated from an ex-post perspective.

One of the few reasons that might remove unlawfulness could be the approval of the client. So, where the lawyer's actions have to be considered as a breach of his obligations due to a lack of corresponding instruction from his client, such behaviour could not be considered as unlawful if later on approved by the client.

Fault

In principle, fault exists if a breach of contract has been committed intentionally or negligently. Intentional breaches of contract do not play too important a role, which is why the following outline deals with negligence only. Acting negligently means to failing to exercise the care as is usual in the ordinary course of business (ordinary care). The requirement to meet a certain objective standard of care is an element of characterising a certain action as unlawful or lawful as well as defining whether the behaviour has been negligent or not. In the context of defining whether an action was lawful or not, one must apply the criteria of the highest possible standard of care.

When it comes to examining whether a lawyer was at fault, the criteria of ordinary care have to be applied to the individual situation of the acting lawyer. However, this does not mean that the standard of ordinary care must be defined according to the individual situation and the individual capabilities of a given lawyer. This is only true in criminal law. As regards civil liability, ordinary care is defined as a standard of care that a reasonable and prudent member of the same profession would have applied in the given situation. As opposed to the element of unlawfulness, the question of fault must be answered by giving an *ex-ante* judgement: The key test is, therefore, what a careful and prudent lawyer would have done in the given situation. It may be worth mentioning that as to the individual lawyer, this standard may be less demanding than his own standards provided that he himself applies an extremely high standard of care.

Referring to the care of a careful and prudent lawyer does, however, not mean that one would have to conform with the standards of an average lawyer. Although this might be true for areas of general practice, different standards may apply as to special fields of the legal profession which one might expect a specialist to be more familiar with than an ordinary practitioner. In addition, higher standards would apply to lawyers asserting to have specific knowledge in these areas. This applies in particular to those lawyers bearing titles showing particular expertise such as lawyers specialised in labour law" (*Fachanwalt für Arbeitsrecht*).

Whether a specific action or non-action could be considered negligent depends on whether a certain risk was foreseeable and/or avoidable. As already explained, filing an appeal which — with retrospect — had no chance of success could be considered to be unavoidable if the deadline for filing the appeal elapsed on the date of receiving the mandate, because the risk of incurring unnecessary costs by filing the appeal is by far smaller than losing the complete case by failing to meet the deadline for filing the appeal.

Similarly, the courts have accepted that a sudden illness could count as an excuse for failing to meet such deadline provided that the illness was not foreseeable.

Origin of default

In day-to-day practice, lawyers collaborate with their staff, other members of their law firm and other law firms. All these persons may be involved in the discharge of the lawyer's obligations *vis-à-vis* the client.

Usually the client confers the mandate on the law firm as a whole. Delegating certain functions or obligations under the mandate to a colleague in the same law firm has no impact on the evaluation of fault, since all acts committed by the second lawyer will be considered equally negligent as would be the case had the delegating lawyer not chosen to delegate the case or certain parts of it.

Under German law, lawyers are usually admitted to the bar only before the district court of their own county. Hence, they have no right of audience in other district courts. If a client has a lawsuit before a district court where his lawyer is not admitted, the services of a local counsel admitted to that particular district court have to be retained. On more than one occasion, a local counsel will be granted a sub-power of attorney by which a direct relationship between him and the client comes into existence. Damages suffered by the client because of negligent behaviour of a local counsel entail a direct claim for damages by the client against the local counsel. A corresponding claim of the client for damages against his lawyer may arise only if he was negligent in selecting the local counsel, which might, for instance, be the case if he should have been aware that the local counsel has a reputation for not being dependable. Besides, direct liability of the lawyer may be based on an unjustified granting of the sub-power of attorney to the local counsel. If there was no need to appoint local counsel and if the client does not approve the retaining of the services of a local counsel, the lawyer himself may be liable for ensuing damages.

Mostly, local counsel will receive not only a sub-power of attorney, which is often insufficient, especially where the lawsuit is pending before a district court, but local counsel will be appointed under a principal power of attorney. Here, the obligations of the client's lawyer, as opposed to the local lawyer, undergo a change to the effect that he must arrange for a smooth correspondence between the client and the local counsel. The local counsel then is the main acting lawyer in court, and he bears the bulk of the responsibilities *vis-à-vis* the client. Nevertheless, a number of obligations remain with the initial lawyer, namely, the obligation to select proper local counsel and to collect and transfer all necessary information. Both, the referring lawyer and the local lawyer are separately responsible for the proper discharge of their obligations *vis-à-vis* the client.

In particular, in larger law firms, a number of associates and/or free lancers are involved in dealing with mandates. They are not parties to a contract between the law firm and the client since they are not partners in the law firm. Since delegation of work within a law firm to an associate is no more than an internal process, a law firm cannot exclude liability by arguing that it was entitled to delegate the mandate to a quasi third party (its associate). Rather, the law firm is responsible for any breaches of contract committed by the associate under Article 278 of the BGB, according to which a law firm must assume liability for negligent behaviour of persons involved by the law firm in the discharge of its obligations.

Similar rules apply to a lawyer's personnel. Their negligent behaviour must be compensated by their employer unless and until their behaviour has no relationship whatsoever to the mandate.

CAUSALITY

It is only justifiable to hold a lawyer liable for a breach of his obligations if such breach of obligations was causal for the damage that occurred. In the first place, causality is a scientific problem. Any breach of any obligation must be considered causal in a scientific sense: The damage would not have arisen, if the respective breach had not occurred? This is the *conditio sine qua non* principle. As a consequence of this, a countless number of reasons would account for the occurrence of the damage since it happened not only because of the breach of a specific obligation but also because a variety of other things had happened before or simultaneously. To narrow down the group of actions or non-actions that, from the legal viewpoint, could be considered as causal for the occurrence of certain damage, additional elements have to be attributed. Causality in a legal sense exists only if, from the viewpoint of an experienced and prudent person, the occurrence of a certain damage as a consequence of a particular action or non-action was foreseeable. Also, damages may only be recovered to the extent that the obligation breached by a lawyer was specifically designed to prevent such damages from occurring. As opposed to that, the realisation of the general risk of life, i.e. those risks against which a lawyer is not intended to protect his client, do not entail his liability for damages.

In a situation where damage occurred with a client because of an omission by his lawyer, the *conditio sine qua non* formula cannot be applied since there was no action of the lawyer without which the damage would not have occurred. In cases of unlawful omissions, causality exists if the required action cannot be added to the theoretical sequence of events without the damage failing to occur. Of course, a number of actions could have avoided the damage although the lawyer was not obliged to perform such actions. The courts, therefore, introduced an element of adequacy by taking into account only such action the performance of which fell into the range of duties of the lawyer.

DAMAGES

Under Articles 249 *et seq.* of the BGB, the obligation to remedy damage in principle must be discharged by restoring a situation that would have existed but for the unlawful action by the lawyer. Alternatively, the client may request payment of the amount of money necessary to restore such situation. The critical point in time is either the rendering of the court decision or the actual satisfaction of the claim for damages. Since there may be a gap between these two, in the case of a court judgement, it may be decided that the defendant must make good all additional damages that may arise after the rendering of the judgement.

The quantum of damages may be reduced by advantages received because of the breach of contract. This may, for instance, apply to costs and expenses saved or other monetary advantages such as tax benefits or interest. However, there must be an adequate relationship between the damage suffered and the advantage related thereto since the obligation to pay damages is to serve as compensation for a particular breach of a contractual obligation or one imposed by law. Voluntary payments of third parties designed to mitigate damages as well as payments of insurance companies will not be credited to the amount of damages.

In case of a lawsuit that has been lost and in the course of which a lawyer has acted incorrectly, the client may be entitled for damages if the lawsuit would have been won in case the lawyer had acted correctly. Sometimes, damages are caused by negligent behaviour both of the lawyer and his client. In this case, according to Article 254 (1) of the BGB, the obligation to make good the damage is reduced in proportion to the client's share in negligence. This may particularly apply to incomplete or delayed rendering of information.

LIMIT TO LIABILITY

There is no statutory limit to liability. Recently, law firms have tried to limit their liability *vis-à-vis* the client by entering into an agreement limiting the law firms' liability. Since limitations in liability are usually laid down in standard business conditions, the Act on Standard Business Conditions (AGBG) comes into play. Recent legislation allows liability to be limited to DM 500.000 by way of standard business conditions, liability may be limited to DM 2 million.

In any case, it is clear that one cannot exclude liability for wilful behaviour. The mainstream attitude in the legal literature is also that a limitation of liability with regard to grossly negligent behaviour is not permissible either. In addition, it is disputed whether exclusion of liability for ordinary negligence in general would be permissible. The majority view is that liability for ordinary negligence cannot be excluded to the extent that it refers to compliance with essential obligations arising from the mandate. As opposed to that, a limitation of liability for ordinary negligence with regard to ancillary duties would probably be upheld.

Claims for damages arising out of a contract between a law firm and a client are time-barred after three years.[7] This provision does not apply to the lawyer's activity as executor, administrator or trustee. It applies, however, to any claims based on the contract. Claims based on tort are also time-barred after three years. The three-year period commences, however, only once the client has obtained knowledge of the damages and the tort feaser. In any event, tort claims are absolutely barred after 30 years. Contrary to that, the time-bar under Article 51 of the BRAO usually commences to run at the end of the mandate. In a number of cases, the time-bar period commences at an earlier stage during the processing of the mandate, in particular when a certain mistake has been committed.

Under German law, lawyers are obliged to advise their clients as to their potential claims against the law firm. In the absence of such advice, a secondary claim for damages comes into existence barring the law firm from resorting to the defence of time-bar. Of course, the secondary claim for damages is also subject to the time-bar commencing at the occurrence of time-bar of the primary claim for damages. Effectively, by the creation of the secondary claim for damages, the time-bar period has been extended from three years to six years.

BURDEN OF PROOF

Due to the fact that in many cases, advice will be given orally, quite often no evidence can be submitted as to the question whether certain advice

7. BRAO, Article 51.

has been given or not. The allocation of the burden of proof is, therefore, of considerable importance. In principle, in a lawsuit each party must establish the elements of those statutory provisions that they seek to rely on. If a client seeks damages on the argument that he lost a lawsuit because of negligent behaviour of his lawyer, the client must establish all those facts which would have resulted in a favourable judgement in the preceding case; the lawyer would have to establish all those facts which would have resulted in a failure to win the case. It has, however, to be borne in mind that a court, when evaluating a lawyer's liability, is not expected to try to deal with the case as similarly as possible as the case would have been dealt with during the unsuccessful lawsuit; rather, the court must try to find the correct decision, irrespective of what the preceding decision was like or was expected to be like.

Once a violation of the obligations under the contract with the client has been established, Article 282 of the BGB establishes a rebuttable assumption for negligent behaviour on the part of the lawyer.

Mostly, the parties quarrel over whether or not a certain piece of advice has been given or not. There is a tendency to place the burden of proof with the client who, hence, must prove the fact that his lawyer has not performed certain tasks which according to the client formed part of his lawyer's duties. There are, however, some deviating court decisions, according to which the obligation to render a certain piece of advice entails also the burden of proof as to whether or not the advice has been given. In any case, it will have to be explained in detail what discussions were held with the client and what advice has been given. Thus, it is not permissible to simply rely on the prospect that the client will not succeed in establishing the facts entailing the lawyer's liability.

Under extraordinary circumstances, the burden of proof may shift. Particularly in cases where one party to the dispute prevents the other party, having the burden of proof, from access to the evidence available, the allegations of the other party may be treated as correct. These cases are, however, fairly rare.

CHAPTER 7

GREECE

CHRISTOS A. PAPACHRISTOU
Law Offices
Athens, Greece

INTRODUCTION

The legal profession in Greece is governed by Legislative Decree 3026/1954, titled "Code of Lawyers", with its subsequent amendments, in conjunction with the "Code of Professional Ethics".

Article 1 of the former Code characterises the lawyer as an unsalaried civil servant. This wording is neither accurate nor literally correct as lawyers in Greece are not directly subordinated to the state. However, the language underscores the public and social function of the legal profession, especially when the lawyer prosecutes cases in the name of the client before the state judicial, administrative and other bodies. Out of court consulting or advising constitutes the liberal nature of the legal profession, but the law makes no distinction. Greek law does not acknowledge various types of legal advisers. The profession is unitary. The capacity of being a lawyer includes both advocacy before courts and out of court advisory work.

In Greece, it takes four years of university study to obtain a degree at one of the three law faculties, after which graduates are required to undergo a further 18 months of training at a law office and in the courts. At the end of the 18 months' training period, the candidate sits the Bar's final qualifying examination.

A candidate may not qualify as a lawyer, and a qualified lawyer's admission may be withdrawn if he or she is sentenced:

(1) To death or life imprisonment;
(2) To imprisonment for theft, embezzlement, fraud, blackmail, forgery, bribery, oppression, disloyalty, malpractice and falsification; or
(3) To imprisonment for a period over three months and the court's decision orders the forfeiture of the capacity to act as a lawyer.

Lawyers who have been admitted and lawfully exercise their profession in the jurisdictional territory of a local district court constitute an association of lawyers or a bar association. Membership of these bodies is obligatory. There are 62 local bar associations, each attached to the local district court, and the law recognises these as the sole official professional body. Lawyers qualified before one bar may not plead before the courts of another bar, but they are permitted to give legal advice.

The bar associations are legal entities governed by Greek public law. They are managed by a council, have their own assets and are subject to civil law regulations with regard to the acquisition of legal rights and the undertaking of civil or contractual obligations.[1]

As legal entities ruled by public law, they supervise the lawful application and observance of the provisions regulating the exercise of the legal profession for the benefit of the public.

Local bars and their councils are responsible for, *inter alia*:

(1) Taking care of the dignity of their members and the respect which the authorities have to pay to them during their practice;
(2) Submitting proposals and opinions regarding the improvement of legislation, its interpretation and implementation;
(3) Voting for its annual budget and the establishment of contribution membership; and
(4) Supervising and monitoring the dignified practice of the legal profession and imposing disciplinary punishment on its members.

Practice structures

Most Greek firms operate on a small-scale, office cost-sharing basis and there are still relatively few firms with more than five partners. Some law firms employ lawyers part-time, and it is possible for in-house lawyers to carry on a considerable private practice simultaneously.

The partnership structure is still in its infancy, since it was not recognised as a legal entity until 1986 by Law 1649. Before that, Article 47(2) of the Code of Lawyers dictated that law practice should be individual, based on the view that the independence of the lawyer — even against its colleagues — is secured by sole practice. In 1986, this Article was amended and the code now admits partnerships as a legal form of practice. However, few have been officially established, partly because the law does not allow the degree of flexibility of operation that Anglo-Saxon firms enjoy. According to the Presidential Decree 518/89, two or more lawyers may form a partnership strictly of a personal — and not of a general commercial — nature in order to provide legal services. Also, partners may only be lawyers who are members of the same local bar association. The legal partnership is governed by Articles 741–784 of the Greek Civil Code, and its activities may not extend beyond the jurisdictional territory of the local district court.

1. Code of Lawyers, Article 194.

Foreign lawyer's practice

By virtue of Presidential Decree 52 of 28 January 1993, which implemented European Community Directive 89/48, lawyers from other Member States may be allowed to practise Greek law in Greece if:

(1) They obtained a law degree after a minimum three-year period of studies at a recognised European Community Law faculty, or have a certified three-year professional experience as a lawyer in their Member State of origin; and
(2) They pass the proficiency examinations in the field of Greek Law. These examinations are oral and written and are conducted in Greek.

FUNDAMENTAL RIGHTS AND DUTIES

According to Article 38 of the Code, the lawyer is an unsalaried civil servant entitled to honour and respect by the courts and the authorities.

Articles 39–42 of the Code stipulate the lawyer's primary task, which is to represent and defend his principal before any court or any authority, committee or disciplinary council and to provide him/her with legal advice. The lawyer is exclusively competent to register trade marks and patents. The utilisation of a lawyer is mandatory for a search at the local real estate registry (mortgages and foreclosures) as well as for the drafting of contracts before a notary public if the contract value is more than 5-million drachma for the prefecture of Attica or 750,000 drachma for the rest of the country.

Article 52 of the Code grants a lawyer the right to issue certified copies from the original or officially certified documents that he has in his possession, thereby assuming responsibility for their accuracy. Lawyers may also certify true translations from foreign language documents.

Articles 46, 47, 48 and 49 of the Code in conjunction with Articles 6 and 7 of the "Code of Professional Ethics" dictate the most important duties with which a lawyer must comply with:

(1) A lawyer must practise conscientiously and exert his best efforts to execute the assigned mandate primarily trying to settle disputes when they are susceptible of thereto;
(2) A lawyer is obliged not to defend illegal and patently unjust cases, to always use legitimate methods of defence, not to neglect his/hers mandate and not to protract trials;
(3) A lawyer is obliged to undertake all cases assigned to them susceptible of defence and not choose clients by criteria of financial background;

(4) A lawyer must refuse to undertake a case if:
   (a) From the evidence, it appears that the case will be dropped;
   (b) In a previous similar case handled by the lawyer, he/she had argued a contrary view that was accepted by a final court judgement;
   (c) For the sake of defence, the lawyer would contradict his/her published theories, opinions or views on the same subject;
   (d) The lawyer will not have adequate time to prepare the case; and
   (e) there is any other conflict of interest.

In the case of felonies, where the defendant is not the able to afford a lawyer and the court orders legal aid, the designated lawyer cannot refuse the appointment. Article 49(1) stipulates the lawyer's duty of absolute confidence regarding any information or document that was entrusted to him/her by the principal.

Thus, a lawyer is strictly prohibited from testifying in a case he has handled. He may reveal, if summoned, any other information of which he became aware during the course of his/her practice and only after he gains permission from the Bar.

Qualified lawyers may lose their capacity as such if at the same they exercise another profession such as workmanship, commerce and brokerage. It is also incompatible with the exercise of the legal profession to be a manager or company representative. However, lawyers may be appointed or elected presidents of the board of directors or financial advisers after having been granted a dispensation from the Bar. Lawyers may not be employed as employees in posts other than that of the in-house lawyer, but they can be active as journalists or teachers of legal and political sciences. Article 9 of the Code of Professional Ethics prohibits of any kind of advertisement in the media or in the press. The lawyer may be introduced only by his/her name, professional, title and address.

Billing practices

Greek lawyers bill by the hourly rate depending on the novelty and urgency of the matter. In certain cases, the hourly rate is substituted by a percentage fee. Billing is governed by the Code of Lawyers, but its guidelines are extremely broad. The minimum percentage fee, which is set by the Code for most non-litigation services, is 1 per cent up to Drs. 5-million and 0.5 per cent on any sums in excess thereof.

PROFESSIONAL NEGLIGENCE

Background

When the lawyer undertakes to pursue a court or extra-judicial matter for a client, and this falls under the professional duties as they are described in Articles 39 *et seq.* of the Code, an agreement is concluded between the lawyer and the client, which normally is concluded informally.

This legal relationship may be characterised either as a stipendiary contract or one of remunerated mandate or even as a contract for the confidential hire of services. However, in the end, its liberal nature most resembles the roman-Byzantine law's contract of unsalaried or stipendiary mandate.

Through this contract, the lawyer undertakes to offer his services to his principal, and he is obligated according to Article 46(1) of the Code of Lawyers to exercise the authority assigned to him with great diligence and conscientiousness.

Also due to the special trust governing the relationship of the lawyer with his client, an additional moral and legal duty is created for the lawyer to take special care and to display a high sense of responsibility during his handling of the cases assigned to him.

It is possible, however, for a lawyer to commit an error — to the detriment of his client — in the performance of his function. Normally, violations of the lawyer's contractual responsibility are not due to intent, and only exceptionally would the lawyer intentionally violate his obligations, either the legal ones emanating from the provisions of the law in force (e.g. the Code of Civil Procedure) or those deriving from the existing legal regime of the bar, that is from the provisions of the Code of Lawyers, of the bar's internal regulation and from the bar council's decisions, as well as the contractual ones emanating from the existing stipendiary or remunerated mandate contract between himself and the client.

The question in the cases of unintentional infringements is whether lawyer's errors give rise to liability for damages at his own expense and in favour of his client. In the cases of intentional infringement, the lawyer's liability arises under penal law and the bar's disciplinary provisions with a corresponding liability to compensate the damage caused to the lawyer's client.

The basis of the lawyer's liability is the "misdemeanour", in other words, his culpable conduct Before any effort to find and analyse the lawyer's misdemeanour, a brief review of what generally applies to the cases of misdemeanour in the Greek Civil Law provisions is appropriate.

Concept of misdemeanour

"Misdemeanour" or culpability (*culpa*) "is a volition offence resulting in the person's liability by law". By the term culpability (or misdemeanour) the law signifies, according to scholarly opinion, the person's mental connection to his action or its result, which justifies reproach at that person's expense. In other words, the kind of behaviour by a person that is deprecated by the law.

There are two degrees of culpability, according to the gravity of the volition of the conduct:[2]

(1) Intention (fraud), which is the graver case; and
(2) Negligence.

Intention exists when the offender sought the unlawful consequence, in other words, when the offender's action "in full consciousness" is directed to the unlawful consequence. Negligence exists when such a wish on behalf of the offender is absent, but he failed to exercise the care he could and should have in order to prevent the unlawful consequence, in other words when his volition proved "inactive".

Both intention and negligence constitute forms of culpability. In theory they are the only ones, and they are mutually exclusive.[3]

The provision of Article 330(2) of the Civil Code provides that "negligence exists whenever the care essential to transactions is not taken". In this way, the initial question arises of what the measure is upon which it will be judged whether the offender's behaviour was intentional or unintentional, and particularly what conduct will constitute the standard in order to decide whether it was possible to predict the unlawful consequence.

Now, an objective criterion prevails in the civil law, according to which the only potentialities to be considered decisive are those of an average, scrupulous, judicious person. For a scrupulous lawyer, specifically, his knowledge of the Supreme Court jurisprudence is considered essential. Any deviation of the offender's behaviour from these standards is to be considered negligence, even if the offender in question is not in a position to display any other kind of behaviour.

The objectification of negligence according to the aforementioned is essentially justified because civil liability does not aim at imposing sanctions (penalties), as does penal liability, but at compensating the damage caused. The Civil Code goes on to distinguish two degrees of negligence (*culpa* in a narrow sense):

(1) Slight negligence (*culpa levis*); and
(2) Gross negligence (*culpa lata*).

2. Civil Code, Article 330.
3. Civil Code, Article 330.

The criterion for this distinction is not stated in the law. However, the terminology used is clear and indicates that it depends on the gravity of the negligent behaviour.

Slight negligence is defined by theorists as "disregard of the care of the diligent family-man" (diligence or *bonus paterfamilias*), whereas the gross negligence is defined as "disregard of the care of the average of person"; in other words, *intelligere quod omnes intelligunt* (to not understand what everybody else does) according to the Regalia.[4]

Negligence means deviation from the average scrupulous man's behaviour. When this deviation is uncommonly high, then it is a case of gross negligence. The point, however, where the deviation exceeds those limits beyond which a negligent act may be characterised as a gross one is only a matter of evaluating the case in question by the judge, who also must take into consideration all the circumstances under which the deviation from diligent behaviour occurred. The Supreme Court, for example, has decided that the lawyer's failure to check public registration books before a real estate transaction is concluded constitutes a gross negligence.

The Civil Code does not acknowledge any form of slighter negligence (*culpa levissima*). Thus, according to the aforementioned criteria, it is either a matter of slight negligence or not.

The distinction between slight and gross negligence has a practical value, since most of the time the law provides for the existence of liability only for gross and not for slight negligence. This normally happens when liability is acknowledged only in cases of intention, which means that the law ranks intention with gross negligence. However, a general rule for such an equation does not exist, and it applies only to the extent that the law provides for it specifically — directly or even indirectly.

In any other case, the law does not accept the behaviour of the average diligent person as a standard for slight negligence. On the contrary, it defines as such the diligence that the person in question displays in his own private affairs.

THE LAWYER'S CIVIL LIABILITY

Background

The lawyer's civil liability in Greece for misdemeanours he commits during performance of his function is restricted as opposed to his disciplinary liability, which is indeed far more extensive. The lawyer's disciplinary liability covers all kinds of violations of his duties and obligations

4. Reg. 2.2.205.

deriving from the provisions of the Code of Lawyers, the internal regulations, as well as from the decisions of the bar council of which he is a member.[5]

The lawyer's civil liability, on the other hand, is restricted to the cases where infringement of the lawyer's duties either general or special, deriving from the lawyer's status and from the existing common legislation or contractually deriving from the lawyer's agreement is due to intention or gross negligence or unjustified refusal to render services provided the lawyer's act or omission caused damages at the expense of the plaintiff.[6] Before expounding on the action for damages against the lawyer, it is necessary to discuss briefly the lawyer's liability deriving from agency principles and applied to the individual cases of the lawyer's misdemeanour. Unfortunately, the present case law is only fragmentary and is not of great help in analysing these issues.

However, in accordance with the comparativist approach of Greek legal scholarship and judicial reasoning, one may resort to the extensive solutions of the German law and legal theory. This source is valuable and renders useful inferences in the cases suited to parallel or converging solutions. The steps of analogy may reveal some deficiencies since they tread virgin legal terrain, but should still serve as a guide for better-founded future dogmatic processes. In this analysis, regard will be had to individual cases of the lawyer's misdemeanour.

Determination of liability

Article 46 of the Code of Lawyers obliges the lawyer during performance of his office to execute diligently and conscientiously the task assigned to him, to try to amicably settle the disputes before him and susceptible to compromise, as well as to contribute to the prevalence of truth and justice. More particularly, he is obliged not to defend illicit and obviously iniquitous cases, to refrain from any devious ("indirect") methods of prosecuting his case, and not to neglect the execution of the mandate assigned to him or protract proceedings.

This general provision may be characterised as a framework provision, mainly including general guidelines, as well as ethics rules applied to the way of performing the lawyer's duties. As to its interpretation, the provisions of Articles 6 and 7 of the Bar's Code of Professional Ethics are of great help.

5. Code of Lawyers, Article 64.
6. Introductory Law of Civil Procedure, Article 73(4).

The general guidelines included in the provisions of Article 46 of the Code of Lawyers must be made more specific in certain cases of lawyer's duties — general or contractual infringement — so as to form the prime basis of the lawyer's liability.

Such a specialisation process is achieved either through the contractual obligations undertaken by the lawyer or through other more specific provisions of the Code of Lawyers, for example, those of Article 47, or even through other provisions of the general legislation in force, for example, those of Article 233 of the Penal Law, the violation of which may constitute a form of lawyer's misdemeanour that may be instituted — regardless of any possible parallel disciplinary or penal liability. It is an independent action for damages against the lawyer.

Mandate or agency liability

Article 46 of the Code of Lawyers discusses the "mandate" and imposes on the lawyer the duty to "conscientiously and diligently execute the mandate assigned to him". In other words, it presupposes the formation of the agreement between the lawyer and his client, a stipendiary or remunerated agency contract. Usually, the agreement between the lawyer and his client is informally formed according to the general principles of the civil law, and on the coincidence of the expression of the parties' volition. The drawing up of the contract does not require any explicit statements, and it may even be formed from the parties' determined behaviour. Actually, this is the commonest form, where the client expounds his case to the lawyer and, in turn, the latter pursues it.

Thus, the duty to render services, which binds the lawyer to his client, is determined by this "contract". When we talk about a lawyer's contract, this expression is a shorthand for the existing relationship between the lawyer and the client, and is used "techno-legally".

The contractually determined performance by the lawyer may also be of a multiple nature, so as an approximating, exhausting enumeration and classification in groups to be impossible. The performance may, for example, consist in merely giving simple advice, in the drawing up of a consultative opinion, a contract draft, or even in the conduct of an entire trial.

Pre-requisites to recover damages

Article 73(4) of the Introductory Code of Civil Procedure restrictively determines the cases that may justify an action for liability against a lawyer, setting at the same time the prerequisites for such a suit to be brought. Thus, for the lawyer's misdemeanour to form the basis of a claim for damages to be paid by the lawyer, the following are necessary:

(1) An act or omission must have occurred to the plaintiff's detriment;
(2) This act or omission must have been the result of intention or gross negligence or denial of justice; and
(3) The plaintiff must have suffered loss due to such an act or omission.

The first prerequisite is to show an act or omission at the expense of the plaintiff. At this point, a brief analysis of the notions of act or omission will be attempted, as they are employed in civil law. The act is a certain human action directed by volition and producing changes to the outside world. The act, in a wide sense, may consist either in a positive action or in an omission.

In both cases, the act may have legal significance, but it may also be of no significance such as a mere social invitation. The omission acquires a legal constellation, not in itself, but when it concerns a certain action, for example, when a person could or should make a statement or positive action or should be observant of a certain behaviour. The law is interested in it not as "inactivity", which is not an action, but as an omission of a certain positive action, which is imposed either by law or by contract.

The second prerequisite is for this act or omission to be based on intention, gross negligence, or denial of justice.

As far as "denial of justice" is concerned, when lawyers are involved, it should be understood as unjustifiable refusal to render services, that is, a violation of the obligation imposed on the lawyer by Article 47(1) of the Code of Lawyers.

The third prerequisite is for this act or omission to have caused damage at the plaintiff's expense.

German legal reasoning in relation to the damage and to its evaluation is widely accepted in Greece. The theory of difference has been adhered to:[7] "As damage we mean any kind of injury caused to a person's material or immaterial goods, in other words any impropitious change of them."[8]

For discovery of the property damage, a comparison between the present (after the harmful event) patrimonial position and that which would exist but for the harmful event is carried out. The difference between the two measures constitutes the damage. The first of the two sizes compared refers to the "present" actual financial position of the

7. First developed by Mommsen, it is also accepted by the Greek legal system; see SC(AM) 172/1969, No. B 17, 836, 807/1973, No. B 22, 321.

8. Stathopoulos, *Law of Contract* (8), p. 243.

damaged person, whereas the second one refers to a hypothetical financial position in which the damaged person would have been if not for the harmful event.

Individual cases of the lawyer's misdemeanour

It is not possible to make a full and *a priori* specialised, analytical enumeration of all the cases of the lawyer's misdemeanour giving rise to the lawyer's obligation to compensate his client. Every violation of the lawyer's duties, meeting all prerequisites quoted above, creates an obligation on the lawyer to pay damages.

The civil offence is not identical with the criminal offence provided for in other areas of the law and must be distinguished from both penal and disciplinary measures.

A wide group of these acts (or omissions) is covered by the provision of Article 233 of the Penal Code, which provides for and punishes the lawyer's malpractice. According to this provision:

"A lawyer, or other legal advocate, who intentionally damages the person whose interests he is legally defending, or is in the same judicial process helping through advice or services rendering to both litigants, is punished with at least three months in prison."

This offence is among the crimes concerning the dispensation of justice and protects legal protection. The above Article includes not only judicial proceedings but also extra-judicial ones, and, in general, any case requiring legal defence. The notion of lawyer also includes trainee lawyers.

There are several examples of such malpractice in the case law. For example, the lawyer who held — after conducting a securities audit — that there was no impediment to purchase, while there was, was considered to have committed fraud and malpractice.[9] Furthermore, a lawyer who in 1960 undertook in his professional capacity to institute legal proceedings in order to achieve ratification of a defective legal transaction, and did not take any further steps up to 1972, was considered to have committed an offence.[10]

On the other hand, a lawyer who offered his legal assistance in one case is not impeded to defend the party adverse to his former client later on in another case.

9. SC(AM) 201/1969.
10. SC(AM) 427/1977.

Other acts similarly constituting a civil and penal offence to the client's detriment and resulting in an obligation for compensation are forgery,[11] fraud,[12] defalcation,[13] and violation of the duty of professional confidence.[14]

A second category of lawyers' misdemeanours also giving rise to the lawyer's civil liability are those committed due to gross or inexcusable negligence. Such misdemeanours include:

(1) The inadequate investigation by the lawyer of securities based on realty. For example, a lawyer who undertakes to investigate the securities of a property must check the securities of a 10-year period, covering regular prescription,[15] and does not have to consult the 20-year period in order to cover extraordinary prescription as well;[16]
(2) Ignorance of the existing legislation or its amendments, resulting in loss of the suit;
(3) The untimely performance of a judicial process, resulting in the oncoming of finality or an irreversible decision against the client;
(4) Failing to observe a strict time limit or non-obstruction of the statute-barring of a client's claim;
(5) The non-taking in time of the proper insurance or precautionary measures;
(6) The untimely notification to the client of a decision served to the attorney-at-law, for the client to decide whether or not to take legal action; and
(7) The non-submission, together with the pleadings, of crucial actual assertions or preliminary objections that would have as a consequence the dismissal of the suit filed against the client or of the legal process taken against the client. The submission of preliminary objections is of particular significance, since they do not simply result in the dismissal of the suit, but also in the reversal of the right subjudice. For example, the non-submission of a statute-barring objection.

It is unclear whether the lawyer's ignorance of the case law of the Greek Supreme Courts' (Supreme Court of Appeal, State Council) amounts to slight or gross negligence in Greece. However, ignorance of significant and widely known decisions of the Supreme Court's jurisprudence,

11. Penal Code, Article 216.
12. Penal Code, Article 386.
13. Penal Code, Article 375.
14. Penal Code, Article 371.
15. Civil Code, Article 1041.
16. Civil Code, Article 1045.

concerning crucial legal issues well known to the great majority of the Bar, may constitute gross negligence and lead to liability in a particular case. The obligation of knowledge on behalf of the lawyer also extends to the State Council's decisions, since a lawyer undertaking a case before the State Council is deemed to have an adequate knowledge of what the position of this court is; otherwise, he is assumed a case without having the appropriate and necessary experience.

The Supreme Court of Appeal accepts that failure to check public registration books constitutes gross negligence. The Greek legal scholar Stathopoulos[17] asserts that, especially for a diligent lawyer, his knowledge of the Supreme Court's jurisprudence is considered essential. He does not state, however, whether this lack of knowledge is considered gross negligence.

The third and final class of lawyers' misdemeanours are those referred to as unjustifiable denial of services. Article 47(1) of the Code of Lawyers obliges the lawyer "to undertake every case assigned to him, which is susceptible of defence". This Article, combined with Article 73(1) of the Introductory Law of Civil Procedure gives rise to civil liability:

> "If a lawyer unjustifiably refuses to act in a case susceptible of defence and this denial causes damage at the client's expense, then the lawyer is obliged to compensate this damage."

Imputation of the misdemeanour to the lawyer

An important factor in claims of lawyer's liability, as well as for any other person's liability, is the culpability of the conduct in question. The term culpability or misdemeanour law refers to the person's mental bond with an action. A person's culpable behaviour (or misdemeanour) is the one allowing personal (direct) reproach for the act imputed to him.

Where there is a breach of a legal obligation and the objective prerequisites for liability are also present, then the act is objectively imputed to the offender. In order for the personal, subjective imputation to be also effected, another element, apart from culpability but likewise subjective, is required: the capacity to impute the act to the defendant, a process which in fact precedes culpability. The same also applies to the cases where an omission is alleged. Imputation is judged by the court as a matter of fact according to the Civil Code obviating further consideration here.

A last prerequisite for compensation liability is the existence of a causal link (*causal nexus*) between a legitimate basis of liability — not merely between the harmful event, iniquitous act or the offender's act in

17. See Stathopoulos, *Law of Contract* I (6), p. 160.

general — and the damage suffered. More specifically, the liability for compensation arises only for that damage which arises from the elements that, according to law, are considered to be the basis of liability. This basis must be the cause of the damage and this damage, on the other hand, is the consequence (causal result) of this basis.

The theory of "conditions equivalent" (*condictio sine qua non* theory) is the application of causality, as it is being perceived by logic and the natural sciences. The theory of the adequate cause (*causa adaequata*) prevails in Greece at present. According to it, the cause can be characterised as "adequate" not simply because it gave rise to the damage by logical causality, but mainly because it generally had the capacity to lead to the occurrence of the damage in the normal course of events. This theory is also supported by the provision of Article 298(2) of the Civil Code. It does indeed achieve the restriction of liability, since it does not accept liability for damages due to an inadequate cause.

According to case law, the presence or absence of a *causal nexus* is a factual matter that is not subject to the Supreme Court's review, but is predominantly decided by the judge of fact at first instance.

As a rule, damages are paid in cash and, exceptionally, in kind. They may include physical and moral (intangible) injuries to persons, the property damage and, only exceptionally, non-physical property damage. They also include indirect damages, to the extent they are connected, through *causal nexus*, with the legitimate basis for liability, as well as future damages. As a rule, the evaluation of the damage is effected specifically and not abstractly.

Article 300 of the Civil Code also applies to the case of lawyer's liability. Thus, the lawyer who causes the damage may prove the existence of his client's culpability or joint liability, if he or she wishes to achieve his release or reduction of his liability, based on Article 300 of the Civil Code.

MISTRIAL SUIT

The mistrial suit may be brought to obtain compensation from legal civil servants such as lawyers, notaries, arbitrators, clerks of the court, and bailiffs.

For the mistrial suit against legal civil servants (members of the State Council, of the Supreme Court of Appeal, of the courts of appeal, the courts of the first instance and their public prosecutor's offices, stipendiary associate judges in the court of the first instance, magistrates, members of the State Audit Council, members of assessor's and other administrative courts), as well as against entire courts, the Special Court constituted according to Article 99 of the 1975 Constitution and Law

407/1914 is competent. The mistrial suit is allowed only in cases of intention, gross negligence and denial of justice (here, unjustifiable refusal to render services).

Mistrial suits may be filed against arbitrators, lawyers, clerks of the courts or public prosecutor's offices, and bailiffs. This is regulated by Article 73 of the Introductory Law of Civil Procedure. The court responsible for the hearing of the mistrial suit is the Multi-Membered Court of the First Instance, which always adheres to regular rules of civil procedure.[18] The suit is drawn up according to Articles 118 and 216(1) of the Code of Civil Procedure and must include, on penalty of being declared null, all reasons on which the plaintiff bases the mistrial suit and an exact account of all probative evidence employed for establishing the charge. On penalty of being declared inadmissible documentary evidence employed to support the suit in the original or certified copies, and a special proxy to the lawyer who signs the suit must be submitted.

A mistrial suit cannot be brought after the passage of six months from the invoked illegal act or omission. As it has been correctly accepted by the case law, the commencement of the six-month time-limit for filing a mistrial suit coincides with knowledge on behalf of the plaintiff of the defendant's act or omission.

The mistrial suit is dismissed, as indefinite, if apart from the invocation of the defendant's omission, no other reason for which the omitted act would prevent damage is stated (lack of the necessary *causal nexus*). In this case, however, the plaintiff may refile the suit, according to Article 263(2) of the Civil Code.

If the mistrial suit is dismissed for any reason, the filing of a new suit as to the same case and for the same or other reasons cannot stand, and the plaintiff is ordered to pay legal expenses, and he may even be punished with a fine, according to Article 205 of the Code of Civil Procedure.

PARTNERS' LIABILITY

Clients with conflicting interests

Lawyers as individuals as well as in a partnership are not allowed to accept instruction of different people with opposing interests. Such an interdiction is harmonised not only with the lawyer's professional ethics, but also with other provisions of the lawyer's legislation imposing directly[19] or indirectly[20] the observance of this obligation. The lawyer is not

18. Introductory Law of Civil Procedure, Article 73.
19. Lawyer's Ethics Code, Article 10.
20. Code of Lawyers, Articles 45(1), 46(1) and (2), 49(1).

allowed to "give advice to or defend a litigant if he has also given advice to the adverse party for the same case" and is similarly not allowed to "directly or indirectly defend both litigants".

Such an interdiction is in accordance with Article 233 of the Penal Law (lawyer's malpractice), and any violation of this Article incurs, apart from disciplinary penalties set out in the Code of Lawyers, the penal measures of this Article as well.

Those who are to suffer penal and disciplinary penalties are the members of the partnership individually, and more specifically those members involved in the violative act. Violation of these provisions may also lead to liability for damages by the partnership itself. The liability for damages is chargeable to the partnership's legal entity as well as to those members individually involved in violation of Article 29(1). This is set out into Article 14, which provides that the culprit or liable members are all "equally" responsible together with the company's legal entity.

Partners' liability to each other

The lawyer who is a member of a partnership and who is not an administrator or assistant administrator of the partnership is liable to the rest of the members and the partnership only in relation to the conduct of his own cases. However, he is also liable for slight negligence to third parties.

Regarding liability to the rest of the partners and the partnership, in accordance with the regulation of Article 746 of the Civil Code, the member is liable only for the conduct of his own cases. In other words, on his dealing with the partnership's cases, the lawyer must pay the same regard he normally spends on handling his own private affairs.

Thus, the relevant standard is slight particular negligence (*diligentia quam in suis*) which is an exception to the general rule of the Civil Law (Article 330(2) of the Civil Code), according to which the debtor is liable for slight abstract negligence. Such negligence arises when the diligence required in transactions is not rendered, namely, the display of the same amount of regard that the average prudent person of the defendant's social circle demonstrates.

This regulation is facultative, and consequently, any contrary agreement making provision for the partners' liability, as well as for abstract slight negligence, in simple accidental events or even in *force majeur* events, is valid. Likewise valid is the contractual release from the member's liability for particular slight negligence[21] or even for gross negligence, when this is exceptionally provided for by general provisions.

As far as liability to third parties is concerned, according to Article 13, the lawyer-partner is also liable for slight negligence. This provision

21. Civil Code, Article 332(1).

introduces exemption from the regulation of Article 73(4) of the Introductory Law of Civil Procedure, which admits existence of the lawyer's liability to his principal only in cases where the act or omission at his client's expense is based on intention or gross negligence or denial of justice. It is only then, according to what is generally in force, when a claim to damages can be founded at the lawyer's expense and a mistrial suit is possible to be filed against him.

Liability of the partnership legal entity

According to Article 14(1) of Presidential Decree 518/89, the partnership legal entity is liable to third parties for the lawyers' acts or omissions, as long as the act or omission was committed in the administration or representation of the partnership and in the handling of the case of a partnership principal. This provision completes the protection of third parties. Parallel to the members' individual liability, the liability of the partnership legal entity is also instituted.

As for the statute-barring of third parties' claims against the partnership's legal entity for the aforementioned acts or omissions of the lawyers-members, the general period of six months would seem to apply since the same the basis of liability is the same in this case.

According to Article 14(2) of the 518/1989 Presidential Decree, the lawyer at fault in the partnership together with the partnership are jointly and severally liable for the former's act or omission. Also, the partnership, in turn, is entitled to indemnification from the culprit-lawyer for the same amount of money defrayed to the third party. However, any possible insurance of the partnership against its civil liability to third parties, is valid in favour of all members. In such a case, the partnership is entitled to indemnification from the culprit-lawyer only for the amount of money that was not covered by the insurance compensation received.

This is the first time that the law in Greece provides for insurance of lawyers' civil liability to third parties. This kind of insurance forms a common ground for most European countries and, for the most part, it is compulsory. In Greece, due to the restricted extent of the lawyer's civil liability for acts or omissions committed in practice, insurance of the lawyer's civil liability is unfamiliar. According to Article 73(4) of the Introductory Law of Civil Procedure, a liability claim against a lawyer can be filed only if it is based on intention or gross negligence or denial of justice (unjustifiable refusal to render services).

However, after the expansion of civil liability for lawyers belonging to law partnerships, the insurance of their professional liability has become necessary.

CHAPTER 8

IRELAND

Edmund Butler And Vanessa Fenton
L.K. Shields & Partners
Dublin, Ireland

INTRODUCTION

The Irish legal profession consists of practising lawyers, legal academics and the judiciary. The liability of these and other professionals for their professional acts or omissions is dealt with in this chapter. Because of the breadth and depth of the area under discussion, this chapter contains only an outline of the main features.

Types of legal adviser

Practising lawyers

Practising lawyers are divided into two branches — barristers and solicitors, the essential distinction between them being that a client must first consult a solicitor for legal advice, as a barrister, with certain exceptions, is not generally permitted to take instructions directly from a member of the public.

A barrister may act for a friend or on an *ex gratia* basis without the intervention of a solicitor, but in such circumstances, he may not act in any contentious matter. A barrister may accept direct instructions from a patent or trade mark agent or from such further parties as may be authorised by the Bar Council.

The judiciary

The principle of judicial independence enshrined in the Constitution of Ireland of 1937[1] strengthens the argument that acts or omissions by members of the judiciary in their judicial capacity are absolutely privileged.[2]

1. Constitution, Articles 35.4 and 35.5.
2. *MacAuley* v. *Power* (1943) 77 ILTR 61.

Judicial immunity from suit is required to maintain public confidence in the judiciary as well as to ensure judicial independence. Therefore it is most unlikely that an individual could successfully sue for damages arising from a judicial decision.

Arbitrators and mediators

Persons conducting quasi-judicial functions such as arbitrators or mediators will be immune from civil actions brought against them due to similar public policy considerations. It is necessary for such immunity that the act complained of be a judicial one.[3] A professional fixing a new rent pursuant to a rent review clause was held to have been relying on his own expert judgement and experience rather than to have decided the matter on the evidence and submissions of the parties and was held not to be immune from liability for negligence.[4]

Community services

Free Legal Aid Centres operate in major cities and are staffed by solicitors and others who give their services on a voluntary basis. Legal advice on many matters may also be available from citizens advice bureaux and other organisations.

Other professions

Ancillary to their particular specialities, professionals including engineers, architects and accountants will have a detailed knowledge of many aspects of law relevant to their specialities and will often advise clients thereon, though such professionals would not ordinarily be regarded as lawyers.

When first drafted, the Solicitors' Bill, 1994 proposed to allow building societies, credit unions, banks and insurance company subsidiaries to provide to members of the public probate and conveyancing services, which can at present be provided only by solicitors. However, recent announcements suggest that the solicitors' monopoly on these areas will not be disturbed.

3. *Siros* v. *Moore* [1975] QB 118.
4. *Palacatts* v. *Flanagan* [1985] 2 All ER 161.

Regulatory framework

Solicitors

Solicitors in Ireland are regulated by the Solicitors' (Ireland) Act, 1898; the Solicitors' Act, 1954 and the Solicitors' (Amendment) Act, 1960 ("the Acts"). The profession is also subject to the European Community (Freedom to Provide Services) (Lawyers) Regulations,[5] the Solicitors' Accounts Regulations[6] and the Solicitors' Professional Practice, Conduct and Discipline Regulations[7] ("the Regulations"). The Solicitors' Bill, 1994 has been published, but has not been enacted as law and is currently the subject of debate. The Incorporated Law Society's Guide to Professional Conduct for Solicitors in Ireland does not have legislative effect and breach of the rules set out therein will be solely a matter for the Disciplinary Committee of the Law Society. However, evidence of such a breach may amount to evidence of negligence in subsequent court proceedings by an aggrieved client.

In the conduct of proceedings in the courts, solicitors are obliged to comply in their conduct with aspects of the Rules of the Superior Courts,[8] as amended, the Rules of the Circuit Court, 1950, as amended, and the District Court Rules,[9] as amended.

Barristers

Barristers' conduct is not regulated by statute. A Code of Conduct issued by the Bar Council of Ireland regulates the conduct of all Barristers (whether practising or otherwise), but this Code has no legislative effect, and breach of the rules will merely render the offending barrister subject to the profession's internal regulatory proceedings.

Professional bodies

Solicitors

The Incorporated Law Society of Ireland is the solicitors' professional body. Its Disciplinary Committee has statutory powers to investigate the conduct of its members and administer disciplinary measures including striking the solicitor's name from the roll of solicitors.[10] The Disciplinary

5. SI Number 58 of 1979, amended by SI Number 197 of 1981 and Number 226 of 1986.
6. SI Number 304 of 1984.
7. SI Number 405 of 1986.
8. SI Number 15 of 1986.
9. SR & O Number 431 of 1947 and SI Number 173 of 1988.
10. Solicitors' Act, 1960, Section 7 (1).

Committee consists of members of the Law Society Council, or past members who are practising solicitors, appointed by the President of the High Court.[11] Statutory grounds on which a person may apply to the Law Society's Disciplinary Committee to have a solicitor disciplined include misconduct likely to bring the profession into disrepute, contravention of provisions of the Acts or Regulations, or conviction of a criminal offence.[12] If the members of the Disciplinary Committee are of the opinion that a complainant has established a *prima facie* case an inquiry will proceed. When the inquiry is completed the Disciplinary Committee's findings will be embodied in a report to the High Court, specifying the nature of the allegation, the evidence laid before the Committee with any other matters which they think fit to report, including their opinion as to the fitness, or otherwise, of the solicitor to be a member of the profession.[13]

The High Court, after consideration of the report, has discretion to make a number of orders[14] including:

(1) Ordering that the name of the solicitor be struck off the roll;
(2) Suspending the solicitor from practice for such period as the Court may fix;
(3) Censuring and requiring the solicitor to pay a money penalty;
(4) Such order as to the costs incurred in the proceedings before it and the Disciplinary Committee as it thinks fit; and
(5) Directing the solicitor to make such restitution to such aggrieved party as the High Court thinks fit.

Barristers

The Honourable Society of Kings Inns is the barristers' professional body. The conduct of the members of the bar is controlled by a non-statutory body called the General Council of The Bar of Ireland, which is annually elected by the Bar Council members, who themselves only are eligible for election.

PRACTICE STRUCTURES

Solicitors

In the Republic of Ireland, solicitors may practise as sole practitioners or form unlimited partnerships of any size governed by contract and the

11. Solicitors' Act, 1960, Section 6.
12. Solicitors' Act, 1954, Section 14.
13. Solicitors' Act, 1968, Section 7 (3).
14. Solicitors' Act, 1960, Section 8.

Partnership Act, 1890. They may not assume corporate status, and furthermore, a body corporate or an officer thereof may not imply that the body corporate is qualified to act as a solicitor.[15]

Barristers

All barristers in private practice are required to be sole practitioners. They may not share premises or facilities without the consent of the Bar Council.[16] In recent years, an amount of co-operation and cost sharing has taken place between barristers who continue to operate as sole practitioners. Unlike England, in Ireland, there is no system of Chambers.

CAPACITIES

Solicitors

The main function of solicitors is to give advice on legal matters and to act on behalf of their clients in legal transactions. They have the task of preparing cases for trial and since the Courts Act, 1971 have the same rights of audience in all courts as do barristers, though in practice, few solicitors avail of this in any but the lower courts. Solicitors may advise clients and act for them in matters that involve commercial investment or other nonstrictly legal considerations.

A solicitor may sometimes be required to act as an intermediary in investing funds or referring clients to a broker for that purpose. A solicitor may offer custodial services, for his clients' documents and property, or he may act as a trustee and would in that capacity be subject to any trust instrument and general trust law.

It is not unusual for solicitors to be members of the Irish Branch of the Chartered Institute of Arbitrators and to act in that capacity. It is also possible for a solicitor to act as a mediator.

Barristers

A barrister acts as a consultant on referral and may not act in a professional capacity except on the instructions of a solicitor or in appropriate cases, those of a patent agent or a trade mark agent.[17] Where a barrister

15. Solicitors' Act 1954, Section 64 (1).
16. Code of Conduct for the Bar of Ireland, Paragraph 14.
17. Code of Conduct for the Bar of Ireland, Paragraph 4.1.

acts as a friend or on a charitable basis, for instance, as a member of a Free Legal Advice Centre, he may act without the intervention of a solicitor, but in such circumstances he may give advice only and may not act in any contentious matter.[18] While barristers are commonly perceived as trial advocates, in practice, much of their time is spent in advising, drafting documents or in legal research. Many barristers would have far wider experience of advocacy at interlocutory stages rather than at trial. A barrister is also permitted to act as arbitrator and many do.[19]

GENERAL DUTIES

Solicitors

Statutory duties pursuant to the acts and regulations

The solicitor has a statutory duty to keep proper books of account to show his dealings with clients' money,[20] to keep such money in a separate bank account and to pay to his client certain interest earned thereon.[21] The solicitor must annually submit an accountant's certificate to the Registrar of the Law Society, stating whether or not the accountant is satisfied on an examination of the solicitor's or his firm's books, accounts and documents that the solicitor or his firm has complied with the Solicitors' Accounts Regulations.[22] Failure to comply with those regulations may result in disciplinary measures being taken against the solicitor by the Law Society's Disciplinary Committee.

Codes of practice

The Incorporated Law Society issued in 1988 a Guide to Professional Conduct for Solicitors in Ireland. Among the duties laid down in this code of practice are:

(1) A duty to ensure that conflicts of interest do not arise;[23]
(2) A duty to do his best for his client using his utmost skill and care;[24]

18. Code of Conduct for the Bar of Ireland, Paragraph 4.2.
19. Code of Conduct for the Bar of Ireland, Paragraph 6.21.
20. Solicitors' Accounts Regulations (SI Number 204 of 1984), Regulation 10(1).
21. Solicitors' Professional Practice, Conduct and Discipline Regulations (SI Number 405 of 1986), Regulation 5(1).
22. Solicitors' Act, 1960, Section 31(1).
23. Code of Conduct for the Bar of Ireland, Paragraph 1.2.
24. Code of Conduct for the Bar of Ireland, Paragraph 1.9.

(3) A duty to be open, frank and honest in dealings with clients;[25]
(4) A duty not to take advantage of the inexperience, youth, want of education, or lack of knowledge or business acumen of a client;[26]
(5) A duty to invest, where he holds a Power of Attorney from a client, monies properly and prudently;[27]
(6) A duty to act promptly and efficiently and insofar as is practicable to explain to a client the procedures to be followed in any particular matter and the length of time the procedures are likely to take;[28] and
(7) A duty not to make secret profits arising from work done on behalf of a client, though where a solicitor acts as an intermediary, he may receive commission from insurance companies and transactions on the Stock Exchange once disclosure is made to the client.[29]

Codes of practice are, of course, without the force of law and cannot create strict legal duties, nor can they alone found an action under the Solicitors' Act, 1954 to have disciplinary measures taken against a solicitor. However, it is submitted that such written standards are likely to carry great weight in the courts as:

(1) Evidence of the general practice of the profession; and
(2) Evidence of what specific steps a reasonably careful and competent solicitor would take.

These standards are likely to lead to a greater uniformity in practice and thus it may become increasingly difficult for solicitors to justify conduct that falls short of that described in the code of practice.[30]

Common Law

The Irish Courts are completely independent from those in England and English precedents are not binding in this jurisdiction, but it is common for English precedents to be cited before the Irish Courts; frequently the Irish judiciary will follow the decisions of their English brethren as well as those of other jurisdictions, although less frequently.

25. Code of Conduct for the Bar of Ireland, Paragraph 1.10.
26. Code of Conduct for the Bar of Ireland, Paragraph 1.11.
27. Code of Conduct for the Bar of Ireland, Paragraph 1.12.
28. Code of Conduct for the Bar of Ireland, Paragraph 1.16.
29. Code of Conduct for the Bar of Ireland, Paragraph 2.10.
30. Jackson & Powell, *Professional Negligence* (3rd ed.), p. 339.

At Common Law, any professional person who makes a statement or omission owes a duty of care to the recipient and may be liable for economic loss suffered due to the recipient's reliance on a negligent mis-statement.[31] This principle has been limited in Ireland so that "the relationship between the person seeking the information and the person giving it must be 'equivalent to contract' before any liability can arise".[32]

However, it is submitted that this limitation will not limit the potential liability of professionals for negligent mis-statement to persons who are not their clients. This is due to the adoption in this jurisdiction of Lord Wilberforce's landmark decision in *Anns* v. *Merton London Borough Council*.[33] In *Anns*, Lord Wilberforce formulated a two stage test for negligence, stating:

"... first one must ask whether, as between the alleged wrong-doers and the person who has suffered damage there is a sufficient relationship of proximity or neighbourhood such that, in the reasonable contemplation of the former, carelessness on his part may cause damage to the latter — in which case a prima facie duty of care arises. Secondly, if the first question is answered affirmatively, it is necessary to consider whether there are any considerations which ought to negative or reduce or limit the scope of the duty or the class of person to whom it is owed or the damages to which a breach of it may give rise."

The Irish Supreme Court has accepted this test[34] and has declined to follow *Anns*' subsequent rejection in England.[35] Thus, under *Anns*, legal advisers may be liable for negligent statements unless public policy can be invoked as a defence. While it must be stated that the Supreme Court's endorsement of *Anns* was *obiter* and that *Anns* dealt with builders', rather than professional's liability, nonetheless the test therein is regarded as a correct statement of the law in Ireland.

The Irish High Court has accepted expert evidence of general practices and it has been stated[36] that though these practices are not rules of law, a solicitor has a *prima facie* duty to adhere to them.

In addition to his duty at Common Law, a solicitor also owes fiduciary duties to his client. Thus, he is under a duty not to make a secret profit and to make full disclosure of any interests he has in a particular transaction and would be liable to account for profit gained by such non-disclosure.[37]

31. *Hedley Byrne & Company Limited* v. *Heller & Partners* (1964) AC 465.
32. *Bank of Ireland* v. *Smith* [1966] IR 646 per Mr. Justice Kenny.
33. [1978] AC 728.
34. *Ward* v. *McMaster and Others* [1988] IR 337.
35. *McLoughlin* v. *O'Brien* [1983] 1 AC 410.
36. *O'Connor* v. *First National Building Society* [1991] ILRM 208 per Lynch J.
37. *Nocton* v. *Lord Ashburton* [1914] AC 932.

Barristers

Code of conduct

Barristers have certain duties imposed on them by the "Code of Conduct for the Bar of Ireland" issued by The Bar Council. This Code does not have the force of law, but failure to comply with the duties set out therein may amount to professional misconduct. The duties of a barrister as stated in the Code of Conduct include:

(1) A duty to uphold the interests of his client without regard to his own interests or those of another person;[38]
(2) A duty to accept instructions in any case in the field in which he professes to practise at a proper professional fee, unless justified by special circumstances in refusing to do so;[39]
(3) A duty not to engage in conduct, whether in pursuit of his profession or otherwise, which is dishonest or which may otherwise bring the profession of a barrister into disrepute or which is prejudicial to the administration of justice;
(4) A duty to be competent in all his professional activities; and
(5) A duty to observe the ethics and etiquette of his profession.

The Barristers' Professional Conduct Tribunal (which is distinct from the Bar Council) has two lay members nominated by the Federation of Irish Employers and the Irish Congress of Trade Unions, and deals with complaints from the public, solicitors, or the Bar Council itself through its Professional Practices Committee. Complaints must be made on a complaints form, which will be forwarded to the barrister against whom the allegation is made. The barrister will have 14 working days from the receipt of the complaint to reply to it. Where the Tribunal upholds a complaint that a barrister has been guilty of a breach of the Code of Conduct or proper professional standards it may:

(1) Take no action save to record the result of the complaint;
(2) Admonish the barrister;
(3) Impose a fine;
(4) Require the re-payment of specified fees by the barrister or order the barrister to forego the payment to him of specified fees;
(5) Suspend or exclude the barrister from membership of the Law Library;

38. Code of Conduct for the Bar of Ireland, Paragraph 3.1.
39. Code of Conduct for the Bar of Ireland, Paragraph 2.2.

(6) Remove the barrister from the Register of Practising Barristers either for a specified period or until a specified act has been carried out; or
(7) Recommend to the Benchers of Kings Inns that the barrister be disbarred.

The complainant or the barrister is entitled to appeal any decision of the Tribunal to the Barristers' Professional Conduct Appeal Board, which is comprised of a retired judge nominated by the Bar Council, a lay person nominated by the Attorney General and the Bar Council's Chairperson.

Common Law

In their capacity as advocates, barristers enjoy immunity from the Common Law duty of care to their client.[40] This immunity is based on a number of policy arguments, including the fact that the administration of justice requires that a barrister should be allowed to perform his duties independently and discharge fully his duty to the court.[41] It is also argued that should a barrister be liable in negligence in his advocacy, subsequent attacks on court decisions could bring the administration of justice into disrepute. However, a barrister's immunity:

"... exists only when particular work is so intimately connected with the conduct of the cause in Court that it can fairly be said to be a preliminary decision affecting the way that cause is to be conducted when it comes to a hearing. The protection should not be given any wider application than is absolutely necessary in the interests of the administration of justice."[42]

In Ireland, this issue has not been decided but it is submitted that the better view is that barristers will enjoy immunity when acting in their capacity as advocates, though they will be liable for their other acts and omissions.[43]

STANDARDS

There can, of course, be no absolute requirement that the lawyer will achieve the desired result, nor will the issue of negligence be judged in accordance with the standard:

40. *Rondel* v. *Worsley* [1969] 1 AC 191.
41. *Rondel* v. *Worsley* [1969] 1 AC 191 per Lord Reid.
42. Per McCarthy P in *Rees* v. *Sinclair* (1974) 1 NZLR 180.
43. Fourteenth Interim Report of the Committee on Court Practice and Procedure: Liability of Barristers and Solicitors for Professional Negligence.

". . . of a particularly meticulous and conscientious practitioner; rather the test is what the reasonably competent practitioner would do having regard to the standards normally adopted in his profession".[44]

Conformity with a widely accepted practice of his colleagues will normally rebut an allegation of negligence,[45] though if the common practice has:

". . . inherent defects which ought to be obvious to any person giving the matter due consideration, the fact that it has shown to have been widely and generally adopted over a period of time does not make the practice any less negligent".[46]

The precise content of the duty of reasonable skill and care will depend on the circumstances. A solicitor is not expected to possess an all embracing knowledge but he ought generally know where and how to find out the law in so far as it affects matters within his field of practice. Furthermore, though a solicitor cannot be expected to guarantee success in contentious litigation:

"Common sense suggests that different tests may be applied to different parts of the solicitor's work: is it too much to expect him to observe with 100 per cent accuracy the relatively simple formalities required for the execution of a Will?"[47]

Broadly speaking, therefore, lawyers should possess a certain minimum degree of competence and should exercise reasonable care in the discharge of their duties.[48]

CIVIL LIABILITIES — SOLICITOR

Contract

The relationship between a client and his solicitor is based on a contract known as a retainer, whereby in return for the offer of a client to employ him the solicitor expressly or by implication undertakes to fulfil certain obligations. At Common Law a solicitor contracts to be skilful and careful, for a professional person gives an implied undertaking to exercise a reasonable degree of skill and care. The solicitor's contractual duty will generally be related to the confines of the retainer, and it has been emphasised that the court should beware of imposing on solicitors' duties going beyond the scope of what they are requested to undertake.

44. Per Oliver J in *Midland Bank Trust* v. *Hett, Stubbs & Kemp* (1978) 3 All ER 571.
45. *Roche* v. *Peilow* [1986] ILRM 189, per Mr. Justice Henchy.
46. *Donovan* v. *Cork County Council* [1967] IR 173, per Mr. Justice Walsh at 193.
47. Professor R. Heuston Lecture (No. 142) to the Society of Young Solicitors (1982).
48. Jackson & Powell, *Professional Negligence*.

Tort

Prior to the Supreme Court decision in *Finlay* v. *Murtagh*,[49] it was felt that a solicitor's liability was solely on the basis of his retainer with the client. However, in this case the Supreme Court held that:

"... the general duty of care created by the relationship of solicitor and client entitles the client to sue in negligence if he has suffered damage because of the solicitor's failure to show due professional care and skill, notwithstanding that the client can sue alternatively in contract for breach of the implied term in the contract or the Retainer".

However, a solicitor will not be liable in tort where the solicitor is not in breach of a general duty but rather of a particular and special term of the contract in respect of which the solicitor would not be liable in contract but for the contract containing such a term.[50] When a solicitor acts in his capacity as an advocate he will enjoy the same immunity from suit as a barrister.

If a solicitor or other professional mislays, destroys or refuses to return his clients' documents he may be liable in tort for an action based on detinue, conversion or trespass to chattels.

Statutory liabilities

Civil liabilities

The Sale of Goods and Supply of Services Act, 1980 provides that the supplier of a service impliedly undertakes to exercise reasonable skill and care in the provision of that service. Professionals provide a service and as such can be held liable for the breach of statutory duty, although in practice breach of this statutory duty tends not to be alleged against lawyers.

A solicitor may also be in breach of statutory duty and liable to penalties should he fraudulently or negligently fail to set out all the facts relevant to an instrument's liability to stamp duty.[51]

If litigation fails to proceed due to the solicitor's failure to make proper preparations, the court may order that the solicitor pay to the other party such costs as the court thinks fit.[52] Likewise, if the court considers that costs have been improperly or unreasonably incurred, the court may order the solicitor to reimburse his client and/or the opposing litigant for

49. [1979] IR 249.
50. *Finlay* v. *Murtagh* [1979] IR 249, per Henchy J.
51. Finance Act, 1991, Section 97.
52. Rules of the Superior Court, 1986, Order 99, Rule 6.

any costs that have been incurred due to his misconduct. Furthermore, the court may order an inquiry into the matter by the Taxing Master of the Court and order the solicitor to attend and take part in such an inquiry.[53]

Criminal liabilities

The solicitor may be subject to criminal liability should he fraudulently sell, transfer or convert the property of his client.[54] Should he be convicted of such an offence he may be liable on indictment to a term of imprisonment not exceeding 10 years or a fine or both.[55]

CLAIMANTS

A current client may take an action for damages both in contract and tort if the solicitor and/or barrister breaches his duty of care. The client would obviously need to engage a new solicitor and a barrister to act in these proceedings.

Where a former client has a cause of action founded in negligence, nuisance or breach of duty, the action must be brought within six years of the cause of action accruing, but the limitation period applicable to actions for slander or damages for personal injuries is three years. After this period the action will deem to be extinguished.[56] Should the action be founded on breach of contract, the client will have six years to bring the action.[57] In the case of concealed fraud, the period of time will not run until the client has discovered, or with reasonable diligence could be expected to discover the fraud.[58]

The Supreme Court has held that the solicitor's liability in tort extends to those:

"... such as beneficiaries under a Will, persons entitled under intestacy or those entitled to benefits in circumstances such as a claim in respect of a fatal injury with whom he has made no arrangements to act but who, as he knows or ought to know, will be relying on his professional care and skill".[59]

Furthermore, it has been held that "a solicitor owes a duty to a legatee named in a draft will to draft the will with such reasonable care and skill

53. Rules of the Superior Court, 1986, Order 99, Rule 7.
54. Larceny Act, 1916, Section 20(1)(iv).
55. Larceny Act, 1990, Section 9.
56. Statutes of Limitations, 1957, Section 11(2)(b).
57. Statutes of Limitations, 1957, Section 11(1)(a).
58. Statutes of Limitations, 1957, Section 71(1); for limitation periods, generally, see Brady and Kerr, *The Limitation of Actions in the Republic of Ireland*.
59. *Finlay* v. *Murtagh* [1979] IR 249.

as to ensure that the wishes of the testator are not frustrated and the expectancy of the legatee defeated".[60] In England, this principle was extended so as to impose a duty of care.[61]

It has been established that persons who are not clients of the solicitor but who have relied on his advice may claim against him for his negligent mis-statement. As already discussed, the limitation of this principle in Ireland renders it unlikely that a company's directors or shareholders would be able to recover against the company's negligent legal adviser. Indeed, the Irish High Court have held that when a financial adviser has discharged his duty of care to a corporate client, he cannot be liable in negligence to its shareholders, notwithstanding that he has been in close consultation with them in the formulation of proposals and they have made a sizeable cash input into the company at his recommendation.[62] However, recovery for shareholders and directors may be possible under *Anns'* two-stage test for negligence.

In England, it has been held under the *Anns'* test, that a solicitor owes a duty to the company's shareholders,[63] director and secretary.[64] Whether the Irish Judiciary will allow recovery under *Anns* has not yet been established as it is eventually a matter of policy to determine at what stage damage incurred will be deemed to be too remote. It is viewed as unlikely that the company's creditors or indeed sub-contractors could claim against their solicitor for negligence.[65]

CLAIMS PROCEDURES

Solicitors

Civil Law

A civil cause of action can be commenced in the District Court, Circuit Court or High Court. No person besides a solicitor is entitled to issue proceedings on behalf of any other party. The court where the action is commenced will depend on the quantum of the claim or, in the case of

60. *Wall* v. *Hegarty* [1980] ILRM 124, per Mr. Justice Barrington.
61. *Smith* v. *Claremont Haynes & Company* in *The Times,* 3 September 1991.
62. *McSweeney* v. *Burke,* unreported, High Court, 24 November 1980, per Justice Carroll.
63. *RP Howard* v. *Woodman Matthews & Company* [1983] BCLC 117, per Justice Staunton.
64. *Re Foster* (1986) 2 PN 193.
65. *Caparo Industries* v. *Dickman* [1989] 1 All ER 789.

actions for recovery of property, rateable valuation.[66] Unless the quantum of the plaintiff's claim exceeds £5,000, proceedings will commence in the District Court. The Circuit Court's jurisdiction extends to amounts of £30,000 though should an action be remitted from the High Court, then like the High Court, the Circuit Court will have unlimited jurisdiction. Likewise, with the parties' consent, the Circuit Court can have unlimited jurisdiction.[67] In advising a client as to the appropriate court in which to bring an action a solicitor must exercise reasonable care so as to protect his client from unnecessary costs.

A charge against a solicitor for alleged criminal conduct in his professional capacity is prosecuted at the suit of the Director of Public Prosecutions in the appropriate court, and the court may convict and fine or sentence the accused, if appropriate. The fact of such conviction and/or penalty does not entitle the victim of the criminal conduct to compensation, but the victim's Common Law or statutory civil remedies will remain.

Professional bodies

SOLICITORS

Where it is proved to the satisfaction of the Law Society that any person has sustained loss in consequence of dishonesty on the part of a solicitor, the Society will make a grant out of the Compensation Fund, subscribed to by all practising solicitors, to indemnify the person for his loss.[68] Furthermore, on receiving the Disciplinary Committee's report the High Court may direct the solicitor to make such restitution to the aggrieved party as it deems fit.[69]

BARRISTERS

An action for negligence or breach of contract can be maintained against a barrister in the appropriate court. The Honourable Society of Kings Inns has not made provision for a compensation fund for persons who have sustained loss due to their barrister's dishonesty, but many barristers will carry professional indemnity insurance that would provide them with indemnity in respect of legal liability for negligence and/or for breach of contract.

66. More or less its property tax value.
67. See, generally, Delaney, *The Courts Acts 1924–1991*.
68. Solicitors' Act, 1960, Section 21(4).
69. Solicitors' Act, 1960, Section 8(1)(b)(i).

DAMAGES

Damages are the principal remedy the courts will grant as compensation for a solicitor's or barrister's negligence and/or breach of contract or of duty. To be recoverable, loss must have been caused by the alleged misconduct and have been reasonably foreseeable. Recoverable loss has included the loss of an opportunity to acquire or renew an interest in property, a decrease in the value of such property, the loss of an opportunity to bring or defend proceedings, the cost of putting right the solicitor's mistake or wasted expenditure and general damages for inconvenience and distress.[70]

SPECIFIC CIVIL LIABILITIES

On-going and once-off representation

It is common to employ a solicitor over an indefinite period, though the retainer in each case is limited to the particular business in respect of which he is employed, and there is no such thing as a "general relationship of solicitor and client of a standing and permanent character for all occasions and for all purposes". A solicitor's authority to act arises from the retainer given to him by his client and his authority to act is limited by any special conditions imposed and supplemented by any special authority conferred by the retainer. It should be noted that if the solicitor acts outside this authority, he may be liable for breach of contract.

While the solicitor will represent his client throughout the period of his retainer, a barrister will be engaged on a once-off basis, either to represent the client in court or to give specialist advice on a particular point of law.

General and specialist advice

If a solicitor fails to attain the standard of a reasonably competent solicitor, he will be potentially liable in negligence. However:

"... if the client engages an expert and doubtless expects to pay commensurate fees, is he not entitled to expect something more than the standard of the reasonably competent solicitor?"[71]

70. Jackson & Powell, *Professional Negligence* (3rd ed.), p. 404, paragraphs 4–172.
71. Per Justice Megarry in *Duchess of Argyll* v. *Beuselinck* [1972] 2 Lloyd's Rep. 172.

It would seem that when a client seeks specialist rather than general advice and engages a specialist for such advice, he is entitled to judge the legal advisor by the standard of "the reasonably competent practitioner" specialising in whatever area of law the lawyer holds himself out as a specialist.[72]

The position of a legal partner and his unqualified apprentice may be different because their qualifications are different, however, the less qualified person may be negligent in not seeking more expert advice, while the firm may be negligent in giving him work which is too difficult or supervising him insufficiently.[73]

Likewise, a barrister who holds himself out as a specialist in a particular branch of law will be liable should he fail to attain the standard of a reasonably competent barrister specialising in that area.

Commercial transactions

The solicitor must protect his client against future possible hazards arising from commercial transactions. If he fails to protect his client by making all proper enquiries and searches, he will be *prima facie* negligent. Where a solicitor's expertise does not extend to all areas of a transaction, he would be expected to obtain or to advise his client to obtain advice on such areas. The High Court has held that a solicitor has a duty to advise the purchaser to have an independent inspection of a property for defects made by a qualified person.[74]

It is, however, no part of the solicitor's duty in the absence of special instructions to advise his clients on matters of business. Thus, a solicitor is under no general duty to advise his client whether a transaction is a prudent one. As Justice Scott stated in *Yager* v. *Fisherman*[75] "it is no part of the solicitor's normal duty to profess the skill and experience for giving such advice". Equally, it would not be prudent for a solicitor to allow his client to believe that the former did possess such skill and knowledge if that were not the case.

The duties of a solicitor, when effecting an investment of a clients' money, flow from the specific nature of the retainer. A solicitor may be employed either to advise the clients on an entire matter, including the prudence of the investment or the sufficiency of any security, or merely to implement the investment chosen by the client.

72. Jackson & Powell, *Professional Negligence* (3rd ed.), p. 341.

73. Jackson & Powell, *Professional Negligence* (3rd ed.), p. 342.

74. *O'Connor* v. *First National Building Society* [1991] ILRM 208, *obiter* per Justice Lynch.

75. (1944) 1 All ER 552.

The Solicitors' Accounts Regulations[76] provide that the client's funds, in the absence of written authority to the contrary, must be invested in banking institutions listed in Schedule I of the said Regulation.

Agreements

It is the duty of a solicitor preparing a document or agreement to explain to his client the nature of the document he is to execute and the consequences to him of the execution, and the solicitor may be liable in respect of legal or other errors in agreements produced by him.

Regulatory compliance

A solicitor may be negligent if he fails to comply with a wide range of statutory requirements which failure results in his client or third parties sustaining loss.

He may be liable to beneficiaries who are denied legacies that the testator intended them to receive if the will fails to comply with the formalities required by the Succession Act, 1965. Likewise, if a solicitor undertakes to perform company secretarial work for a corporate entity that subsequently incurs fines or suffers loss due to the solicitor's failure to comply with statutory requirements of the Companies Acts 1963–1990, the solicitor may be liable for his negligence.

Litigation conduct

Both a barrister and solicitor when acting in their capacity as advocates are immune from civil action being brought against them by a client.[77] However:

> ". . . the duty of a solicitor with regard to the conduct of a case in Court where he has briefed Counsel is firstly, to brief appropriate and competent Counsel and secondly to instruct them properly with regard to the facts of the case which he has obtained from his client, and to make provision for the attendance of appropriate witnesses and other proofs".[78]

Where litigation is in prospect, it is the duty of the solicitor to make proper investigation into the cause of action, to enable him to form an opinion as to whether or not it will succeed. If in consequence of the

76. SI Number 204 of 1984.
77. *Rondel* v. *Worsley* [1969] 1 AC 191.
78. Per Lynch J in *Finlay* v. *Gannon* [1988] ILRM 193.

solicitor's failure to perform this duty, the action is stayed or dismissed, he may be unable to recover his costs. It has been held in England that a solicitor will only be liable for the costs of litigation if he actually knew both that the client's action would not succeed and that it was being brought in bad faith as an abuse of the process of the court.[79]

Administration

Trust

A solicitor may be appointed as a trustee, though he ought not charge costs to the trust for legal work done by him in relation to the trust, unless the other trustees agree to that course of action or it is permitted by the trust instrument.[80] The Solicitors' Accounts Regulations[81] state that a solicitor who receives trust money is obliged to pay the sum without delay into a trust account[82] and must keep proper Books of Account to show his dealings with the trust fund.[83]

Company

It is not uncommon for a solicitor to perform administrative company secretarial work for its corporate clients. This will include preparing the company's annual accounts and filing them with the Companies Registration Office. The solicitor will also prepare any documentation necessary to effect any changes in the constitution of the company as well as notices and minutes necessary to hold the company's Annual General Meetings. This administrative work is regulated by the Companies Acts 1963–1990 and companies, and in some cases, their directors may be penalised for failure to comply with the relevant provisions.

Conflict of interest

The relationship of solicitor and client is fiduciary and, thus, the solicitor must make full disclosure of any interest he may have in his client's transaction, else he may be liable for breach of duty.[84]

79. *Orchard* v. *South East Electricity Board* [1987] QB 565.
80. *Guide to Professional Conduct of Solicitors in Ireland*, Paragraph 2.5.
81. SI Number 204 of 1984.
82. Regulation 11, SI Number 204 of 1984.
83. Regulation 19 SI Number 204 of 1984.
84. *Nocton* v. *Lord Ashburton* (1914) AC 932.

Likewise, where a solicitor acts for two clients and a conflict of interest arises between them, he should cease to act for both.[85] Neither a sole practitioner nor solicitors acting in partnership should (subject to some exceptions) act for both the Vendor and Purchaser in a transfer of property.[86]

Confidentiality

Barristers and solicitors have a duty not to disclose or make use of confidential information communicated to them by clients or by third parties at the instance of clients.[87] This duty continues after the relation of lawyer and client has ceased, and information may only be divulged when the client consents to such communication.

A lawyer enjoys legal professional privilege and he cannot be compelled by a court to disclose communications either oral or documentary passing between him and a client or a person who consults with him with a view to becoming a client. The privilege exists only when the relationship between client and lawyer is on a professional basis and does not exist where advice or information is given to assist the client in carrying out an unlawful act.

DEFENCES

Acting as advocate

As already discussed, where a barrister or solicitor acts as an advocate he does not owe a duty of care to his clients and an action for negligence cannot be sustained.[88]

Acting on counsel's advice

If the solicitor acts in accordance with the advice of counsel, when he has properly instructed such counsel then usually he will not be held negligent, even if the advice proves to be mistaken or misconceived. However, "he is not entitled to rely blindly or with no mind of his own on Counsel's views".[89]

85. *Guide to Professional Conduct of Solicitors in Ireland*, Paragraph 1.2.
86. *Guide to Professional Conduct of Solicitors in Ireland*, Paragraph 1.3.
87. *Boardman* v. *Phipps* (1967) 2 AC 46.
88. *Rondel* v. *Worsley* (1969) 1 AC 191.
89. Per Justice May in *Davy Chiesman* v. *Davy Chiesman* [1984] Fam 84, at p. 63 E.

Acting on client instructions

Where a solicitor's act or omission is due to adherence to his client's informed instructions, he will have a defence to a subsequent action for breach of duty.[90]

Exclusions

A professional may exclude or limit his contractual or tortious liability by an exclusion clause. The clause must be incorporated in the retainer, reasonable and in case of ambiguity, it will be construed *contra proferentum*. The doctrine of privity renders exclusion clauses ineffective against persons not party to the contract.[91]

EXTENDED LIABILITY

The law does not generally recognise a firm as distinct from the partners composing it. Partners can sue and be sued in the firms name.[92]

Partners are jointly and severally liable[93] for any wrongful act or omission of any partner acting in the ordinary course of the business of the firm or with the authority of the partners.[94] Furthermore, a firm will be liable for the fraud of one of its members while acting for the firm and the innocent partners cannot divest themselves of responsibility on the ground that they never authorised the commission of the fraud.[95] If the firm is party to the contract, the partners will be sued jointly. However, should the contract be entered into by a partner in his personal capacity that partner alone should be sued.

If a partner, being a trustee, improperly employs trust property in the business or on the account of the partnership, the other partners are not liable for the trust property to the persons beneficially interested therein.[96]

The firm will be liable vicariously and in agency for the tortious actions of its staff and associates.[97]

90. Jackson & Powell, *Professional Negligence* (3rd ed.), at p. 348.
91. *Chitty on Contract*, Sweet & Maxwell, Ch. 14 .
92. Rules of the Superior Courts, 1986, Order 14.
93. Partnership Act, 1890, Section 12.
94. Partnership Act, 1890, Section 10.
95. *Lindley & Banks on Partnerships* (16th ed.), at p. 280, paragraph 12.96.
96. Partnership Act, 1890, Section 13.
97. *Lynch* v. *Palgrave Murphy* [1964] IR 150.

An incoming partner is not liable for anything done before he became a partner, unless there is some agreement express or implied between himself and the person with the cause of action.[98]

If a person ceases to be a partner, he will no longer be the agent of his co-partners. However, a retired partner ought be joined, in every action to which, had he not retired, he would have been a necessary party. This will be the case even where the contract is entered into before and breach of it occurs after his retirement.[99]

INSURANCE

Professional indemnity policies have become common in all professions. Insurance is not yet compulsory for solicitors. The Incorporated Law Society recommends that each practitioner have a minimum cover of IR£150,000. Policies will afford cover in respect of negligence on the part of the insured or his employees, though indemnity will generally not be granted for loss arising out of a claim in respect of any dishonest, fraudulent or criminal act or omission on the part of the insured or his employees.

Many solicitors are members of a Mutual Defence Fund, which provides indemnity to them subject to conditions of membership, similar in many respects to conditions applicable to contracts of insurance. It is the duty of the solicitor to disclose to the Fund all facts that would influence a prudent insurer in determining whether to accept the risk and the appropriate premium.

The Incorporated Law Society through its Compensation Fund also undertakes to reimburse persons who suffer loss due to solicitor's misconduct. The enactment into law of the Solicitors' Bill, 1994 is expected to improve a cap of IR£250,000 on amounts the Law Society will be obliged to pay to any client of a solicitor, subject to a discretionary power to grant larger amounts if satisfied that grave hardship would otherwise be caused.

Barristers are obliged by their Code of Conduct to have Professional Indemnity Insurance. The Code states that it is professional mis-conduct for any barrister who is not so insured to advise on the law, draft legal documents or pleadings, or act as an advocate.[100]

While claims against solicitors are relatively common, such claims against barristers are rare in the jurisdiction.

The cost of professional indemnity cover has, over the past number of years, increased at a rate in excess of the national inflation rate, reflecting

98. *Lindley & Banks on Partnerships* (16th ed.), at p. 388, paragraph 14.15 and the Partnership Act, 1890, Section 17.

99. *Dobbin* v. *Fraser* (1844) 1 Car and K 323.

100. Code of Conduct for the Bar of Ireland, Rule 2.13.

a greater willingness by the public and the legal professional to prosecute such claims than in the past. The fact that most lawyers are seen as being indemnified against claims has encouraged claims that might not otherwise have been made and — in common with other areas — public policy considerations appear to be broadening the range of circumstances in which the judiciary is willing to impose liability on lawyers.

INTERNATIONAL PRIVATE LAW ASPECTS

To establish the Common Market, the European Communities is committed to achieving free movement of services.[101] To facilitate the free movement of lawyers the European Council issued Directive 77/249 which provides that lawyers qualified to practice in their own member state may practise in Ireland, subject to the Rules of Professional Conduct here, though without being required to be resident or registered with the Incorporated Law Society of Kings Inn or hold a Practising Certificate under the Solicitors' Acts, 1954 to 1960.[102]

Lawyers from countries that are not members of the European Communities will be required to qualify here as solicitors or barristers before they are entitled to practise as such in Ireland.

CONCLUSION

The upsurge in the number of claims made against the legal profession since the 1970s is reflected by the increasing cost of insurance for solicitors and barristers. This is reflected by the Solicitors' (Amendment) Bill, 1994, which will introduce compulsory insurance for solicitors. The Bill, when enacted, may establish the office of an independent adjudicator who will monitor the activities of solicitors and investigate complaints made by the public.

Greater emphasis than before is now placed by the legal profession and its indemnifiers on risk management against the background of a rising tide of claims. Technological advances and further legal education have assisted greater control of risk. A growing number of solicitors are seeking accreditation with the "Q Mark", a national standard, or the internationally recognised ISO 9000.

Traditionally, the bulk have arisen out of property transfer and litigation matters, and while the more common type of claims continue to arise, one area seen as likely to spawn many future claims is that of drafting wills, capital taxation and estate planning.

101. Treaty of Rome 1957, Article 48.
102. Directive 77/249, Article 4.

CHAPTER 9

ITALY

GIANNI MANCA
Piergrossi Villa Manca Graziadei
Milan, Italy

INTRODUCTION

There are approximately 45,000 practising lawyers in Italy including 7,000 in Rome and 4,300 in Milan. The titles by which lawyers are known in Italy reflect the number of years they have been in practice, though there are special examinations that can be taken to quicken the ascent up the title tree.

Procuratori are newly qualified lawyers who, having completed two years' apprenticeship and passed the state examination, are allowed to appear and represent clients only in courts within the district of the Court of Appeal where the Tribunal of their residence is situated. There are 26 Courts of Appeal.

After six years in practice, a *procuratore* becomes an *avvocato*, and whilst he/she retains the right to represent the client within the district of the Court of Appeal as defined above, he/she is able to appear in courts throughout Italy and can charge higher fees.

Avvocati cassazionisti are those lawyers who, after 12 years as *avvocati*, are allowed to appear before the Court of Cassation and the other courts of the highest jurisdiction.

The professional bars in Italy are the *Consiglio dell'Ordine* (discharging at the same time the functions of Bar Councils and Law Societies), of which there are 159. They are organised, and their officers are elected, locally. However, there are national rules[1] which govern ethics and fees, although their enforcement is left entirely to each local *Consiglio dell'Ordine*. Disbarment is the ultimate sanction exercised by local councils over their members. The *Consiglio Nazionale Forense*, the national advisory council, also acts as an appellate court for disciplinary decisions of the local bar councils.

There is a fixed scale of fees for litigation; contingency fees are not allowed. For non-litigious matters, the maximum fee which can be charged by law is 6 per cent of the value of the matter (e.g. contract, settlement). The percentage declines as the value of the matter increases.

1. See also Capacities, Duties and Standards, below.

Thus, when the amount is approximately US $3,000,000 or more the maximum fee may not exceed 1 per cent. However, among "international" law firms, it is usual for fees to be calculated on a time basis, ranging from about L30,000 per hour for young paralegals to L500,000 per hour for experienced lawyers. Many firms charge corporate and private clients different hourly rates and vary their charges according to the degree of technical complexity or the risks and liability the work exposes the firm to. Statements of fees are sometimes accompanied by a more or less detailed breakdown of work undertaken.

There are perhaps 50 firms in Italy that deal with legal transactions or matters involving non-Italians. Their sizes range from a minimum of two or three partners, with the same number of legal assistants and/or associates to a very rare maximum of perhaps around 15 partners, with an equivalent number of legal assistants and/or associates. Some of these firms also have part-time associates, usually academics, who provide specialist advice.

PRACTICE STRUCTURES

Sole practice is still, to a very large extent the usual form favoured by the profession in Italy. The law graduate joins an established lawyer as an assistant, eventually passing his/her bar examination and after a certain period, sets up his/her own practice.

There are, of course, some "professional associations" as they are defined in the Act,[2] which is still in force, which are basically partnerships as understood in the Anglo-Saxon system. However, because of the 159 separate bars, it is quite impossible to obtain reliable statistical information as to the number and size of these partnerships; many of the bar councils, including notably the Milan Council, do not publish a separate list of partnerships in their official registers. Accordingly, the estimate of the number of firms with international practice already mentioned (50) is also matter of deduction. The total number of partnerships in the country may conceivably be three or four times greater.

As regards the size of firms, once more the lack of records makes accurate figures difficult to establish. Additionally, even firms the existence of which is known may present an outward image as to the number of partners which is different from the actual one, some of the "apparent" partners not fully exercising this function as it is normally understood. On the basis of educated guesswork, there are perhaps a dozen firms with more than six genuine, unlimited partners. It might perhaps be noted that — especially in large cities — the sole practitioner frequently shares office expenses with one or more other sole practitioners. This type of arrangement

2. Law No. 1815 of 23 November 1939.

is purely financial in the sense that all the firm's "members" are sole practitioners, who act independently from each other and do not in any way share their respective professional duties and liabilities.

There are no professional corporations. As the law stands at the moment, they are not permitted and therefore, all lawyers have unlimited liability.

A final background point which is perhaps worth making, is that relating to Multi Disciplinary Partnerships (MDPs). Although, under the current rules, MDPs are forbidden, a number seem to be in existence, especially between lawyers and accountants. This situation arises from the laxity of the bar councils, which one does not, regrettably, expect to change in the present environment. One of the effects of MDPs is that the rules on confidentiality which are very protective in the case of lawyers, but are not nearly so strict in the case of other professions (except for medical practitioners), will not protect the client's confidentiality where information is shared between members of other professions in the MDP.

CAPACITIES, DUTIES AND STANDARDS

The Italian lawyer's principal functions are advocacy and advice. Advocacy includes functions such as acting as a receiver in bankruptcy, as an executor or as an arbitrator. Unlike in other countries, lawyers may not act as intermediaries and are in fact prevented by ethical rules from receiving commissions of any kind; this includes referrals to another lawyer.

There is no statutory or other code of ethics for lawyers, although the body of disciplinary decisions has been compiled by some authors,[3] and these compilations are used as guides to the lawyer's conduct. The basic statutory rule from which the body of disciplinary *dicta* stems is at present Law No. 36 of 22 January 1936, as amended, which includes a provision to the effect that a lawyer's conduct must, somewhat quaintly, be *specchiatissima ed illibata* (absolutely flawless and spotless). Therefore, the source of disciplinary rules of conduct is effectively case law as administered by each of the 159 bars and reviewed on appeal by the National Bar Council.

It is worthy of note that, under Italian law, lawyers are not subject to bankruptcy proceedings which are limited to entrepreneurial activity: In other words the insolvency of a lawyer, due to the lawyer's failure to pay his debts regardless of whether such debts arise from his professional liability, can only give rise to the ordinary remedies of judicial pursuit but cannot lead to the lawyer's bankruptcy. Nor has the Italian profession established a compensation fund such as that which exists in other countries, notably in France and in the United Kingdom.

3. Notably, Danovi, *Corso di Ordinamento Forense e Deontologia,* Giuffrè 1992.

The standard to which a lawyer is held in the performance of his/her services is set down in the Civil Code in respect of all professions. The rule is set out in Article 2236, which reads as follows:

"If the services require the solution of technical problems of particular difficulty, the professional is not answerable for damages except in the event of wilful or gross negligence."

This rule is the principal reason why, in Italy, clients' claims against professionals in general and lawyers in particular, have been few and far between. In brief, the standards of a lawyer's services are as follows:

(1) The services of a lawyer are not designed to obtain a result; a lawyer must only perform his/her services in a manner consistent with the diligence of an expert in his profession;
(2) This degree of diligence, though of an expert, is an ordinary diligence and not an exceptional diligence: thus, for instance, a lawyer must warn the client of the deadline for an appeal, but his/her views as to whether or not an appeal should be made, and on which grounds, are largely irrelevant from the viewpoint of diligence; and
(3) Whilst the position as to damages in an ordinary matter is that set out in (2) above, if a matter or case can be argued to be "especially difficult", the onus would be on the client to prove wilfulness or gross diligence, the tests for which are of necessity quite high.

CIVIL AND ADMINISTRATIVE LIABILITIES

The basis of the lawyer's civil liability is the contract with the client. This is normally an oral contract, as written agreements are exceedingly rare. The contract is with the client and no one else. Therefore, it is only the client who can raise an action in respect of the lawyer's civil liability; if the client is a company, it is only the company which is entitled to seek redress, although, in this case and where the injury to the company is reflected on its directors, the damages might include those suffered by the directors in their capacity as representatives of the company.

The damages which a client can recover are only his/her actual losses, as there are, in substance, no "punitive" damages available to the claimant.[4] Hence, the lawyer's liability can extend to parties other than the client only to the extent that the client is responsible for such parties' injuries arising from the lawyer's act or omission, for no such parties have a direct action against the lawyer, unless it is predicated on a tort.

4. See also Insurance, below.

Procedurally, a lawyer's liability can be pursued only through the ordinary courts. As stated above, disciplinary proceedings can be instigated by a client, but the Council has no power to award damages, its sanctions being only of a disciplinary nature such as a warning, suspension or disbarment.

There is no special liability arising from specific matters handled by a lawyer and, accordingly, the principles summarised above apply regardless of the matters dealt with. Thus, it is irrelevant if the liability arises in relation to a one-off client or one whom the lawyer serves on a continuous basis; or in respect of general or specialist advice (though it is difficult to conceive of specialist advice, as Italian lawyers are not allowed to advertise specialisation in any particular branch of the law). There are perhaps two points worth noting:

(1) Conflict of interest is a breach of conduct and as such gives rise to a breach of discipline, which is subject only to sanctions imposed by the Bar Council. Of course, if a conflict of interest is found by the Bar Council, this finding can be used as evidence in any civil proceedings which may be instituted by the client.
(2) Confidentiality, unlike in many other countries, is again part of the rules of conduct and, accordingly, a breach thereof is subject to disciplinary proceedings; of course, if and to the extent that a breach of confidentiality has injured a client, the latter is entitled to pursue the lawyer in respect of any damages suffered as a result of such breach.

Since the lawyer's liability arises from a contractual obligation, the statute of limitation follows the normal rule and is, therefore, ten years, beyond which time a defence is available to the lawyer that the claim is time-barred.

LIABILITY

The partners of a firm are liable jointly and severally in respect of any obligations incurred by the firm. At present, lawyers may not incorporate and, therefore, none of the partners can have limited liability. This is the position also with respect to a new partner, who pursuant to Article 2269 of the Civil Code, is jointly and severally liable for the partnership's obligations incurred prior to his/her joining the partnership. Conversely, a former partner is jointly and severally liable only for the partnership's obligations incurred until the date of his/her ceasing to be a partner.

Nevertheless, the joint and several liability of all the firm's partners requires that a creditor of the firm pursue in the first instance the firm's assets if, in accordance with the provisions of Article 2268, there are assets on which any such creditor can levy execution without undue difficulty.

No other members of a firm, namely associates or staff, have any liability whatsoever, other than to the firm itself, in respect of the diligent performance of their respective duties.

INTERNATIONAL PRIVATE LAW ASPECTS

The basic rule is that to the extent that a lawyer's work is performed in Italy, the applicable standards are those prevailing in Italy also with respect to the damages arising from any breach of those standards.

As regards the work performed by a lawyer abroad, the key aspect of this problem is the determination of when an Italian lawyer's work is in fact performed abroad. Clearly this question does not arise in respect of judicial work for this is, by definition, fully performed within the country. An exception to this rule may be argued in respect of a lawyer's work before an international tribunal, for instance, the European Court of Justice. One is unaware of any claim for professional liability ever having been raised at this level and one doubts that the standards required of an Italian lawyer and the damages claimable for breach of those standards would be other than those applicable for work performed in Italy.

When it comes to advice, a lawyer may direct it to a client abroad, though it would by definition concern only Italian law and matters in Italy governed by Italian law. Whether or not advice so rendered can be viewed as work performed abroad has never, reportedly, been raised heretofore, judicially or otherwise, but it appears that both the standards of diligence and the damages arising therefrom would be governed by Italian law, if for no other reason than because it would seem exceedingly difficult, if not altogether impossible, for an action to be raised anywhere but against the lawyer in Italy. It is difficult to imagine on what grounds an Italian Court would adjudge a claim other than under Italian law, unless, of course, the client and lawyer had expressly agreed to apply another law.

Finally, an Italian lawyer may perform his/her work from an office located outside Italy; in this event, an action would legitimately be raised against the lawyer in the country in which the office is located and, although it may be arguable whether the standards of diligence should be the Italian ones, there is no doubt that the damages would be awarded in accordance with the laws of such country.

The reverse question of a non-Italian lawyer performing work in Italy must have the same answers as those outlined above. In cases of litigation work and advice, the non-Italian lawyer would be subject to his own domestic standards and compensation of the damages arising from the breach thereof, whilst in case a foreign lawyer advising from an Italian office, the Italian standards and damages would apply.

INSURANCE

Insurance is not compulsory in respect of lawyers' professional liability and, indeed, it is understood that very few lawyers bother to take up appropriate policies. Insurance for professional liability is, of course, available. It has a limit of approximately US $3,500,000 and its cost is quite small, in that the annual premium amounts to less than US $10,000. Within the liability limits, it provides cover for the insured which is, relatively speaking, low in cost. Any extra cover must be obtained from non-Italian insurers.

Insurance of this nature covers risks of professional liability incurred anywhere in the world provided that it is actionable, and is so actioned, in an Italian jurisdiction. The liability covered is normally that arising from the acts or omissions of any of the members of the firm, including associates and para legals. Although there is no standard policy, a typical policy would cover damages suffered by third parties, including clients, in the course of the firm's professional work; it would also provide cover for:

(1) Death, injuries and damages to property suffered by clients by reason of accidents occurred within the firm's office premises;
(2) The negative tax consequences to a client; and
(3) The acts or omissions of the firm's outside correspondents.

Damages are always the actual loss sustained by the injured party. So-called "punitive" damages are not claimable under Italian law. This fairly stringent test of damages is perhaps the main reason why claims for the professional liability of lawyers are very rare indeed.

CONCLUSIONS

The upshot of the foregoing is that in Italy, claims for professional liability against lawyers are not an exercise on which it is easy or profitable to embark; the corollary is that there have been, and still are, exceedingly few such claims. In any event, the prudent lawyer can take out insurance cover against any risk, such being available at a reasonable cost. The Italian lawyer working from an office located outside Italy would be wise to evaluate the local scene and obtain the insurance cover consistent with his findings.

CHAPTER 10

NEW ZEALAND

GREGORY C. EVERARD
Kensington Swan
Auckland, New Zealand

INTRODUCTION

Regulatory framework

The most important statute that relates to the legal profession is the Law Practitioners Act 1982. This Act has Sections that cover the Law Society, the Council of Legal Education, admission and enrolment, practice in the legal profession, intervention in solicitors' practice, solicitors' trust accounts, discipline within the legal profession, practitioners' costs, the solicitors' fidelity guarantee fund and the partners' protection fund.

Other rules and regulations that govern the handling of clients' money are:

(1) Solicitors Trust Account Rules 1969;
(2) Solicitors Audit Regulations 1987; and
(3) Solicitors Nominee Company Rules 1988.

Other rules of relevance are the Rules of Professional Conduct for Barristers and Solicitors and the Code of Ethics.

Professional bodies

The most important professional bodies are the New Zealand Law Society and the District Law Societies.

The New Zealand Law Society is constituted by Section 3 of the Law Practitioners Act 1982. Its functions are, *inter alia*:

(1) To promote the interests of the legal profession and interests of the public in relation to legal matters;
(2) To promote and encourage proper conduct among the members of the legal profession;
(3) To suppress illegal, dishonourable or improper practices by members of the legal profession;
(4) To preserve and maintain the integrity and status of the legal profession;

(5) To assist in and promote the reform of the law; and
(6) To provide means for the amicable settlement of professional differences between members of the legal profession.

The powers of the Society are those which are reasonably necessary or expedient for the exercise of any of its functions. These powers include the power to:

(1) Provide or arrange for the provision of services and facilities for practitioners, including seminars and educational and training services and facilities;
(2) Publish such material as it may consider of benefit to the public or practitioners in relation to the practice of the law;
(3) Oppose any application made for admission as a barrister and solicitor;
(4) Institute prosecutions against practitioners for breach of any statute, rules or regulations relating to the practice of the law; and
(5) Appoint any practitioner to perform any work or services for the Society.

District Law Societies have within their own districts the same functions and powers as the New Zealand Law Society except the power to impose levies. In addition, District Law Societies have the function of providing and maintaining libraries. These libraries are used by the High Court and practitioners.

The legal profession

The legal profession can be divided into "barristers and solicitors" and "barristers sole". In New Zealand the legal profession has been described as "fused".[1] The reason for this is that a practitioner may practise both as a barrister and a solicitor. This description is not strictly correct, and it would be more accurate to describe New Zealand as having a "split" bar. This is in contrast to the English "separate" bar because the delineations between the work of a barrister, on the one hand, and a solicitor on the other, are less clearly marked than they are in England. In *Rees* v. *Sinclair*, it was stated that there is probably only one material difference between the status of barristers in New Zealand and the status of barristers in the United Kingdom. That difference is that barristers and solicitors are on the same roll in New Zealand.[2]

1. *Rees* v. *Sinclair* [1974] 1 NZLR 180.
2. Law Practitioners Act 1982, Section 49.

Section 62(2) of the Law Practitioners Act 1982 provides that no barrister of the rank of Queens Counsel shall practise as a solicitor, and no practising certificate as a solicitor shall be issued to him. A Queen's Counsel and a practitioner practising solely as a barrister must be instructed by a solicitor, and there is a rule of professional etiquette that they are precluded from receiving instructions from a lay client. Practitioners who practise both as barristers and solicitors, however, are entitled to be instructed directly by a lay client even in respect of work that is exclusively barristers' work.

A barrister should not normally file documents in court or, in the course of proceedings, show his or her rooms or chambers as the address for service. There may however, be exceptional circumstances where it is practicable and necessary to do so. One exception would be where the barrister is not instructed by a solicitor in accordance with the rules of professional conduct.

PRACTICE STRUCTURES

Law firms

Law firms or partnerships are probably the most common practice structure in New Zealand. Law firms are unincorporated, and are partnerships with unlimited liability. To be a partner, or to go out in sole practice, it is necessary to comply with Section 55 of the Law Practitioners Act. Basically, this involves acquiring experience of legal work for at least three years.

Partnerships employ solicitors. Solicitors must be admitted to the bar and must also have a practising certificate. The requirements for admission to the bar are set out in Section 44 of the Law Practitioners Act. A candidate for admission must have attained the age of 20 years, must have completed a law degree and the law professionals, which are a three-month practical skills course conducted by the Law Society.

Partnerships also employ para-legals such as legal executives.

Other practice structures include sole practitioners and barristers' chambers. Barristers in chambers effectively share word processing and other office facilities. There are also a number of lawyers who are in-house solicitors in companies, and who practise in the public sector.

Capacities

Most large firms are divided into commercial and litigation departments. Within those divisions, some firms are divided into further teams, which are engaged in specialist areas of work such as insurance, intellectual property, banking, employment, property, taxation, estates and so on. It would be fair to say that lawyers engage in work as advisors, intermediaries, advocates and custodians.

DUTIES

General

The basis for the duties of lawyers is contained in the regulatory framework referred to above. The relevant statutes are:

(1) The Law Practitioners Act 1982;
(2) Solicitors Trust Account Rules 1969;
(3) Solicitors Audit Regulations 1987;
(4) Solicitors Nominee Company Rules 1988.

The relevant code of practice for solicitors is the Rules of Professional Conduct for Barristers and Solicitors. The remainder of solicitors' duties are derived from case law. These duties can be divided into the following categories:

(1) Contractual;
(2) Tortious with duties of care:
  (a) To a client; or
  (b) To a third party; and
(3) Fiduciary.

Note that the position of barristers is slightly different. Barristers enjoy immunity from suit when appearing in court and also for pre-trial work, but only where that pre-trial work is so intimately connected with the conduct of the cause in court that it could fairly be said to be a preliminary decision affecting the way that the cause is to be conducted when it comes to a hearing.[3]

Case law

The leading cases dealing with the contractual and tortious liabilities of solicitors are *MacLaren Maycroft & Co.* v. *Fletcher Development Co. Limited*,[4] *Day* v. *Mead*,[5] and *Mouat* v. *Clark Boyce*.[6]

3. See *Rees* v. *Sinclair* [1974] 1 NZLR 180.
4. [1973] 2 NZLR 433.
5. [1987] 2 NZLR 443.
6. [1992] 2 NZLR 559.

In *McLaren Maycroft*, it was held that where a professional's relationship with his or her client is contractual, the true nature of an action brought against the professional for damage caused by lack of professional skill and care is an action founded upon a contract alone. Although liability in contract can be reduced under the New Zealand Contributory Negligence Act 1947, to date the courts have refrained from confirming any reduction in damages or apportionment of responsibility in a situation where there has been contributory negligence. Instead, the courts prefer to use the most appropriate remedy, be that damages, compensation or a restitutionary remedy. This approach is said to have been adopted by the courts as a result of the mingling of Common Law and Equity.

In *Day* v. *Mead*, it was held that while liability for non-disclosure may be fixed at the initial stage in a relationship (that is any action for damages is based on contract), damages may be reduced if a solicitor is able to point to equitable apportionment considerations analogous to contributory negligence factors.

In *Mouat* v. *Clark Boyce*, it was held that even though an action for damages is based on contract, contributory negligence on the part of the client can be taken into account.

Fiduciary duties

The most important duties for law practitioners are set out in the Rules of Professional Conduct. These include:

(1) The relationship between practitioner and client is one of confidence and trust which must never be abused;
(2) A practitioner must not act or continue to act for any person where there is a conflict of interest between the practitioner on the one hand, and an existing or prospective client, on the other hand;
(3) A practitioner shall not act for more than one party in the same matter without the prior consent of both or all parties;
(4) A practitioner must not act against a former client of a practitioner when through prior knowledge of the financial or other affairs of the former client which may be relevant to the matter, to so act would be to the detriment of the former client;
(5) Information communicated to a practitioner by a client or otherwise received by a practitioner on behalf of a client, is confidential and, with certain statutory exceptions, privileged from disclosure; and
(6) In most circumstances, a practitioner is bound to disclose to the client all information received by the practitioner which relates to the client's affairs.

Sims v. *Craig Bell and Bond*[7] and *Collier* v. *Creighton*[8] were both cases of conflict of duty and interest in a solicitor and client context. The general rule is that a solicitor may not make a profit from a transaction that has involved a conflict of duty and interest. This is not the case where a solicitor obtains the consent of his client to his private dealing after making full disclosure, and the solicitor demonstrates that no thing he could have done would have obtained a better bargain for his client.

Duty of care to client

The relationship between the solicitor and his client is based upon the contract of retainer. In order to avoid confusion, the terms of the retainer contract ought to be recorded in writing and communicated to the client. In all cases, a general duty to exercise the skill and care of a reasonably competent solicitor will be implied into the retainer. In the current economic climate, judicial attention most regularly focuses on:

(1) Commercial advice given by solicitors; and
(2) Conflicts of interest.

Commercial advice

In *Candoola Investments Limited* v. *Cavell Leitch Pringle & Boyle*,[9] the court, in considering a claim against the plaintiff's former solicitors following the collapse of their business, held that it is a solicitor's duty to advise his clients as to the wisdom of a contract they have entered into.

The recent Privy Council judgement in *Mouat* v. *Clark Boyce* has clarified a solicitor's duty in relation to commercial advice. The Privy Council held that:

> "When a client in full command of his facilities and apparently aware of what he is doing seeks the assistance of a solicitor in carrying out a particular transaction that solicitor is under no duty whether before or after accepting instructions to go beyond those instructions by proffering unsought advice on the wisdom of the transaction. To hold otherwise could impose intolerable burdens on solicitors."

7. CA 262/90, 6 June 1991.
8. High Court, Christchurch, 7 May 1991, CP 13/89, Roper J.
9. High Court, Christchurch, 15 December 1992, CP 313/88, Holland J.

Conflict of interest

There has been a trend in New Zealand in recent years for claims to be made against solicitors where solicitors act for more than one party to a transaction, for instance, where solicitors act for the borrowing company and the director is a guarantor or a mortgagor and mortgagee. In *Mouat* v. *Clark Boyce*, the Privy Council held that:

"A fiduciary duty concerns disclosure of material facts in a situation where the fiduciary has either a personal interest in the matter to which the facts are material or acts for another party who has such an interest. It cannot be prayed-in-aid to enlarge the scope of contractual duties. Thus, there being no contractual duty on Mr. Boyce to advise Mrs. Mouat on the wisdom of entering into the transaction, she cannot claim that he nevertheless owed her a fiduciary duty to give that advice. Furthermore, any duty of disclosure can only extend to the solicitor's knowledge of the facts and not his lack of knowledge thereof."

In *Grove Darlow & Partners* v. *Rusden*,[10] the interests of one client conflicted with the interests of another. The solicitor failed to make full disclosure or to obtain consent to his acting for both clients. The court took the view that disclosure alone would not have been sufficient because the solicitor could not fairly and adequately act for both.

In *Hammington* v. *Ross*,[11] the court affirmed the principles set out by the Court of Appeal in *Farrington* v. *Rowe McBride*[12] that:

"The relationship between solicitor and client carries with it obligations on the solicitor's part to act with absolute fairness and openness towards his client. Like any other agent, but to a higher degree because of his position as an officer of the court and the privileges which the law attaches to legal professional confidence, he is found to observe the utmost good faith .... It follows that a solicitor must not without the informed consent of his client stand to make any profit or receive any benefit other than his professional remuneration from the transaction which he is retained to carry through. It is no defence that his interest is indirect — as where the transaction is between his client and company in which he is a member or his family has a significant shareholding or where he otherwise has an indirect financial interest in the transaction."

The court held that in any financial transaction between solicitor and client, there is a presumption that it should not be upheld unless the solicitor can establish that it was effected by free exercise of the client's will and without influence by the solicitor. The onus is on the solicitor to show informed consent. The relationship automatically gives rise to the duty, with the reposing of trust by the client automatically assumed. The solicitor must be dedicated to the best interests of the client, and if the solicitor is to have business dealings with a client, "the requirements of the law" are rigorous.

10. High Court, Auckland, 17 December 1992, CP 48/91, Wallace J.
11. High Court, Wellington, 11 November 1991, CP 73/90, McGechan J.
12. [1985] 1 NZLR 83.

In all cases involving a conflict of interest, the paramount question is the informed consent of the client. If a client is fully aware of what he is doing and has rejected independent advice, there is no duty on a solicitor to refuse to act.

Duties of care to third parties

The leading case in this area is *Hedley Byrne* v. *Heller.*[13]

The concept of assumption of responsibility by a solicitor and reliance by a third party, implicit in the judgement of *Hedley Byrne* v. *Heller,* is reflected in two cases where solicitors were successfully sued by third parties — *Allied Finance & Investments Limited* v. *Haddow & Co.*[14] and *Connell* v. *Odlum.*[15] In both those cases, the solicitor gave a certificate that was relied upon by a third party to its detriment. In the *Haddow* case, the certificate was to the effect that the yacht of the solicitor's client was unencumbered, whereas in fact it was. In *Odlum* v. *Connell*, the solicitor's certificate was to the effect that his client had been properly advised of her rights under the Matrimonial Property Act when signing a pre-nuptial agreement. Mrs. Odlum was successful in having the agreement set aside upon the grounds that she had not been properly advised as to the effect and implications of the agreement. Mr. Odlum succeeded in the claim against his former wife's solicitor for the loss of the benefit he would have achieved had the pre-nuptial agreement been valid.

In *Gartside* v. *Sheffield Young & Ellis*,[16] solicitors were held liable to third party beneficiaries for failing to promptly prepare a will and have it executed by the testatrix.

In all the above cases, the court held that there was a sufficient degree of proximity to give rise to a duty of care. However, it is only in these very narrow circumstances that solicitors have been held to owe a duty of care to someone other than their client.

STANDARDS

The standard owed by a solicitor is that of a reasonably competent solicitor.[17]

13. [1964] AC 465, where it was held that those who give advice that they know other identified or identifiable parties will or must rely on are liable if they give that advice negligently.
14. [1983] NZLR 32 (CA).
15. [1993] 2 NZLR 257 (CA).
16. [1983] NZLR 37.
17. *Nocton* v. *Lord Ashburton* [1914] AC 932, *Day* v. *Mead* [1987] 2 NZLR 443.

In *Geddes* v. *Lane Neave Ronaldson*,[18] the court found that the standard of care expected of a solicitor is the same as that stated in *Halsburys*:

"A solicitor holds himself out to his clients as possessing adequate skill, knowledge, and learning for the purpose of properly conducting all business that he undertakes, whether contentious or non-contentious. If, therefore, he causes loss or damage to his client owing to want of such knowledge as he ought to possess or the want of such care as he ought to exercise, he is guilty of negligence giving rise to an action for damages by his client. Where an action is brought by the client against his solicitor for negligence, the client must prove that there was such a want of skill or care on the part of the solicitor as to amount to a breach of contract .... A solicitor is not guilty of negligence if he has merely acted upon his client's instructions in the reasonable belief that they were correct, or if he has fully explained the position to his client and is nevertheless instructed to proceed, or merely because he has committed an error in judgement, whether on matters of discretion or of law such as, for instance on points of new occurrence or of doubtful construction."

Liability

Partners are jointly and severally liable for the negligent acts, errors or omission of their partners and employees. Legal staff could conceivably be liable in tort for negligence causing loss to clients of the firm or third parties. Normally however, a claim is brought against the firm in respect of its vicarious liability for the acts of its partners or legal staff and, particularly as the cause of action generally arises in contract, it would be unusual for a claim to be made against a staff member personally in tort. Usually, employees are covered under the definition of the insured in the firm's policy so that there is no need to sue them separately. Also, it is usual for the insurer to waive its right of subrogation in respect of a claim by the firm against an employee.

Partners are only liable for acts, errors or omissions (which include breaches of fiduciary duties), which arise at the time they are partners in the firm. Accordingly, a new partner's exposure to liability is limited to occurrences that arise after the partner joins the firm, and conversely, a former partner's liability relates only to occurrences that arose prior to the date of resignation. There have been cases where former partners have been liable for subsequent acts of the firm where they have allowed, or acquiesced in, the firm holding them out as partners of the firm. For example, in *Estate of McElwain* v. *Hamlin and Others*,[19] a partner remained on the firm's letterhead after the date of resignation and thereby exposed himself to liability.

18. CP 157/88, 15 November 1990.
19. High Court, Wellington, CP 66/92, 3 April 1992, Williams QC.

INSURANCE

Professional indemnity insurance for lawyers is maintained on a voluntary basis. Traditionally, voluntary compliance has been high, with well over 90 per cent of the profession (which comprises about 6,400 lawyers, including both barristers and solicitors) carrying some form of insurance. The profession has given a very clear indication that it does not want to be involved in a Master Policy scheme. However, the New Zealand Law Society is now looking to implement a compulsory scheme on a "minimum terms" or "approved policy" basis. Negotiations are in train with four of the leading brokers, and it is anticipated that during 1994, professional indemnity insurance for the legal profession will become compulsory. Of course, it will be compulsory only as to minimum requirements, and it is expected that many, if not most, law firms will voluntarily carry cover in excess of the minimum requirements. The New Zealand Law Society is also investigating the possibility of fidelity insurance, which would substitute for the present statutory Fidelity Fund. If implemented (and this is much more conjectural than compulsory PI insurance because of the need for statutory amendment and, therefore, Government acceptance of the proposal), it would include dishonesty cover, which would negate the need for some dishonesty extensions commonly carried by lawyers holding PI insurance policies.

Insurance cover is available from the local market (which includes Australia) and from the London market. Currently, the London market is "hardening", although the Austral-Asian market appears a little "softer". However, it would be fair to assume that some firms may be finding difficulty in obtaining cover and in many cases, terms such as the cost of insurance, the limit of cover, the number of automatic reinstatements and extensions (e.g. for fraudulent conduct by partners and/or staff), may be less favourable to the insured than in previous years. There is also a trend towards higher deductibles.

Common exclusion clauses apply to claims arising out of the following circumstances:

(1) Claims by the insured, or members of the insured's family;
(2) Loans to the insured or the insured's family or to entities in which such persons have an interest;
(3) Prior claims or notification of circumstances likely to give rise to a claim;
(4) Undertakings;
(5) Dishonesty (of staff and/or employees); and
(6) Investments in nominee companies.

CONCLUSION

Liability trends

Since the New Zealand share market crash in October 1987, there has been an increase in the number of claims against solicitors. Largely, these claims arise out of failed business ventures but, in part, they reflect an increasingly litigious society. A great many claims are based on allegations of conflict of interest and lack of advice as to the risks involved in a commercial venture.

Nominee companies have, until recent times, been operated by most law firms, often as an important adjunct to a conveyancing practice. Unfortunately, the operation of the nominee company gives rise to an inherent conflict of interest, in that investors in the nominee company are usually clients of the firm, as are the borrowers from the nominee company. The advantage of a nominee company, from a borrower's point of view, is that it is interest-only finance, which is generally capable of being rolled over. From the law firm's point of view, the ability to provide finance to clients wishing to consummate a commercial transaction can be significant in terms of the flow-on effect in generating fees from conveyancing and commercial transactions. This inherent conflict of interest can, and sometimes does, give rise to a lack of objectivity in advising investors about the prudence of a proposed mortgage investment. There have been some spectacular cases involving the use of clients' funds to prop up failing property ventures in what turn out to be a vain attempt to recover losses, which would have arisen on an earlier mortgagee's sale. Unfortunately, in some of those situations imprudence has given way to dishonesty.

Prior to its reversal by the Privy Council, the Court of Appeal's decision in *Mouat* v. *Clark Boyce* spawned a number of claims by guarantors. When called to account by the financier or bank, guarantors have turned upon the solicitor who acted for them (or simply witnessed their signature). In some situations, directors who guaranteed the obligations of their company have contended that they ought to have been given the opportunity to receive legal advice that was independent of the company. In those cases, the plaintiffs attributed some magical quality to the "conflict of interest" concept, which they believed was inherent in their dual capacity as director and shareholders. The identification of a conflict of interest, if only arising out of a split personality, was seen by some as guaranteeing recovery from the solicitor's insurers. To a degree, their faith was not misplaced in that in *Simperingham* v. *Skeates*,[20] Thorp J held that where there was a conflict of interest between the clients for whom

20. CP 292/89 Auckland, 3 June 1993.

the solicitor was acting, giving rise to a breach of fiduciary duty, the onus was on the solicitor to prove that the loss was not caused by the conflict of interest.

Other more credible claims have involved allegations that the solicitor failed to explain the difference between joint and in several guarantee circumstances where only one guarantor turned out to be "worth powder and shot".

Vendor and purchaser cases, where the solicitor acted for both parties or, at least, for more than one party to the transaction have also given rise to a number of claims.

There is still a general reluctance by plaintiffs and their advisors to closely analyse the *causal nexus* between the alleged negligent act and the loss complained of. Although it was not part of the *ratio decidendi* in either of the Privy Council's decisions in *Deloitte Haskin & Sells* v. *National Mutual Life Nominees Limited*[21] or *Mouat* v. *Clark Boyce*,[22] the fact that their Lordships held in both cases that there was no loss flowing from the alleged acts of negligence should give future plaintiffs and their advisors reason to pause.

The decision of the Privy Council in *Mouat* v. *Clark Boyce* will go some way to reversing the trend towards greater liability for solicitors, but perhaps more importantly, the current recovery from a long recession should do more to reverse that trend because business ventures have an increasing prospect of success rather than failure.

Prevention measures

The Law Society, on behalf of its members, negotiated with the government for a reduction in the availability of claims against the Fidelity Fund. The Law Practitioners Act 1993 provides that clients no longer have recourse to the Fidelity Fund if they lose money through investment in a solicitors' nominee company, although they continue to be protected against theft by a solicitor of funds belonging to a client (e.g. from the proceeds of sale of a property or the collection of assets in an estate).

There has been a steady trend, particularly by the medium-sized and larger law firms, to close down nominee companies all together. However, they are still a reasonably important component of smaller and provincial practices.

The *Mouat* v. *Clark Boyce* decision has generally made solicitors much more aware of the risks involved in acting for two or more parties in a

21. Lords Keith, Bridge, Griffiths, Jauncey and Mustill; PC 28/92; 10 June 1993.
22. Lords Goff, Jauncey, Lowry, Mustill and Slynn; PC 49/93; 4 October 1993.

transaction even where one of those parties has been offered the opportunity to obtain independent advice. While there is no empirical evidence available, it is likely that solicitors will record their advice, either by way of file-note or letter, more often than they may have done in the past.

Note: The author wishes to acknowledge the assistance provided by Kim Burkhart, Michael Robertson and Lucy Riddiford.

CHAPTER 11

SPAIN

HÉCTOR RODRÍGUEZ MOLNAR
Membrillera & Rodríguez Molnar
Madrid, Spain

INTRODUCTION

The relevant Spanish statutory provisions applicable to the legal profession are found in Articles 436 to 442 of the Organic Law of the Judiciary Power 6/1985, dated 1 July 1985 (LOPJ), and the General Statute of the Legal Profession enacted by means of Royal Decree 2090/82 of 24 July 1982. These two instruments set forth the regulatory framework of the legal profession in Spain. According to Article 436 of the LOPJ:

"[T]he title and functions of the lawyer are vested exclusively upon the holder of a degree in law, (*Licenciado en Derecho*) who conducts the professional defence of the parties in any kind of proceedings, and renders legal advice and/or undertakes legal counselling work."

On the basis of the foregoing provision, we can distinguish two main issues:

(1) The requirements established by Spanish Law, in order for a person to become a lawyer; and
(2) The professional scope of activities of lawyers in Spain.

Turning to the first point, the general pre-emptive requirement established by Article 10 of the General Statute of the Legal Profession is that lawyers must apply for membership to a professional bar association. Under our legal system, an attorney can become a member of a professional bar either as a "practising" or "non-practising" member. The latter enjoys many of the benefits of being a member (e.g. medical assistance and pension plans) but is not allowed to practice. In order to become a member of a professional bar, Article 15 of the General Statute of the Legal Profession establishes the following requirements:

(1) Spanish nationality (although the waiver of such requirement, certificate of dispensation/exemption, can be obtained in certain cases);
(2) The applicant must be of age (18 years) and have a degree in law;
(3) No criminal record;

(4) Payment of the incorporation fee; and
(5) Incorporation to the Mutual Fund (*Mutualidad General de Previsión de la Abogacía*).

Concerning the professional scope of activities of lawyers in Spain, we can distinguish two general areas of work: conduct of the case of parties to judicial proceedings and legal counselling or advice. Both kinds of activities are reserved in Spain exclusively to lawyers, that is, to the holders of a degree in Law who have joined a bar association. The first area of work is divided into two branches: conduct of the defence (reserved to lawyers/solicitors) and the representation of the parties in court (entrusted to barristers).

While both barristers and lawyers/solicitors hold a degree in law (*Licenciado en Derecho*), there remains in force a prohibition to act as a lawyer (*Abogado*) and barrister *(Procurador de los Tribunales*) at the same time: This is because in the Spanish legal system, they are regarded as distinct and incompatible professions, having different rules and bar associations.

Bar associations are the governing bodies of the profession and the general assembly of their deans constitutes the supreme executive body. The General Council of the Legal Profession (*Consejo General de la Abogacía*) is the executive, co-ordinating and representative body of the different bars.[1] There is a bar association in each province, with exclusive competence within its jurisdiction and with its seat in the provincial capital. It is forbidden to exercise the legal profession without being affiliated to the corresponding professional bar. Nevertheless, certain bars have entered into specific agreements establishing the possibility for lawyers of one jurisdiction to practise in another jurisdiction without having to join the professional bar of such other jurisdiction.

Bar associations are governed by:

(1) The General Statute of the Legal Profession;
(2) Their specific by-laws;
(3) Their regulations on internal organisation; and
(4) The resolutions of the General Council of the Legal Profession and of the Meetings of Deans.

The aims of the bars are:

(1) The control and co-ordination of the requirements for the practice of law;

1. The General Statute of the Legal Profession, Article 1.

(2) The exclusive representation of the legal profession;
(3) The defence of the professional interests of their members;
(4) The fulfilment of the social function of the legal profession; and
(5) To co-operate in the promotion and administration of justice.

In particular, bars are vested with the exclusive representation and defence of the profession before the administrative bodies, institutions, courts, entities and individuals, and have the capacity to be a party in any proceedings that may affect the professional interests of the bars or their members. In pursuance of their goals, the bars are entitled to establish minimum suggested fees, organise activities and educational services for their members and, above all, monitor and ensure that lawyers act in accordance with the required honesty and ethical standards. The bars are entitled to impose disciplinary sanctions on their members.

LAWYERS AND VARIOUS LIABILITIES

The General Statute of the Legal Profession devotes a full title (Title VI) to dealing with liabilities of professional bar members. Apart from the General Statute of the Legal Profession, other legal rules also foresee different kinds of professional liability. We can distinguish the following:

Criminal liability

Article 100 of the General Statute of the Legal Profession sets forth that lawyers are subject to criminal liability for offences and faults they commit in the course of their practice.

The bar associations or the General Council, as the case may be, are entitled to bring criminal actions in cases of alleged professional misconduct[2] pursuant to Article 321 of the Criminal Code setting forth:

"... a person who carries out actions which are inherent to a specific profession without having the corresponding official degree, will be punishable with minor imprisonment [jail term ranging between six months and one day to six years]".

The offender can also be subject to fines, ranging between 100,000 and 1-million pesetas if he publicly represents himself as a professional.

Article 41 of the General Statute of the Legal Profession sets forth the duty and the right of lawyers to maintain confidentiality about their professional secrets, which implies the obligation and the right of the lawyer not to disclose any fact or document known to him as a result of

2. The General Statute of the Legal Profession, Article 101.

his profession and which may adversely affect his client. In accordance with the above, Article 360 of the Criminal Code establishes that:

"... the lawyer or barrister who, with malicious abuse of his duties or with inexcusable ignorance or negligence, damages his client or reveals secrets he came to know as a result of his profession, will be punished with suspension and fines from 100,000 to 500,000 pesetas."

Finally, Article 361 of the Criminal Code sets forth that:

"... any lawyer or barrister who, having assumed the defence or representation of one party, would subsequently defend, represent or advise, without the first party's consent, the adverse party in the same case, will be punished with disbarment and fines from 100,000 to 500,000 pesetas."

Civil liability

Civil liability is dealt with in Articles 102 to 106 of the General Statute of the Legal Profession, establishing the following general rules: Lawyers will be subject to civil liability in the exercise of their profession when, due to either fault or negligence, they prejudice the interests of their clients. The foregoing civil liability can only be claimed by the damaged person, its successors or assignees, in accordance with the general rules of private law. This will only apply if civil liability is not attached to criminal liability, which is pursued through a separate criminal action introduced by either the prosecutor (*Ministerio Fiscal*) or a private plaintiff.

Disciplinary liability

Serious mistakes committed by a lawyer in the course of his practice or that might affect same, may result in serious disciplinary liability, including the suspension from practice for a period of up to two years, or even disbarment. Should criminal and/or civil liability arise, the relevant professional bar may bring proceedings to ascertain the existence of a disciplinary liability. Article 442.2 of the LOPJ provides that:

". . . disciplinary liability concerning lawyers' behaviour before the Courts will be governed by this Law and the Codes of Procedure. Disciplinary liability resulting from professional behaviour is governed by the relevant Statutes, and proceedings undertaken thereunder must respect the guarantees of defence."

As a result of the above, two different kinds of disciplinary authority exist and, consequently, two different sanctioning procedures can be followed. Nevertheless, their respective boundaries are not always clear due to the fact that specific conduct can be subject to either the provisions of the General Statute of the Legal Profession or to those of the procedural codes and the LOPJ. Case law has in some ways contributed to clarifying this point by establishing that:

"... from the jurisdictional point of view such authority (disciplinary authority) is only an instrument that allows the procedural rules to carry out their function, while from the point of view of the bar associations, penalties have the more general aim of contributing to maintain a certain ethical level in the actions of the professionals."[3]

Disciplinary authority of judges and courts

Lawyers and barristers may be sanctioned by judges or courts whenever they, for example, show lack of respect, or do not appear in court without justified reason.[4] Punishment may consist in either a specific warning or a fine, the amount of which will be determined pursuant to the provisions of the Criminal Code on the subject.

Disciplinary authority of bar associations

Article 107 of the General Statute of the Legal Profession establishes that lawyers are subject to disciplinary liability in the event of a breach of their professional duties. The General Statute of the Legal Profession lists a number of faults which are classified as very serious, serious and minor. Sanctions may range from the suspension in the practice for a period between three months and two years, to disbarment.

CIVIL LIABILITY OF PRACTISING LAWYERS

Legal nature and sources of liability

In general terms, civil liability may have a contractual, a non-contractual or criminal origin. In any case, several elements or conditions must concur before civil liability can arise; these elements are common to all of the three types of civil liability (contractual, non-contractual and criminal) and involve the existence of an action or omission infringing:

(1) A legal provision;
(2) A contractual commitment; and/or
(3) The due diligence normally expected from an individual in light of the nature of the values at risk or the nature of the profession itself.

3. Supreme Court, 3 April 1990.
4. Organic Law of the Judiciary Power 6/1985, Article 449.

Real damage (duly proven) and adequate causation (with no third party interference) must be shown.

Upon this basis, we will first try to describe what should be the proper behaviour of a practising lawyer, and then review the lawyer-client relationship as well as other ways of practising law.

Practising lawyer

Due diligence

The principle of civil liability of lawyers and/or other professionals stems from Article 1104 of the Civil Code. This Article applies to either contractual or non-contractual obligations and reads as follows:

"Fault or negligence of the debtor consists in the omission of the diligence required, by the nature of the obligation, and by the circumstances of persons, time and place. When the obligation does not set the level of diligence to be observed, the diligence of a good head of a family shall be required."[5]

Based on the above, diligence has been defined by legal scholars as "the minimum, unrepealable level of commitment and effort that every debtor is generally obliged to guarantee to the creditor".[6]

Therefore, when the person under an obligation is a professional (lawyer or otherwise) who has been engaged precisely in such capacity, then the objective applicable standard will be that of an average professional. Such standard will allow one to evaluate if the concrete behaviour, in accordance with those rules, is appropriate to achieve the result foreseen, regardless of whether such result is actually achieved or not. With regard to lawyers, the due diligence standard is always the one described in Article 1104 of the Civil Code, but we must narrow down such principle further. We have seen that the basic responsibility of the lawyer is to defend his client's interests in addition to giving him legal advice or counselling. These are very technical services; the lawyer must be aware that his duties are very specific and that a significant degree of diligence is required. Such degree is usually higher than that applicable in other walks of life.

Considering that the relationship between lawyer and client is, most of the time, embodied in a contract, the relationship shall also be governed by Article 1258 of the Civil Code. It states:

5. "Diligence of a good head of a family" (*bonus pater familias*) has been understood by case law as the diligence of an individual who is normally careful within the scope of his activity.

6. Munoz Campos, *La Responsabilidad Civil de Abogados y Procuradores*, Madrid, 1988.

"Contracts . . . oblige not only to comply with their terms, but also to bear any consequences that, depending on its nature, are in line with *bona fides*, usual practice and the law."

With regard to the practising lawyer, the "law" is the General Statute of the Legal Profession, and he will have to observe very closely the provisions of the same; in particular, Article 53 of the General Statute of the Legal Profession provides that the "lawyer must fulfill his duties with maximum devotion and diligence".

Legal nature of the lawyer-client relationship

Sources of the relationship

In general terms, the relationship between any professional and his client implies the absence of subordination. Nevertheless, it is becoming more and more usual for lawyers to be subject to some degree of dependence on a principal. Therefore, we find two different ways to practice law:

(1) As an independent practitioner, thus accepting the risk of having or not having income; or
(2) The professional placing his knowledge and skills at the disposal of a third person in the form of a labour or administrative contract for services.

Initially, the first kind of practice will be considered, reviewing the nature of the relationship and its consequences with regard to a lawyer's liability. Then, the second kind of practice, where the lawyer has no independent relationship with a client, as well as other special cases such as partnership and office sharing and the consequences of such practice on the principles of liability will be reviewed.

Contractual or non-contractual relationship

The practical consequences of whether the relationship is contractual or non-contractual are important, due to the differences existing between these two kinds of liability; first, because under the applicable Statute of Limitations, actions derived from contracts prescribe in fifteen years,[7] while actions derived from a non-contractual relationship prescribe in one year;[8] second, because of the kind of liability involved. From a contractual

7. Civil Code, Article 1964.
8. Civil Code, Article 1968.2.

viewpoint, joint and several liability of debtors only exists if specifically agreed upon.[9] While the technical solution should be the same in the case of non-contractual liability, our case law has consistently ruled in favour of joint and several liability of the persons responsible in tort, based on the principle of due protection of the victims. Finally, concerning the territorial competence of judges and courts, claims demanding contractual liability must be brought at the place where the defendant is domiciled or at the place where the contract was executed, at the option of the plaintiff; in the case of (non-contractual) liability in tort, claims must always be brought at the place where the damaging events took place.

Although some authors have considered that the liability of a professional is non-contractual regardless of whether a contract actually exists, the most reasonable attitude, which in fact has been the one followed by case law and by most of legal scholars,[10] is to consider that the source of the relationship is always a contractual one and most of the time, this is a contract for the rendering of services. In any case, the lawyer can still eventually incur non-contractual liability, for example, when the lawyer becomes in liable to the party adverse to his client.

Moreover, it is possible that both kinds of liability appear together. For instance, if the lawyer loses some documents entrusted to him, he might cause damage to both his client and to persons other than his client.

Kind of contract

In general terms,

> ". . . services rendered by lawyers, as well as by other individuals exercising liberal professions, can be regarded as requiring a quality in excess of what the legal tradition and our Civil Code have identified as a contract for the rendering of services."[11]

Nevertheless, this is not a general rule, as there are other situations where the lawyer enters into the so-called contract of works (*contrato de obra*) with his client. This leads us to the traditional distinction between obligations of activity and obligations of results proposed by Demogue in 1925.[12]

In most instances, the professional obligates himself only to carry out a certain activity directed to obtaining a certain result which, nevertheless, is not guaranteed (e.g. defence of the client in court proceedings); these are obligations of activity, where liability is based only on diligence;

9. Civil Code, Article 1137.

10. Yzquierdo Tolsada, *La responsabilidad Civil del Profesional Liberal*, Madrid, 1988.

11. Supreme Court, 16 February 1935.

12. Demogue, *Traité des obligations en general*. I. *Sources des obligations*, Paris, 1925.

this is the case of the contract for the rendering of services.[13] On the contrary, in other instances, the lawyer must achieve a specific result and if such result is not achieved, the contract will have been breached, no matter the reason for the breach (e.g. the contract by means of which the lawyer has to prepare a report on a certain subject). These are obligations of result, where liability is based on the result; this is the case of the contract of works.[14]

These two kinds of obligations have different consequences with regard to liability. In obligations of result, the debtor (lawyer) assumes all risks of loss until the delivery of the result (product) to the creditor (client), but even if a breach of contract is actually proved by the creditor, the debtor may be held free from liability if he proves that the breach was due to an act of God or *force majeure* (e.g. lawyer who has to deliver a report, his office is destroyed by fire). Conversely, in obligations of activity, the creditor has to prove that the debtor was negligent while the latter has to prove his own diligence; and if negligence is effectively proved, the debtor will end up being liable. In obligations of activity, the onus is on the creditor, thus putting him in a difficult position; for this reason, case law has considered that it is not necessary to have a complete or definite proof of negligence, which can simply be deducted from facts that would allow to assume that negligence existed.

In any event, the contract for the rendering of services is the most common one. This solves the problem of its legal nature, but not that of ascertaining the applicable provisions, because Articles 1583 to 1587 prove insufficient to such effect. The Supreme Court[15] clearly expresses this idea:

> "[S]aid services [lawyer's services] exceed, in many instances, the scope of the simple rendering of services, featuring aspects pertaining to the management and representation mandate and even those of the contracts of works; notwithstanding, this does not mean that such kind of activities are devoid of juridical and legal protection."

Lawyers and employment contracts

If the lawyer is employed by a private company, for example, by an insurance company, or as a civil servant, this sort of professional regime excludes any kind of contractual relationship between lawyer and client. Although the case of private companies and the employment by the public

13. Civil Code, Articles 1583 to 1587.
14. Civil Code, Articles 1588 *et seq.*
15. Judgement of 24 June 1991.

administration employing lawyers will be reviewed separately, we may advance that in both cases, the employer bears the consequences of the lawyer's professional liability.

Regarding employment by private companies, Article 1903.4 of the Civil Code sets forth that:

"The owners or managers of establishments or companies are liable for damage caused by their employees in the course of the activities for which they are employed, or when carrying out their duties."

At the same time, employers are ancillarily liable for civil damages that may be assessed as a result of a criminal action[16] although in this case it is necessary for the offender to be found liable under civil law and convicted as a result of the criminal action.[17] The victim can claim against either the employer or the lawyer, as both actions are independent from each other. The lawyer and his employer are jointly and severally liable, but the latter can subsequently bring an action for recovery against the lawyer. In practice, victims will choose to bring action against the employer and the lawyer at the same time.

Regarding employment by the public administration, liability of the employer is based in Article 1903.5 of the Civil Code and, most of all, in Article 40 of the Law on Juridical Regime of the State Administration, which establishes a principle of objective liability of the administration for any damage caused to individuals and/or to their assets and/or rights as a result of the operation of the public services. Unlike in the previous case, the administration incurs indirect (not ancillary) civil liability that may derive from a criminal action. However, here also the administration may claim restitution from the lawyer responsible for the damage. In this case, the victim may bring his claim against the administration and the responsible individual, but in practice, the injured party will claim only against the administration.

Other special cases

LAW PARTNERSHIPS

Article 34 of the General Statute of the Legal Profession foresees the possibility that several lawyers may practise law in a collective manner. Conditions for establishing such a partnership are the following:

(1) The partnership will have not more than 20 partners, and partners will not be allowed to have an office independent from the collective one; and

16. Criminal Code, Article 22.
17. Criminal Code, Article 19.

(2) Registration of the office with the relevant bar association, following prior authorisation by the bar of the covenants governing the activities of the firm.

Concerning the legal nature of these collective offices and the problems that may arise with regard to liability, it is interesting to review the position of the Bar Association of Madrid:

"It is not possible to practise law through collective offices having the form of corporations or limited liability companies, nor under the form of commercial associations or firms."

The Madrid Bar states that "liability demanded from lawyers, whether or not they are a part of a collective office, is individual and is determined *ex lege*".

This position has been reaffirmed by the Directorate General of Registers and Public Notaries, by the Resolution of 2 June 1986, declaring that:

". . . whenever a professional or similar degree is required, it is clear enough that it is not possible to practise through a commercial company, due to the fact that the company 'per se' and as an ideal entity is not capable of carrying out this kind of service directly."

Should more than one lawyer be liable for the damage, the problem would be to determine if the liability is only joint or joint and several. It is possible to establish the following rules. In the presence of a contractually based relationship, joint liability will be the rule.[18] If there was no contract, the position of case law has been to impose joint and several liability. In fact, since 1964 the Supreme Court has consistently ruled that joint and several liability existed in all cases where Articles 1902 and 1903 of the Civil Code (non-contractual liability) applied to actions of several individuals, being all of them responsible in the commission of an illicit action. Case law has based this position strictly on equity, as there are no other arguments within our legal system to support this trend. However, some authors consider that the same criteria should apply to cases of contractual and non-contractual liability; in both cases, the facts that give rise to liability are the same or similar, and it seems unfair to apply different criteria thereto. Likewise, the most advanced legal systems, consistently apply the principle of joint and several liability.[19]

OFFICE-SHARING

Under the concept of office sharing one can envisage in principle both a situation where a single, principal lawyer works with subordinate

18. Civil Code, Article 1137, and case law.

19. Yzquierdo Tolsada, *La Responsabilidad Civil del Professional Liberal*, Madrid, 1988.

collaborators and assistants and a situation where different lawyers work independently from each other.

Article 35 of the General Statute of the Legal Profession sets forth that a collective office will not exist if a single lawyer has collaborators or assistants, or in the situation where ascendants or descendants of the principal lawyer practice in the office. The Spanish Civil Code does not regulate these sorts of situations, which are specifically foreseen in other European codes.[20] We can only find a similar provision in Article 1596 of the Civil Code concerning the contract of works establishing that "the contractor shall be responsible for the work carried out by other persons whose services he may use to comply with his obligation".

Certain authors admit that when the debtor acts through third persons, he must be liable for their actions.[21] The grounds for this position are similar to those we have seen above with regard to the liability of the employer for the actions of his employees. The debtor uses collaborators and assistants for his own benefit and "it is therefore a principle of equitable justice to make him liable for their activities".[22]

In the situation where different lawyers work independently from each other in the same office, it is clear that liability will be individual for each and every lawyer.

CONSEQUENCES OF CIVIL LIABILITY

The concern about professional liability of lawyers is fairly recent in Spain; the increasing number of claims and the protective trend of case law with regard to the victims of damage have bought with them the logical concern of professionals. Insurance companies have proliferated accordingly. In fact, legislation, case law, social habits, and economy, *inter alia*, are different factors that have gradually derived in an increased number of "accidents" and in claims for much larger amounts. The draft EEC Directive on Liability regarding the Rendering of Services may help to clarify this situation, if and when approved.

Insurance

Until very recently, the Madrid Bar Association, as well as other Spanish bars have entered into agreements with several insurance companies in

20. For example, in the Italian, Swiss, Portuguese and German codes.

21. Yzquierdo Tolsada, *La Responsabilidad Civil del Professional Liberal*, Madrid, 1988.

22. Larenz, *Derecho justo. Fundamentos de ética jurídica*, translated by Díez-Picazo, 1985.

order to cover certain risks involved in the practice of law. Unlike other professions (e.g. doctors), it is not compulsory for lawyers to take out insurance. We shall examine, as an example, the main features of the insurance policy subscribed by the Madrid Bar Association.

Coverage

The contract covers the financial consequences of civil liability that may be attributed to a lawyer with the occasion and as a result of the rendering of his professional services.

Technical definitions

For the purposes of the insurance contract, "professional error, fault or negligence" is understood to mean the conduct of the insured person which causes a patrimonial damage that may subsequently result in claims for compensation. Patrimonial loss or damage suffered by third parties as a consequence of professional faults, errors or negligence is that loss resulting in:

(1) The annulment of rights;
(2) The interruption of a service carried out by a person or the inability to use personal property or real estate; or
(3) Loss of profits.

Risks covered by the policy

The policy covers the following risks:

(1) Indemnifications for which the lawyer or his dependants may be held liable under the policy and under civil law;
(2) Damage caused by actions carried out in any part of Spain, even if out of the jurisdiction of the Madrid Bar (except when the lawyer has any other policy covering professional civil liability taken out at the place where the damaging event occurred);
(3) Indemnifications payable as a result of bodily or other physical injury that may derive from the use of business premises by the lawyer, either as owner, tenant or user; and
(4) Claims arising from damages to loss or misplacement of files and documents kept by the insured person in the course of his practice.

Risks excluded

Various risks are excluded, such as:

(1) Claims derived from bodily or other physical injury, other than those foreseen in point (3) above;
(2) Claims derived from an activity other than the practice of law;
(3) Claims brought before foreign courts, derived from the infringement or non-observance of foreign law (except when the said law should be legally applied in Spain and by Spanish Courts) or derived from a professional activity carried out abroad;
(4) Claims derived from loss or misplacement of money, money orders or instruments to the bearer, endorsed in blank;
(5) Claims for cash shortages, errors in payments, or disloyal actions of persons under the surveillance or control of the attorney;
(6) Intentional actions, premeditation (*dolus*) or fraud; or
(7) Claims derived from breach of professional confidentiality.

Time limits

Insurance covers damages due to errors and/or faults committed from the date of execution of the policy until its termination. This coverage is subject to the condition that the claim against the insured person and the subsequent notification of the claim to the company take place while the policy is in effect or within a term not exceeding one year after the termination of the policy, for any reason whatsoever.

Previous conduct

Claims concerning actions taken during the one-year period immediately preceding the execution of the policy are covered by the same provided the insured person had no knowledge of the existence of such claim at the time the policy was executed and such claim is brought and notified while the policy is in effect.

Defence of civil liability and criminal actions

The costs of civil defence are automatically guaranteed by all civil liability insurances, pursuant to Article 74 of Law 50/1980 of 8 October 1980 on Insurances.

With respect to criminal defence, for those persons whose civil liability is already covered by the policy, the following guarantees are included:

(1) Handling of any subsequent criminal proceedings by lawyers and barristers appointed by the insurer (even if the claim for civil liability is previously settled);
(2) Furnishing of bail deposits; and
(3) Payment of all judicial expenses that may be incurred as a result of criminal proceedings that may result from an action for civil liability.

Deposits or bail bonds must not exceed the maximum limits fixed within the special conditions of the policy. Payment of judicial expenses does not include those resulting from a personal sanction. In the case of conviction, the insurance company will decide whether or not it is appropriate to appeal to the competent appellate court. If it decides that an appeal is not convenient, the company notifies this decision to the insured person, who is then free to appeal at his own expense.

Claim for lawyer's own losses

Physical damages suffered by the insured person or his dependants within the scope of the risks covered by the policy are subject to indemnification. The insurer obliges itself, on behalf of the insured person, to claim indemnification directly from the responsible third party. The compensation obtained shall correspond entirely to the damaged party.

Coverage limits

The Madrid Bar Association has contracted with the Insurance Company a maximum limit of indemnification of Ptas. 5-million. This amount refers to either a single loss derived from different professional errors or to all the consequences of one and the same error.

At present, lawyers are entitled to contract with the Insurance Company individual coverage in excess of amounts contracted by the Bar as follows:

Excess Cover over Ptas 5-Million up to	Total Annual Additional Premiums
Ptas. 20-million	Ptas. 6.004
Ptas. 45-million	Ptas. 11.500
Ptas. 70-million	Ptas. 18.714
Ptas. 95-million	Ptas. 23.981

Other policy aspects

The coverage extends to accidents that the insured person may suffer as a passenger of any vehicle, whether public or private, which occur within the relevant territory in the course of a professional activity.

Disputes are subject to the decision of an arbitration board. The insurer agrees to accept the resolutions of the arbitration board concerning disagreements that may arise on the interpretation and scope of the risks covered by the policy and the existence, if any, of liability, provided however that disputes must arise from claims relating to damages caused by professional error, fault or negligence of the attorney. The board is formed by three members, representing the insured person, the Madrid Bar Association and the insurer respectively and acting in accordance with the Law on Arbitration of 5 December 1988 and other applicable legal provisions.

Any notices of damage addressed to the insurer are to be previously notified in writing to the bar and the latter will produce a report on the merits of the matter.

European perspectives

Free rendering of services

Council Directive 77/249 of 22 March 1977 provides the legal frame for the free rendering of legal services in other member States. It has been implemented into Spanish law by means of Royal Decree 607/86 of 21 March 1986, partially modified by Royal Decree 1062/1988 of 16 September 1988. According to these provisions, any person entitled to practice the legal profession in another member State shall be able to render occasional services in Spain. This means that while European lawyers will not be able to open an office in Spain, they can render various legal services such as counselling, giving legal advice and conducting of court cases.

Royal Decree 607/88 sets forth that the visiting lawyer must appear before the dean of the bar association of the place where he intends to act in order to furnish certain professional information. Likewise, the visiting lawyer will have to act in concert with a national lawyer. In rendering the services, the foreign lawyer is subject to the rules governing professional practice in Spain, including the provisions concerning ethical behaviour. This is without prejudice to the provisions applicable in his home country.

Right of establishment

Council Directive of 21 December 1988 establishes the requirements that are necessary in order to develop a permanent professional activity (as a lawyer or otherwise) in a permanent way in a member State other than the one where the individual obtained his degree in law. In order to benefit from the Directive, studies must have a duration of at least three years. The underlying principle is that a European Union citizen who is capable of practising a profession in a member State should also be considered capable of practising that profession in another member State. Certain provisions aim to overcome the existing differences in the duration of the professional training and the specific subjects studied in each country.

The Directive has been implemented into Spanish law by means of Royal Decree 1665/91 of 25 October 1991. In order to practise the legal profession in Spain, the foreign lawyer is required to take and pass a test of aptitude. The bar associations must put in place the educational programmes necessary to allow the foreign lawyer to pass such a test. The additional provisions necessary to implement Royal Decree 1665/91 have still not been enacted, and the practical consequences of this regime are still to be seen.

Note: The author acknowledges the valuable assistance of Begóña González del Tángo, which was material in preparing this chapter.

CHAPTER 12

SWEDEN

THOMAS TENDORF AND LARS SANDBERG
Advokatfirman Södermark
Stockholm, Sweden

INTRODUCTION

This chapter, which has been written primarily for lawyers outside Sweden, does not by any means attempt to be exhaustive in any respect with regard to the subject matter of lawyers and professional liability. Some of the sections such as those which give an outline of the legal profession, practice structures and procedures before courts and professional bodies only serve the purpose of setting out the main features with respect hereto. Other chapters, although providing a fair degree of details as to a number of legal issues, are intended to outline what have appeared to be the main issues involved. Finally, the reader should neither forget the maxim "*non est regula quin fallet*" (there is no rule without an exception) nor the fact that each particular case may have and often does have its peculiarities and that the law is a difficult subject.

The legal profession

The legal profession in Sweden is not divided into different branches. There is only one branch made up of *Advokater* (*Advokat* in singular form in Swedish), who are members of the Swedish Bar Association (the Bar). The *Advokater* in Sweden deal with both contentious as well as non-contentious legal work. There are, of course, *Advokater* who specialise in litigation (civil and criminal), commercial and family law as well as other areas of the law. However, it is not unusual to come across a commercial *Advokat* who undertakes both litigation work and who also acts as a legal adviser on a variety of commercial transactions. It is a criminal offence under Swedish law for someone who is not a member of the Bar to pass himself off as being an *Advokat*.

A person applies to the Bar in order to become an *Advokat*. An eligible applicant from Sweden is required to have a law degree from a Swedish University (*jur.kand*) and a record of five years of practice. A diploma from a faculty of law in Sweden indicates in English that the degree is an LL.M and not an LL.B although it is only a first degree in law. The LL.M programme requires four and a half years but the average student appears to graduate in approximately five and a half years. Participation in a three-day course arranged by the Bar is also mandatory prior to becoming a member.

Many applicants have worked as law clerks within a traineeship programme of, presently, two years at a court of first instance. Today, this is available to about 30 to 40 per cent of graduate students based on examination results from the University. They may thereafter apply for membership after an additional period of three years of practice with a law firm. An applicant must indicate in the application form, *inter alia*, references to other *Advokater* in support of the application. All applications are notified to the members of the Bar as well as to the courts so that anyone with objections against an applicant may come forward.

As a result of the European integration process, the Bar recently adopted rules that allow foreign lawyers from a number of European countries to become members subject to certain requirements.

Types of legal advisers

A Swedish law firm (normally referred to as *Advokatbyrå* or *Advokatfirma* in Swedish) can be made up of *Advokater* and lawyers who are not yet eligible for membership of the Bar. The lawyers forming part of the latter category are normally referred to with reference to their law degree (that is, *jur.kand*) or as assistant lawyers (*biträdande jurister*). *Advokater* are either partners or associates whereas assistant lawyers are associates only. There are today approximately 2,900 members of the Bar, of which more than a third are practising in the Stockholm area. There are approximately 700 assistant lawyers.

Other types of legal advisers that one would come across in Sweden are, for example, in-house lawyers working for companies and banks. Many in-house lawyers have started as assistant lawyers with a law firm and might also have become members of the Bar. However, if an *Advokat* leaves a law firm to join the industry, as it were, he cannot then any longer continue to be a member of the Bar. Other types of legal advisers also exist such as lawyers working for the Trade Unions and Associations of Employees.

Regulatory framework

The regulatory framework for *Advokater* consists mainly of three sets of rules. The principal source is to be found in Chapter 8 in the Code of Procedure which deals with the subject matter of *Advokater*. These rules are applicable to all members of the Bar, irrespective of whether they are engaged as counsel in litigation or not. A second set of rules is represented by the Regulations of the Bar adopted by the Assembly of the Bar and confirmed by the Swedish Government (hereinafter referred to as the Regulations). A third set of rules are those which set out guidelines on professional conduct and etiquette (*God Advokatsed*) adopted by the Board of the Bar (hereinafter referred to as the Guidelines).

Professional bodies

The profession is supervised by the Bar, which was established in 1887. It grew out of the variety of practitioners who operated in different capacities in the legal system throughout the country since, it is believed, the 17th century. The Bar is both the professional association concerned with the advancement of the interests of *Advokater* and the governing body responsible for dealing with complaints against *Advokater* and disciplinary and other matters.

To summarise, the Bar is organised as follows. The members elect an Assembly which holds an ordinary meeting every year. The Assembly elects a Board. The Bar is divided into sections based on geographical structure and each section has its own board. The sections hold meetings with their members, that is those members practising within the region of each Section respectively.

Charges of professional misconduct are heard and determined by a Disciplinary Committee, which is composed of nine members of which seven are elected by the Bar and two by the Government. Complaints alleging misconduct by an *Advokat* received by the Bar can either be dismissed by the Board of the Bar or referred to by the Board of the Bar to the Disciplinary Committee. If the Board of the Bar decides not to refer a complaint to the Disciplinary Committee, then the Attorney General (*Justitiekanslern*) may do so within a limited period of time.

In respect of any complaint, the Disciplinary Committee may decide either that no disciplinary action should be taken or that the *Advokat* should be subject to a disciplinary action pursuant to the remedies available, the most severe of which is to expel an *Advokat* from the Bar. A decision to expel an *Advokat* is subject to a right of appeal to the Supreme Court on the part of that *Advokat*. The Attorney General has the right to refer a complaint to the Disciplinary Committee if the Board of the Bar has dismissed the complaint. He is also always entitled to bring an appeal before the Supreme Court with respect to all decisions made by the Disciplinary Committee irrespective of whether complaints have been referred to the Disciplinary Committee by the Board of the Bar or the Attorney General.

During 1992, there were 427 complaints filed with the Bar, and the Board of the Bar dealt with a total of 435 complaints during the same year, of which 325 did not result in any action (one complaint was withdrawn). The remaining 109 complaints were referred to the Disciplinary Committee which dealt with a total of 99 complaints during 1992. Disciplinary actions of some kind were taken in 50 of those cases.

PRACTICE STRUCTURES

Before providing a brief outline of the various practice structures in existence in Sweden today, it should be noted that the principal rule is that an *Advokat* is an individual and is responsible for his own work as an individual.

Advokater practise in firms. An *Advokat* may practise his profession alone or together with other *Advokater* by the use of a limited liability company (*Aktiebolag* or AB, in abbreviated form) with the permission of the Bar. However, the Companies Act makes provision for personal liability of an *Advokat* in his capacity as owner or co-owner of a limited liability company for liabilities towards clients incurred by the company. The business name registered must indicate that the company is an *Advokataktiebolag*.

Advokater who practise their profession independently from each other (not in partnership) may share offices, that is share the services of assistant lawyers, office expenses such as rent, secretarial facilities, library and other costs.

Advokater may form partnerships and are allowed to do so by means of incorporating a partnership company which is a separate legal entity in Swedish law. All members of the partnership company are jointly and severally liable for the liabilities of the partnership company (unless the members make use of a partnership company with limited liability in which case different rules apply). An *Advokat* may be a member of the partnership company through a limited liability company. The partnership members are allowed to agree to share fees.

There are also in existence in Sweden legal firms set up by lawyers who are not members of the Bar (*Juridiska byraer*). Nevertheless, as a general rule, they are subject to the same standards in terms of professional conduct (but perhaps not with regard to etiquette in all respects) as members of the Bar. Such a lawyer would normally be expected to apply for membership with the Bar after five years of practice and would, upon becoming a member of the Bar, continue to practise but then as *Advokat* in the same firm that would then become known as *Advokatbyrå* or *Advokatfirma*.

Finally, it should be mentioned that a number of *Advokater* are employed by the state as part of the legal aid system. The main difference in making a comparison with *Advokater* in private practice is that they are under a duty to provide legal services to those who are entitled to legal aid under the Legal Aid Scheme, whereas *Advokater* in private practice do not have a duty to take any assignments offered. This rule applies irrespective of whether a client would be entitled to have legal representation and/or advice paid for by the state under the Legal Aid Scheme.

CAPACITIES

An *Advokat* may be found practising his profession in a great variety of different capacities. The most common today in Sweden are perhaps the following (which listing is not made in rank of importance or frequency):

(1) As legal adviser to individuals in connection with such issues as family law matters, conveyancing, tax advice and other private law oriented matters;
(2) As legal adviser to the business community on a variety of commercial matters;
(3) As advocate before the courts and other tribunals including arbitral tribunals and panels;
(4) As party nominated arbitrator, chairman or umpire in arbitration proceedings;
(5) As bankruptcy administrator by appointment of the courts;
(6) As guardian for a minor to, for example, administer gifts given by parents of a minor and as guardian for the administration of an estate after a person has deceased, either by appointment under a will or by the courts; and
(7) As legal opinion writer.

With respect to (3) above, it is worth noting that there is no need for intervention of another lawyer in connection with litigation in Sweden. Counsel would therefore see and advise clients directly and accordingly appear as advocate on behalf of clients without intervention of another lawyer. Some have specialised in appearing as advocates before arbitral tribunals in connection with commercial disputes. Advocates who act as counsel in criminal cases are either funded by the clients or from public funds through the legal aid system.

Regarding bankruptcy, the profession in Sweden engaged as bankruptcy administrators is *Advokater* and not firms of chartered accountants as in some other countries. *Advokater*, of course, are normally assisted by chartered accountants, stock and real estate brokers and others in the course of administrating bankruptcy estates.

The typical opinion-drafting situation is, for example, where the client of an *Advokat*, in connection with a litigation matter or a non-contentious issue such as the drafting of a commercial contract, wishes to obtain a second opinion from another *Advokat*. Legal opinions are also given by

Advokater, for example, to overseas clients who are about to engage in business activities in Sweden and who seek opinions on Swedish legal matters from local counsel.

DUTIES

Statutory

The most fundamental rule for *Advokater* is statutory and is set forth in Section 8(4) of the Code of Procedure. Pursuant to this rule, an *Advokat* owes a duty to discharge all assignments entrusted to him in a fair and diligent manner and to observe professional conduct and etiquette in all respects. An additional set of statutory rules in the Code of Procedure apply to *Advokater* appearing before the courts.

Regulations

The Regulations (as defined in this chapter) contain a separate chapter dealing with professional duties. The first rule therein is the same as that set out in the Code of Procedure referred to above. A number of other duties are also set out, for example, the duty to hold moneys received or other assets owned by a client separately from the *Advokat's* own assets. Another rule which perhaps should be mentioned is that a member of the Bar is not allowed to conduct any activities the nature or extent of which would adversely affect the independence of the member or would otherwise be considered as incompatible with the member's position as an *Advokat*.

Codes of practice

The code of practice applicable to *Advokater* is represented by the Guidelines and those in existence today were adopted by the Board of the Bar on 9 November 1984. The Guidelines are of a consolidated nature in that they, at the time they were first adopted on 18 June 1971, represented to a greater or lesser extent unwritten rules as confirmed by decisions by the Board of the Bar and the Disciplinary Committee. The Board of the Bar has also adopted CCBE's ethical rules or code of conduct for cross-border activities regarding the EC countries, Finland, Norway, Switzerland and Austria.

The introductory part of the Guidelines indicates that there are no statutory rules nor any other rules in the Regulations which explain any further the meaning of professional conduct and etiquette. However, norms with respect hereto have been developed among *Advokater* and have furthermore been expressed in decisions by the Board of the Bar and the Disciplinary Committee.

The Guidelines serve the purpose of providing guidance for the members of the Bar. It is emphasised in the Guidelines that it is impossible to provide written rules dealing with the variety of circumstances and all questions that may arise in the course of practising as an *Advokat*. In other words, the Guidelines are not exhaustive, and not even a deviation from the rules would by implication need to result in a disciplinary action. That is a matter which needs to be resolved in view of the facts in each particular case. The Guidelines contain the following main headings:

(1) General rules governing practice at the Bar;
(2) Organisational aspects of practising as *Advokat*;
(3) Refusal of and withdrawal from assignments;
(4) The relationship with the client;
(5) The relationship with the adverse party;
(6) The relationship with the courts;
(7) The relationship with other authorities;
(8) The relationship with other members of the Bar; and
(9) The relationship with the Bar.

Those rules in the Guidelines which perhaps are regarded as more important than others, from a general point of view, may briefly be summarised as follows:

(1) The principal duty of an *Advokat* is to use his best efforts to act in the interest of the client within the limits of the law and in compliance with professional conduct and etiquette;
(2) An *Advokat* shall act in a factual and correct manner and in such a way that the confidence of the Bar is maintained;
(3) An *Advokat* owes a duty to be faithful and loyal to his client;
(4) An *Advokat* shall give legal advice upon having carried out necessary investigations of the law;
(5) An *Advokat* shall pursue assignments with care, attention and reasonable promptness and with the consideration not to incur unnecessary expense to the client;
(6) An *Advokat* may not, of course, knowingly mislead the adverse party or the court either as to the facts or as to the law; and
(7) An *Advokat* is not allowed to disclose to the courts an offer made by an adversary party to settle a dispute without consent from the adversary party.

Case law

Case law on professional duties is to some extent available through law reports. The most important and useful series is *Nytt Juridiskt Arkiv* (NJA).[1] It makes available judgements and decisions in cases brought before the Supreme Court. The judgements and decisions given by the inferior courts in those cases are also reported.[2]

The most important source with respect to the interpretation of professional conduct and etiquette is made available through the monthly publication *Advocater*, which was first published in 1935, contains a section of reports on decisions made by the Board of the Bar and the Disciplinary Committee.

The writings of legal scholars are also an important source of law in Sweden, and a number of books and articles have been published in recent years on or relating to the subject matter of professional liability of *Advokater*.

Custom

Custom might, in a particular case, become a relevant source in determining, for example, whether or not an *Advokat* is in breach of his duties. Custom may also become relevant for purposes of future codification, that is for implementation into the Guidelines but, of course, only if and to the extent any such custom is viewed upon by the Bar as reflecting professional conduct and etiquette.

STANDARDS

The standard laid down pursuant to the Guidelines is that an *Advokat* owes a duty to use his best efforts to act in the interest of the client within the limits of the law and in compliance with professional conduct and etiquette. Whether this standard is satisfied by an *Advokat* or not in a given case depends on the facts involved. The ultimate standard in relation to liability for damages is, at the end of the day, set by the Supreme Court in negligence cases.

1. *New Legal Archive*, if literally translated; it was first issued in 1874. Six issues are published every year.

2. When a case reported in this series is referred to in the legal literature or if reference is otherwise made, this is done not by reference to the names of the parties but by reference to the year and the page on which the case begins.

CIVIL AND ADMINISTRATIVE LIABILITIES

Civil liabilities

Basis

The subject matter dealt with under this heading only concerns liability for financial loss in contractual relations and liability for financial loss without connection to personal injury or damage to property in non-contractual relations (*ren förmögenhetsskada*). Reference hereinafter made to financial loss in non-contractual relations means financial loss caused without connection to any such injury or damage.

Initially, it should be stated that the fundamental principle on liability in Swedish law, as expressed under the Act on Torts of 1972, is that of *culpa* or negligence. This principle is said to apply generally to contractual relations as well, without the support of a statutory provision. A person is accordingly, as a rule, liable to another for financial loss when there exists a contractual relationship if such a person has caused the financial loss as a result of negligence (or wilful misconduct) in the course of performance or non-performance under a contract. Such liability may also arise on grounds of breach of promise or guarantee without fault.

Pursuant to Section 2(4) of the Act on Torts of 1972, a person can recover damages, when there is no contractual relationship, for financial loss suffered as a result of a criminal offence committed by another. In other words, an action in tort for financial loss is available pursuant to this rule only if a criminal offence has been committed provided also that the financial loss results from, or has been caused by, the criminal offence. The requirement of a criminal offence does not exist in contractual or so-called quasi-contractual relations to be further discussed below. Here, even such loss is recoverable in case of negligence and in some additional situations provided that a contractual relationship exists, irrespective of fault such as in case of breach of promise or guarantee.

As a result of the distinction between contractual and non-contractual relations the question of whether a contract exists and how the law determines the existence of a contractual relationship could become important in a given case.

Although the provision in Section 2(4) of the Act on Torts of 1972 makes no explicit exception, the history of this piece of legislation, which is an important source of interpretation with respect to this and other Acts of Parliament, made it clear that case law had allowed actions for the recovery of financial loss in certain instances in the absence of a criminal offence, where no contractual relations could really be said to have been established (by some legal authors referred to as quasi-contractual relations) provided, however, that the loss was caused by negligence, and that there was no intention either to discontinue this case law nor to prevent it being further developed by the courts.

In a ruling in 1987,[3] the Supreme Court confirmed this exception in a case concerning the liability for financial loss caused to a lender by a valuer of real property who had acted upon instructions from a third party (the owner of the real property who had been granted a loan from the lender with security in the real property). The Supreme Court ruled that a valuer is liable for financial loss caused to a third party provided that:

(1) The valuer has provided a certificate of valuation in his professional capacity;
(2) The valuer has acted with negligence;
(3) The third party who has suffered a financial loss as a result hereof has with reason relied upon the certificate of valuation;
(4) The valuer has been aware of the fact that his client could make use of the certificate of valuation for different purposes towards different persons; and
(5) The valuer has not made express provision for the exclusion of liability.

It remains to be seen if and to what extent this rule may become applicable to an *Advokat* in a negligence case involving a third party relationship.

Two other issues, mitigation of loss and contributory negligence ought to be mentioned. There is a duty under Swedish law to mitigate, that is to take reasonable steps to minimise a loss. A plaintiff cannot recover anything in respect of loss due to failing this duty. Contributory negligence might arise as an issue in two instances: where the plaintiff who alleges that he has suffered a loss, has allegedly, negligently contributed to that loss and where the plaintiff alleges that a third party has negligently contributed in an act by another (in relation to a contract or in a so-called quasi-contractual relationship) which has caused a recoverable loss to the plaintiff. In the latter case, the plaintiff would perhaps try to bring an action not only against his immediate adversary (the contractual party) but also against that third party (or as a practical matter only against the third party in the event the contractual party appeared incapable of paying adequate compensation).

The law on contributory negligence on the part of the plaintiff is clear under Swedish law in that it will have an impact on the question of liability of the defendant. The law on contributory negligence on the part of a third party insofar as it relates to financial loss, whether in relation to a contractual relationship or not, appears, however, to be unclear in Sweden. There are some Supreme Court cases, that perhaps could be used in support of such a claim (for example, where A and B have made a contract and B is in breach thereof to which C has negligently contributed).

3. Reported in NJA 1987, p. 692.

Their discussion would stray from the narrow purpose of the present chapter as would the related issue of whether there is a distinction in law and the relevance of such (if any) between a situation of contributory negligence and a liability case referred to above as quasi-contractual.

Claimants

A claimant alleging professional liability on the part of an *Advokat* would normally be a client or a former client, but a claimant could equally be outside of this category. Whether the claimant, in a given instance, would have a reasonable cause of action or, in other words, a litigable claim and, even more importantly, could succeed in an action depends on a number of circumstances. The section below illustrates this with respect to specific civil liabilities.

Procedure

There are three different levels of courts for civil and criminal cases in Sweden: District Courts, as courts of first instance, Courts of Appeal, as appellate courts, and the Supreme Court. The District Court has jurisdiction to hear both civil and criminal cases. To date, there are 97 District Courts throughout the country; each with its own territorial jurisdiction. In civil and criminal cases heard before a District Court, there is a right of appeal (with a few exceptions) to one of the six Courts of Appeal. Which one of these six appellate courts hears the appeal depends upon which District Court heard the case. The Courts of Appeal are trial courts as well, so that, as a rule, an appeal case starts afresh as if it had not been heard before. There is a right of appeal from the Courts of Appeal to the Supreme Court, but a case will only be heard with leave of the Supreme Court. Leave is, as a rule, granted only if a case involves a point of law of importance as guidance to the legal community. Some different rules apply to matters of leave in criminal cases. No leave is required with respect to an appeal against decisions made by the Disciplinary Committee of the Bar.

The Swedish machinery of justice is adversarial in nature, and this applies to both civil and criminal cases. There is in both a clear distinction between pre-trial proceedings and trial. A brief description is given below with respect to the procedure in civil cases before a court of first instance. It is regrettably not possible to even touch upon, within the framework of this chapter, the procedure in civil cases in the appellate courts or in criminal cases at any level.

An action in a civil case before a District Court is commenced by way of the plaintiff issuing a writ of summons (*stämningsansökan*) to the court, which then issues a writ (*stämning*) to the defendant (enclosing the writ of summons) with a request to submit a defence. After the defence is served, the parties continue to exchange written pleadings through the court. A judge will normally summon the parties to a preliminary hearing the purpose of which is to make sure, *inter alia*, that the case is ready to be set for trial.

The trial is divided into three main stages. The first is for the plaintiff to open and present his case. The plaintiff must, *inter alia*, state the relief requested and the material facts on which he relies. The next step is for the defendant to open and present his case along the same lines. The second stage is for the parties to produce the evidence such as testimonies by witnesses and documentary evidence which must have been disclosed prior to trial. The final stage is for the parties to give their final speeches. A civil case in a District Court is heard before either one or three professional judges subject to a few exceptions depending on the nature of the case. The successful party is as a general rule, awarded costs.

Briefly, the procedure before the Disciplinary Committee at the Bar is as follows. Prior to rendering a decision the Disciplinary Committee must give the *Advokat* an opportunity to defend himself. The Disciplinary Committee has powers which provide great flexibility with respect to the procedure to be adopted in each case. The *Advokat* may be summoned to appear before the Disciplinary Committee, to disclose required documents or to make submissions in writing. These are but a few of the powers vested in the Disciplinary Committee. It is also possible, if required, to have counsel appointed to defend the *Advokat*. The Disciplinary Committee must state the reasons for imposing disciplinary measures against an *Advokat*.

Damages recoverable

In case of a breach of contract, that is when liability arises in a contractual relationship, the plaintiff is entitled to recover the loss he has suffered as a result thereof, including loss of future profits or earnings. The idea is that the plaintiff should be awarded damages as if the contract had been fulfilled according to its terms and conditions without breach on the part of the defendant. Assessment of damages in tort, or, more broadly, when liability arises outside a contractual relationship, is undertaken on the principle that damages should be awarded on the basis that the tort had never occurred. There is no general statutory rule in existence with respect to assessment of damages in case of financial loss (whether in contract or not), and assessment of damages would, therefore, have to be determined on the basis of general principles of law under which, however, certain statutory provisions, rules with respect to assessment of damages in the Sale of Goods Act of 1990 could become a relevant source. Punitive damages are not awarded as a matter of Swedish law.

Specific civil liabilities

It is a difficult task to discuss specific civil liabilities along the lines of a clear distinction between on-going and one-off representations, general and specialist advice, commercial transactions and agreements. All of these items will therefore be discussed generally under one heading. Certain specific rules may apply to each.

Liability in contract (when no breach of promise or guarantee or any other ground is alleged which does not require fault for liability) is a question of negligent conduct, loss and causality. When ruling on questions of negligence, the courts will generally compare the conduct of an *Advokat* with the professional standard required in each particular case. The courts often obtain written opinions from the Bar in negligence cases. In particular, the Guidelines are important as a source when the courts determine whether or not an *Advokat* has satisfied the required standard in a given case. A critical issue is if and to what extent non-compliance with a rule in the Guidelines also constitutes negligence.

An *Advokat* is subject to a number of rules in the Guidelines that are of particular importance for his conduct *vis-à-vis* a client some of which may be summarised follows:

(1) An *Advokat* is under a duty to decline forthwith an invitation to give legal advice if he is not willing to do so. If an *Advokat* wishes to withdraw from an assignment or if he wishes not to comply with instructions given by the client previously accepted by the *Advokat*, he has to produce a valid reason and if such is the case secure that the legitimate interests of the client are not jeopardised as a result thereof.

(2) The client is entitled to be informed about the progress of the matter(s) entrusted to the *Advokat*. Questions from the client in this respect are to be answered promptly. An *Advokat* may not, as a rule, settle a matter with the adverse party without the consent of the client.

(3) Funds owned by clients must be held separately from funds owned by the *Advokat* and statements of account have to be arranged in a clear and intelligible manner in accordance with, *inter alia*, the Rules on Accounts adopted by the Bar.

(4) Where final accounts show a balance in favour of the client, the balance shall be paid to the client without delay.

Some sources of the law suggest that breach of any of these rules would normally constitute negligence on the part of the *Advokat*.

The more general duties of the *Advokat*, that is to use his best efforts to act in the interest of the client and to give legal advice only upon having carried out necessary investigations of the law, have been substantiated by court decisions, primarily regarding negligence cases, and by legal writers.

One of the leading Supreme Court cases on liability for a lawyer having given negligent advice resulting from a failure to conduct the requisite investigation of the law was rendered in 1957.[4] In that case, a lawyer (not being a member of the Bar) had given legal advice to a client on the creation of a security in connection with a contemplated loan transaction which advice later turned out to be wrong causing a loss to the client as a result of a subsequent bankruptcy of the borrower. The Supreme Court ruled (confirming the judgement of the District Court) that the lawyer was under a duty to consult a standard legal work, widely known by lawyers, on a particular issue prior to rendering advice to the client. This was based on the view that particulars of the relevant facts known to the lawyer should have made him suspicious with respect to the feasibility of creating a legal and valid security interest, with respect to which the client was seeking advice. If the lawyer had so consulted that standard legal work, it would have become apparent to him that it was not possible to accomplish the client's aims.

To satisfy the standard with respect to carrying out investigations of the law (and thus avoiding an allegation of negligence), one may assume that an *Advokat* has to make a thorough study of the best available sources of the law. If in view of the circumstances of a case, a statutory rule would appear to indicate the possibility of two (or more) answers to a specific legal question, the *Advokat* is under a duty to make further investigations of the relevant sources of the law such as the history of the statutory rule, relevant published court cases and standard legal works. If a preliminary study would indicate that a legal issue is unclear, the *Advokat* is under a duty to make further investigations unless the situation allows him to inform the client of the unclear legal situation without any such further investigations. If legal advice is sought on a matter of significant value, the requirement of, for example, thoroughness would be expected to increase.

A client or any other claimant seeking compensation for financial loss must prove the alleged loss and the extent thereof as well as causality. The burden of proof in this respect rests with the plaintiff claiming compensation in accordance with general principles of Swedish law. This is illustrated by two leading Supreme Court cases. In one,[5] two lawyers (not

4. Reported in NJA 1957, p. 621.
5. Reported in NJA 1929, p. 343.

being members of the Bar) had been instructed by their client to bring an appeal against a court decision. Due to a mistake, the lawyers did not bring the appeal within the prescribed time limit. The Supreme Court ruled for the laywers since the client had not been able to prove that he had suffered a loss as a result of the mistake by the lawyers. The difficulty for the client was to prove that an appeal would have brought his case to a successful end.

In the other leading case,[6] the Supreme Court referred to the burden of proof by stating that a sufficient degree of probability was required which had not been satisfied in respect of the financial loss alleged by the plaintiff. This case and subsequent negligence cases reported with respect to professional liability of others indicate a development contrary to the Supreme Court case of 1929, under which less is required by a plaintiff in order to discharge the evidential burden with respect to loss resulting from negligence.

When instructions are given to an *Advokat* relating to a specific task in an assignment of an *ad hoc* nature, it appears that the same relevant standards would apply as those which would apply to ongoing representations. There is, as a rule, no difference. Even if an *Advokat* were instructed by a client to reduce his efforts, the *Advokat* would owe a duty to satisfy the minimum requirements of the relevant standards applicable. An *Advokat* has the opportunity and often is under a duty not to accept assignments or instructions if it would not be possible for the *Advokat* to act in a professional manner.

Matters of liability in relation to general advice would normally arise with respect to alleged wrongful advice due to lack of necessary investigations of the law, in which case the standard already discussed in relation to the leading Supreme Court cases would have to be satisfied.

A specialist is subject to a higher standard than a non-specialist. The leading Supreme Court case with respect hereto (also of interest because it provides, *inter alia*, statements generally on the requirements regarding investigations of the law) was decided in 1981.[7] A lawyer (not being a member of the Bar) had, in a litigation case regarding a situation similar to expropriation, claimed indexation of the principal amount up to a date which was less favourable to the client in contrast to a claim up to another future date which had been possible for the lawyer to make. The Supreme Court found that the lawyer's firm was specialised mainly in a field of the law of which the actual case formed part. Thus there was an expectation that the lawyer was well-acquainted with this area of the law and the client could accordingly justify a claim relying on the lawyer as a specialist in that field. The lawyer was required to have knowledge with regard to the particular question of indexation and of the relevant sources

6. Reported in NJA 1949, p. 271.
7. Reported in NJA 1981, p. 1091.

of the law. Although the Supreme Court appears to have indicated that the particular matter of indexation involved a delicate task on the part of the lawyer, he was nevertheless found liable for the loss suffered by the client.

A wide variety of questions of both legal and non-legal nature often arise in commercial transactions. With respect to matters which do not involve legal considerations, for example, whether or not a client ought to buy a business or when seeking professional services on drafting a sale and purchase agreement, the question arises whether the *Advokat* owes a duty, depending on the circumstances, to inform the client that although any such matter is not of a legal nature, it would not be in the best interest of the client to pursue the matter according to his wishes. Although it could be argued that a prudent commercial *Advokat* should give his opinion to a client as to the commercial soundness of a transaction or any particular aspect thereof, if justified in a given case and if capable of doing so, it would nevertheless require a great deal to suggest that a failure in respect hereof would constitute a breach of duty and negligence on behalf of the *Advokat*. There seems to be a general consensus in legal literature that no specific duty is imposed upon an *Advokat* with respect to advice on issues of a non-legal nature.

Legal advice with respect to agreements, whether or not of a commercial nature, also often involves an assessment of possible risks and how to deal with such risks; for example, the legal consequences upon either party becoming insolvent in the future and how to minimise any such risks (if possible) by means of giving advice on suitable contractual provisions. There is a duty of the *Advokat* to make a reasonable analysis under the circumstances with respect to such matters. However, the required standard, in particular regarding the innovative ability of the *Advokat*, appears to be fairly low, but it varies from case to case.

If a specific requirement has to be satisfied in order to create a valid contract, for example, written form, or if a specific action has to be taken in compliance with a statutory rule for the purposes of maintaining a valid claim, a mistake by an *Advokat* is likely to be viewed upon as negligent by the courts. This is illustrated by a Supreme Court case reported in 1939[8] where a lawyer (not being a member of the Bar) was instructed by his client to undertake an act similar in nature and effect to probate of a will in Common Law jurisdictions. The lawyer failed to file the relevant documents with the proper court, and the will was subsequently found invalid, which resulted in economic loss for the client, who was a beneficiary under the will. The Supreme Court ruled that the lawyer was liable for that loss since he had not diligently carried out his assignment.

8. Reported in NJA 1939, p. 374.

Regulatory compliance

The Disciplinary Committee has in several cases expelled *Advokater* who have committed criminal offences, and in a few cases it has expelled *Advokater* who have wilfully acted unlawfully in various respects. Statutory compliance is generally an absolute requirement, and of course looked upon by the Bar as most important to, *inter alia*, maintaining the reputation of the profession.

Litigation conduct

An *Advokat* who appears before the courts is subject to a number of specific rules relating to litigation conduct. He should, whilst acting with all due courtesy to the court before which he is appearing, uphold the interests of his client. He must not, of course, knowingly mislead the court, either on the facts or on the law. Questions of liability would normally arise in a situation where an *Advokat* has not brought an action before the courts or an appeal against a judgement or a decision by a court within any prescribed time-limits applicable, which is illustrated by the Supreme Court case[9] discussed above. The difficulty and problem, however, is to successfully argue and discharge the evidential burden of proof to the effect that an appeal would have reversed a judgement or a decision by an inferior court or that an action brought before the courts in the first place had resulted in a favourable final judgement.

Conflicts of interest, disclosure, withdrawal

According to the Guidelines, an *Advokat* must decline an assignment where a conflict of interest arises in relation to another member of his firm or an associate of his firm or someone with whom he shares the office.

An *Advokat* may assist two or more clients who jointly seek advice on a matter where they share the same interest. However, if the *Advokat*, after having accepted such an assignment becomes aware of any circumstances which, if known at the outset, would have compelled him to decline acceptance, he must withdraw from the assignment. This might be so, even if any such circumstances arise later in the course of the assignment.

9. Reported in NJA 1929, p. 343.

Confidentiality

An *Advokat* owes a duty of confidentiality with respect to the affairs of his clients and may not, without permission — unless there is a contrary statutory duty, disclose anything entrusted to him as legal advisor or which he has acquired knowledge of in connection therewith. An *Advokat* is under a duty to impose the same degree of confidentiality on his staff. A breach of the confidentiality rule causing a client financial loss will most probably impose civil liability upon the *Advokat*.

Defences, exclusions, time-bars

A defendant (an *Advokat*) could make a number of submissions in defence of a claim for damages on the ground of wrongful advice including but not limited to the following:

(1) He could deny that he has been negligent in rendering advice;
(2) He could deny that the plaintiff has not suffered any financial loss as a result of him rendering advice, whether negligent or not; or
(3) He could deny that the plaintiff has not suffered any financial loss as a result of (including a defence that even if causation would be established, it would still not satisfy the so-called adequacy requirement or the requirement as to foreseeability) him rendering advice, whether negligent or not.

Whether a defendant would also be successful in making any such submissions will, at the end of the day, depend on the circumstances in each particular case.

A party to a contract may, as a matter of Swedish law, rely on a clause excluding or limiting his liability, and accordingly, such clauses are usually valid and will be upheld by the courts in Sweden. This was recently confirmed by the Supreme Court in its ruling in the case reported in 1987[10] However, a clause purporting to exempt a party from liability could become ineffective in view of the circumstances on grounds of statutory unreasonableness. The effectiveness of a clause excluding liability could also come into question if a party would attempt to exclude liability for gross negligence (without any statutory support but by some authors and other sources of the law suggested to be supported by an unwritten rule). However the law is not entirely clear on this final point. As suggested by a number of legal writers, it appears that an *Advokat* would not be able to make use of a clause purporting to exempt liability

10. Reported in NJA 1987, p. 692.

generally with respect to his duties. Still, an *Advokat* might achieve the same consequences in law, at least with respect to opinions given, by means of making reservations in the course of advising a client.

A claim for damages in tort is usually time-barred after ten years from the date of the negligent act. Specific contractual provisions may apply with respect to time-limits in case of an action based on contract. Some assignments which satisfy certain requirements of the law are time-barred within one year from the date when the assignment was accounted for to the other party.

LIABILITY

Liability for partners, associates and staff

Pursuant to Section 3 (1) in the Act on Torts of 1972, an employer is liable for financial loss (in a non-contractual relationship) caused by a criminal offence of an employee in the course of his employment. Associates and other staff may be employed by a partner, a partnership company or a limited liability company. Liability of a partner for financial loss caused by an associate might also arise in a situation where a partner has been entrusted with an assignment by a client and has used an associate for that assignment. The typical issue that would arise in connection with work carried out by an associate is whether or not the partner has provided reasonable means of supervision.

Joint and several liability

A principal rule under the Act on Torts of 1972, Section 6 (3) is that two or more tortfeasors who are liable for the same loss are jointly and severely liable.

New partner's exposure to liability arising from firm's prior acts

With respect to the assumption of liability ties upon becoming a partner, it is sufficient to indicate herein that pursuant to the Act on Partnership Companies of 1980, a member of a partnership company is exposed to liability for commitments that the partnership company has made prior to him becoming a member.

Former partner's exposure for subsequent liability

With regard to continuing liability once a partner has left a practice, one need only bear in mind that pursuant to the Act on Partnership Companies of 1980, a member is not liable, as against third parties, for subsequent acts provided that any such third party has actual or constructive notice to the effect that the partner was not a member at the relevant time.

INSURANCE

Advokater and their assistant lawyers are covered by, *inter alia*, a third party group insurance through the Bar. The coverage is world-wide provided that the *Advokat* practises in an office located in Sweden, Denmark, Finland, Iceland or Norway, irrespective of where the duties are actually performed or where advice is actually given in a particular case. Economic or financial loss is compensated for with the exceptions of, *inter alia*:

(1) Liability for damages which is not based on general principles of torts;
(2) Loss which is caused by wilful misconduct; and
(3) Loss which is compensated for through another insurance.

The insured amount for each damage is presently limited to SEK 3-million.

Advokater may obtain additional coverage through a number of insurance companies.

INTERNATIONAL PRIVATE LAW ASPECTS

According to Swedish international private law the applicable law with respect to a contractual dispute between an *Advokat* and a client on the question of liability is governed by the proper law of the contract.

To determine the proper law of the contract Swedish courts often use a *prima facie* rule by which the applicable law is the law of the country of the party whose performance signifies the contract.

However, the rule is not without exceptions. If an individualised evaluation of the particulars of the contract (for example, the place where the parties are situate, where the contract was negotiated and signed, currency of payment, where the contractual obligations are to be performed) would disclose a closer connection to a country or jurisdiction other than the country indicated by the *prima facie* rule, that may determine the applicable law.

The issues of compliance by a Swedish *Advokat* with foreign standards and exposure to liability, on the one hand, and, on the other, by a foreign lawyer with Swedish standards and liability appear to represent a "grey area" in Swedish law. However, it seems reasonable to suggest that a Swedish *Advokat*, as a rule, would always be subject to Swedish standards in terms of professional conduct and etiquette. Whether a foreign lawyer who in a given case would be in breach of Swedish standards but not similarly in breach under the relevant foreign standards is exposed to liability for damages, is a matter yet to be determined by the Swedish courts.

CONCLUSION

The courts in Sweden appear to be reporting an increasing number of tort cases including cases involving accountants, lawyers and other professionals who have been brought before the courts on alleged grounds of lack of and/or wrongful advice. The damages sought, represent in some instances, significant amounts. This development is likely to be a result of the previous decade where a great many and significant number of commercial transactions on mergers and acquisitions of companies, real property and capital market instruments were entered into at great speed. It was at the same time difficult to predict adverse changes in the relevant market places, if at all anyone did believe that would ever happen, as it afterwards appears. The number of companies and individuals in bankruptcy is now extremely high in Sweden.

It seems that plaintiffs and defendants have come across significant difficulties in the course of these proceedings with respect to drafting statements of claim and defences respectively. The reason is the difficulty involved in trying to understand and establish what the law actually says on professional liability; one must bear in mind that this is a somewhat new field for the litigation lawyer. Is relief sought on grounds of breach of a contractual relationship? What constitutes negligence? Has the loss been suffered as a result of wrongful legal advice? These and many other legal issues will most likely be clarified during this decade as a result of the increasing number of cases brought before the courts in this area of the law. Many lawyers have now also become aware of the actual risks in becoming exposed to liability for rendering wrongful advice. Although this awareness has most likely brought insurance issues to the attention of *Advokater* and other professionals as never before, the only source available which at the end of the day would satisfactorily protect the lawyer seems to rest with the lawyer himself in giving the necessary care and attention to assignments entrusted to him also keeping in mind, *inter alia*, that the law is not a science but an art no matter the extent to which clients request or desire firm statements on legal matters.

CHAPTER 13

SWITZERLAND

REBECCA G. BRUNNER-PETERS
Umbricht Badertscher & Roesle
Zurich, Switzerland

INTRODUCTION

The legal profession

The Swiss legal fraternity is relatively small, considering only those engaged in the private practice of law. Most private practitioners in Switzerland are members of the Swiss Law Federation (SLF), the umbrella organisation for the cantonal law societies.[1] As of January 1993, there were around 4,700 SLF members.[2] It may be fairly said, however, that the Swiss legal profession has been growing at a rapid pace, with the current number of SLF members representing an increase of more than 50 per cent over the past decade.[3]

More than one-fourth of all current SLF members are members of the Zurich law society.[4] Canton Geneva is the Swiss canton with the second highest attorney populace, while the Cantons of Ticcino, Berne and Basle also rank high in terms of numbers of attorneys.

Most Swiss attorneys practise alone or in a small firm and may be described as generalists, able to service more or less all of their clients' needs. In recent years, however, the trend in many Swiss law practices has been towards an increase in both size and internationalisation, including through mergers with other firms.[5]

Types of legal advisers

The introduction of Roman law during the middle ages brought about in many European countries a division of legal advisers into two categories,

1. *SLF Bullet*in No. 95, 3/1985, p. 1.
2. "Mitgliederstatistik SAV 1983–1993", 143 (1993), *Der Schweizer Anwalt*, p. 17.
3. "Mitgliederstatistik SAV 1983–1993", 143 (1993), *Der Schweizer Anwalt*, p. 17.
4. "Mitgliederstatistik SAV 1983–1993", 143 (1993), *Der Schweizer Anwalt*, p. 17.
5. Bachmann, "Berufshaftpflichtversicherung für Anwälte", 129 (1990) *Der Schweizer Anwalt*, p. 31; "Will Swiss Lawyers Miss the European Boat?", *International Financial Law Review*, December 1992, pp. 9–10.

those responsible for preparing court filings and giving instructions (*Advokat, avocat, avvocato*) and those entrusted with court litigation (*Prokurator, avoué, procuratore*).[6]

In Switzerland, this type of division never gained a foothold.[7] However, the so-called "attorney monopoly" does exist: In every canton except Canton Solothurn,[8] strict cantonal licensing rules prescribe who may or may not professionally represent clients in courtroom litigation and define the exact scope of the work reserved for licensed attorneys. On the other hand, with a few exceptions, such as in Canton St. Gallen,[9] none of the cantonal laws, regulations or professional codes of conduct in Switzerland prevent anyone, including foreign lawyers, from advising under federal or local Swiss law on a professional basis to the extent that the client matter in question does not involve court litigation (and, in the case of a foreign lawyer, provided that the required work permit has been obtained). Further, representation before federal and cantonal administrative tribunals may, in many cantons, be undertaken by anyone, including non-lawyers.[10] Thus, non-licensed legal counsel at Swiss accounting firms may often represent their clients, for example, in tax administrative proceedings.

Qualification in a particular canton may only be obtained after that canton's licensing examination has been successfully completed (or, if applicable, an exception has been granted). The prerequisites for being admitted to sit for the licensing examination vary from canton to canton. Generally, however, the cantons require at a minimum that the candidate:

(1) Possess Swiss citizenship (exceptions — the Cantons of Basle Land and Wallis);[11]
(2) Have a clean certificate of standing from the Swiss police authorities;
(3) Have completed a basic law diploma at a Swiss university (exceptions — Cantons Basle City, Schaffhausen, Graubünden, Appenzell and Obwalden);[12] and

6. Brunner, *Die Anwaltsgemeinschaft* (Arlesheim, 1977), p. 3.
7. Brunner, *Die Anwaltsgemeinschaft* (Arlesheim, 1977), p. 3.
8. Auer, "Die Ausbildung der Anwälte in der Schweiz", 129 *Der Schweizer Anwalt,* p. 9 (1990).
9. Grand, "Der St. Gallische Anwaltsverband", 117 *Der Schweizer Anwalt,* p. 15 (1988).
10. Brunner, *Die Anwaltsgemeinschaft* (Arlesheim, 1977), p. 59.
11. Kunz, "Basellandschaftlicher Anwaltsverband", 133 (1991), *Der Schweizer Anwalt,* p. 24.
12. Auer, "Die Ausbildung der Anwälte in der Schweiz", 129 (1990), *Der Schweizer Anwalt,* p. 9.

(4) Have completed a prior period of training, ranging in length from six months (Canton Obwalden) to two years (Cantons Geneva and Waadt).[13]

Although many attorneys in private practice also complete a dissertation and obtain a doctorate in Swiss law, only one canton (Canton Waadt) requires a published dissertation (in conjunction with a basic law diploma or a doctorate) as a prerequisite for the licensing exam.[14]

An attorney licensed to appear in the courts of one canton must apply for and be granted a reciprocal licence by another canton before he is entitled to litigate in the courts of that canton.[15] While Article 5 of the Transitional Provisions under the Swiss Federal Constitution requires Swiss cantons to recognise proof as to expertise in a particular field, such as law, which is issued by another canton, reciprocal attorney licences may nonetheless be denied if the personal prerequisites for a licence in that canton are not fulfilled.[16] As a general rule, reciprocal licences will be granted to attorneys of Swiss nationality who have obtained a licence in one canton by means of a licensing exam.[17]

Pursuant to a recent decision of the Swiss Federal Supreme Court, it appears that in the future non-Swiss citizens may also claim reciprocal licences to the extent that they possess a permanent residence permit and have already passed a licensing exam in one of the few Swiss cantons not requiring citizenship.[18] This decision, however, is expressly limited in scope to reciprocal licences and appears to leave intact the practice of most cantons of restricting the initial licensing exam to Swiss citizens. Subsequent to Switzerland's rejection of membership in the European Economic Area (EEA) on 6 December 1992, plans to introduce a federal law requiring the inter-cantonal and international recognition of attorney licences held by citizens of EEA countries have at least temporarily been abandoned.[19]

13. Auer, "Die Ausbildung der Anwälte in der Schweiz", 129 (1990), *Der Schweizer Anwalt*, p. 10.

14. Wolffers, *Der Rechtsanwalt in der Schweiz* (Zurich, 1986), p. 66; Rusconi, "L'Ordre des Avocats Vaudois", 120 (1989) *Der Schweizer Anwalt*, p. 40.

15. Wolffers, *Der Rechtsanwalt in der Schweiz* (Zurich, 1986), p. 66, at 64.

16. Wolffers, *Der Rechtsanwalt in der Schweiz* (Zurich, 1986), p. 27.

17. Cf. Judgement of the Second Public Law Division of 7 June 1985, Decisions of the Swiss Federal Supreme Court (BGE) 111 Ia 108, 110.

18. See Judgement of the Second Public Law Division of 29 January 1993, published in: Oesch, "Zulassung ausländischer Staatsangehöriger zum Anwaltsberuf in der Schweiz", 144 (1993) *Der Schweizer Anwalt*, pp. 14–17.

19. Zimmerli, "Das 'Nein' des Schweizervolks zum EWR und die Folgen für die Schweizer Anwälte", 144 (1993), *Der Schweizer Anwalt*, pp. 18–21.

While Swiss attorneys generally hold both a cantonal licence and more than one reciprocal cantonal licence, this does not necessarily mean they will appear in court in all cantons in which they hold licences. The co-existence of three different official languages in Switzerland, German, French and Italian, together with the complexities presented by rules of civil procedure differing from canton to canton mean that, typically, a matter to be litigated in another language region will be referred to an attorney in the relevant canton or language region.

Certain professional titles are reserved for use by licensed attorneys, and use of any of these titles is strictly regulated as a matter of cantonal law.[20] A licensed attorney in Zurich, Zug and St. Gallen is a *Rechtsanwalt*, but is a *Fürsprecher* in Canton Berne and a *Fürsprech* in Canton Aargau.[21] In the French-speaking cantons such as Geneva, the professional title is *avocat*, while a licensed attorney in Italian-speaking Ticcino is an *avvocato*.

A special category of lawyer in Switzerland, the notaries, are granted a separate monopoly with respect to certain official acts outside the context of litigation, in particular, the authentication of corporate documents, real estate deeds and wills. Apart from a normal law education, notaries are required to fulfil certain specialised notary training and licensing requirements imposed by the cantons. Depending on the canton, the notaries may be State officials or be independently employed.

The title of "federally-recognised tax expert" is reserved for tax attorneys (and non-attorneys, such as accountants) who meet the strict qualification requirements. The tax expert exam is administered by the SLF in conjunction with the Swiss Trustee and Auditors Chamber and the Conference of Public Tax Officials.[22] Candidates for the tax expert examination must have practised for a minimum of four years specialising in the area of tax, at least two of which must be spent at a tax accounting firm or as a tax official for the public administration or at a private company.[23]

Regulatory framework

The regulatory framework governing lawyers in Switzerland does not readily lend itself to a brief overview. Regulation of attorneys in Switzerland is primarly at the cantonal level, with Swiss lawyers estimated to be subject to cantonal regulation under more than 100 different substantive, administrative and procedural laws, rules, ordinances, decrees and

20. Brunner, *Die Anwaltsgemeinschaft* (Arlesheim, 1977), p. 3.
21. Brunner, *Die Anwaltsgemeinschaft* (Arlesheim, 1977), p. 3.
22. "Die Steuerexperten-Prüfungen 1986", 106 (1987), *Der Schweizer Anwalt*, p. 14.
23. "Die Steuerexperten-Prüfungen 1986", 106 (1987), *Der Schweizer Anwalt*, p. 14.

regulations.[24] In addition, scattered provisions of Swiss federal civil, criminal and procedural laws also apply to Swiss attorneys.[25]

Civil liability under the attorney/client relationship is mainly governed by the Thirteenth Chapter of the Swiss Federal Code of Obligations, Articles 394 *et seq.* and 97(1). The former chapter regulates the rights and duties of, among others, legal advisers and clients in connection with an ordinary mandate, while Article 97(1) deals with compensation for the non-performance or improper performance of an obligation. The provisions of Swiss tort law[26] are also, in some instances, relevant.

As a matter of public law, licensed attorneys in Switzerland are subject to supervision under the so-called cantonal "attorney laws". The cantonal attorney laws are substantively similar to one another.[27] The only canton lacking an attorney law is Canton Solothurn, which, as mentioned above, imposes no licensing or other requirement as a prerequisite to courtroom representation.[28] The cantonal attorney laws apply by their terms to all licensed attorneys engaged in the relevant canton in activities subject to the attorney monopoly, regardless of law society membership.[29] The attorney laws subject such attorneys to the disciplinary control of either the cantonal court of appeals or a supervisory authority subject to the court of appeals.[30]

The cantonal attorney laws list, among other things, the most important professional duties and disciplinary norms. Often, the cantonal attorney laws merely set forth broad, generalised standards of conduct, the concrete interpretation of which is left up to the relevant cantonal courts.[31] Provisions prescribing the prerequisites for the licensing examination and regulating the attorney tariff structure in connection with activities in the administration of justice, i.e. client representation in court and out-of-court settlements,[32] are included in separate decrees or in the text of the law itself.[33] Sanctions which may be imposed for violations of the attorney law range from a warning or fine to the temporary or permanent withdrawal of the attorney licence, depending on the nature of the violation and the cantonal law in question.

24. Wolffers, *Der Rechtsanwalt in der Schweiz* (Zurich, 1986), pp. 28–29, citing Blass, "Standes pflichten der Rechtsanwälte", 42 (1944) *Schweizerische Juristenzeitung*, p. 323.

25. Wolffers, *Der Rechtsanwalt in der Schweiz* (Zurich, 1986), p. 21.

26. Code of Obligations, Articles 41 *et seq.*

27. Wolffers, *Der Rechtsanwalt in der Schweiz* (Zurich, 1986) p. 29.

28. Studer, "Solothurnischer Anwaltsverband", 127 (1990), *Der Schweizer Anwalt*, p. 29.

29. Schwarz, "Standesregeln", 119 (1989), *Der Schweizer Anwalt*, p. 8.

30. Schwarz, "Standesregeln", 119 (1989), *Der Schweizer Anwalt*, p. 8; Schwander, "Einige Gedanken zur Anwaltshaftung", 104 (1986), *SLF Bulletin*, p. 14.

31. Wolffers, *Der Rechtsanwalt in der Schweiz* (Zurich, 1986), p. 29.

32. Wolffers, *Der Rechtsanwalt in der Schweiz* (Zurich, 1986), p. 160, n. 21.

33. Wolffers, *Der Rechtsanwalt in der Schweiz* (Zurich, 1986), p. 29.

In interpreting the general duties applicable to licensed attorneys under the attorney laws, Swiss courts frequently look to the rules for professional conduct issued independently by the cantonal law societies.[34] The rules issued by the various cantonal law societies do not vary significantly from one another in most respects[35] and typically include detailed standards for compliance with a particular prohibition or rule.

The law society rules are merely ethical standards of conduct which are limited in application to the members of the respective law societies[36] and are intended to protect the interests of the legal profession; the cantonal attorney laws, on the other hand, serve to ensure the correct practice of law by licensed attorneys in the public interest.[37] Thus, conduct which is determined not to violate a certain standard under the attorney law may nonetheless be determined to violate an identical law society code of conduct.[38] The law societies publish general tariff rules which apply to all legal work performed by member attorneys which is not regulated by the public tariffs.

Cantonal and federal procedural codes in civil and criminal matters often regulate the attorney compensation to be awarded in particular court proceedings and the procedural rights of attorneys in litigation, including their right to refuse to testify as to attorney secrets.[39]

Last but not least, legal advisers in Switzerland are also subject to certain substantive provisions of the Swiss Penal Code.

Professional bodies

There are 24 different law societies in Switzerland, representing Switzerland's 22 full cantons and the four half-cantons. As an exception, the law societies in the Cantons of Ticcino and Jura are organised as public corporations, with the result that the law society rules in these two cantons apply by force of law.[40] Most Swiss law societies, however, are private law entities organised in the form of an association,[41] such that the individual attorney chooses whether to subject himself voluntarily, through membership in the law society, to the particular law society's

34. Schwarz, "Standesregeln", 119 (1989), *Der Schweizer Anwalt*, p. 8; Schwander, "Einige Gedanken zur Anwaltshaftung", 104 (1986) *SLF Bulletin*, p. 8.

35. Wolffers, *Der Rechtsanwalt in der Schweiz* (Zurich, 1986), p. 29.

36. Brunner, *Die Anwaltsgemeinschaft* (Arlesheim, 1977), pp. 17–18.

37. Schwarz, "Standesregeln", 119 (1989), *Der Schweizer Anwalt*, p. 8; Schwander, "Einige Gedanken zur Anwaltshaftung", 104 (1986), *SLF Bulletin*, p. 8.

38. Schwarz, "Standesregeln", 119 (1989), *Der Schweizer Anwalt*, p. 9.

39. Wolffers, *Der Rechtsanwalt in der Schweiz* (Zurich, 1986), pp. 28–29.

40. Schwarz, "Standesregeln", 119 (1989), *Der Schweizer Anwalt*, p. 8; Christe, "L'Ordre des Avocats Jurassiens", 116 *Der Schweizer Anwalt* (1988), p. 15.

41. Wolffers, *Der Rechtsanwalt in der Schweiz* (Zurich, 1986), p. 29.

rules for professional conduct. However, as mentioned above, the law society rules may be used to interpret cantonal attorney law and therefore may be indirectly applicable even to non-members.

While the SLF (*Schweizerischer Anwaltsverband, Fédération Suisse des Avocats, Federazione Svizzera degli Avvocati*) serves as an umbrella organisation for the cantonal law societies, it has no power to bind or discipline member law societies.[42] The development and issuance of rules of professional conduct is left entirely to the discretion of the cantonal law societies.[43] However, the rules for professional conduct of the SLF member law societies generally conform to the SLF's official guidelines for conduct rules.[44]

Most licensed attorneys are members of a cantonal law society, although such membership is not mandatory (other than in Tessin and Jura, where the law societies are public corporations).[45] The law societies may impose monetary sanctions and take other disciplinary measures, including expulsion from membership, but are not, in contrast to the cantonal supervisory authorities, authorised to divest an attorney of his licence. The law societies typically appoint various committees to supervise compliance with the law society rules, decide as to fee disputes between clients and members and deal with other individual problems that may arise.

PRACTICE STRUCTURES

The sole practice represents the traditional legal practice structure in Switzerland. As numerous companies have a tradition of using sole practitioners for their legal work in Switzerland, the size of the legal practice in Switzerland is not necessarily indicative of the quality or scope of the practice. Many of Switzerland's attorneys practise as sole practitioners (*Einzelanwälte*) and run their practise alone, rather than sharing offices with lawyer colleagues.[46]

On the other hand, a large number of Swiss attorneys practise together in an office-sharing arrangement (*Büro- oder Kanzleigemeinschaft*). Pursuant to such an arrangement, the relevant attorneys share a common infrastructure in order to reduce office expenses but nonetheless practice law independently.[47] There is a joint law firm plaque, the law firm premises are jointly rented, the office personnel are jointly hired and paid,

42. Schwarz, "Standesregeln", 119 (1989), *Der Schweizer Anwalt*, p. 9.

43. Schwarz, "Standesregeln", 119 (1989), *Der Schweizer Anwalt*, p. 8.

44. Wolffers, *Der Rechtsanwalt in der Schweiz* (Zurich, 1986), p. 29 and Appendix I.

45. Riva, "Die Unabhängigkeit des Rechtsanwaltes im Tessin", 115 (1988) *Der Schweizer Anwalt*, p. 16; Christe, "L'Ordre des Avocats Jurassiens", 116 *Der Schweizer Anwalt* (1988), p. 15.

46. Brunner, *Die Anwaltsgemeinschaft* (Arlesheim, 1977), p. 4.

47. Brunner, *Die Anwaltsgemeinschaft* (Arlesheim, 1977), p. 39.

and the other necessary professional expenses, such as for computer equipment and publications are shared equally among all law firm members. In most essential respects, however, each firm member in an office-sharing arrangement engages in the practice of law for his own account, as a sole practitioner. The attorney acquires and advises his own clients, maintains separate bank accounts, accepts powers of attorney in his name only and issues invoices in his name only.[48]

The law partnership (*Anwaltsgemeinschaft*) is a relatively recent development in Switzerland and may be encountered in the major urban areas such as Zurich, Basle and Geneva.[49] In a law partnership, a contractual relationship joins together several attorneys who represent themselves to the public as a unity and practice law on a collective basis, using the jointly-owned firm equipment and furnishings in the interest of and for the account of all partners and accepting powers of attorney in the names of all partners.[50] Law partnerships in Switzerland generally fall into one of three categories:

(1) The two-man partnership with a junior and a senior partner;
(2) Partnerships with two or more partners of approximately the same age (without associates); and
(3) Partnerships of more than five attorneys, with or without associates.[51]

Applicable attorney laws and/or rules for professional conduct may, depending on the canton, prohibit licensed Swiss attorneys from practising together in a law firm (partnership or office-sharing arrangement) with non-licensed attorneys or non-law society members.[52] In Canton Zurich, the law society rules were revised in late 1989 to allow law society members to practise together with non-member lawyers and even non-attorneys, provided that the majority of persons in the firm are member attorneys, the unlimited liability of each such person is ensured and the activities engaged in by the non-attorneys are closely related to those of the attorneys.[53]

Cantonal attorney laws and/or law society rules may impose restrictions on the types of name which may be used by law firms.[54] A law firm

48. Brunner, *Die Anwaltsgemeinschaft* (Arlesheim, 1977), p. 39.
49. Brunner, *Die Anwaltsgemeinschaft* (Arlesheim, 1977), pp. 54, 80.
50. Brunner, *Die Anwaltsgemeinschaft* (Arlesheim, 1977), p. 38.
51. Brunner, *Die Anwaltsgemeinschaft* (Arlesheim, 1977), p. 40.
52. Brunner, *Die Anwaltsgemeinschaft* (Arlesheim, 1977), p. 81.
53. Articles of Association of the Zurich Law Society, Section 2 (4); see Umbricht, "New Zurich Bar Rules Welcome Foreigners", *International Financial Law Review*, January 1990, p. 3; Schiller, "Verein Zürcherischer Rechtsanwälte", 124 (1990), *Der Schweizer Anwalt*, p. 21.
54. Brunner, *Die Anwaltsgemeinschaft* (Arlesheim, 1977), pp. 81, 115.

may, for instance, be prohibited in some cantons from retaining the names of deceased partners or partners who have left the firm on the firm's letterhead or plaque. A similar prohibition was eliminated by the Canton of Zurich law society in 1989.

There do not appear to be any Swiss law firms which are currently organised as stock corporations.[55] Whether or not such a form of practice would be permissible depends on the canton. In some cantons, such as Geneva, practising law in the form of a stock corporation would be prohibited under applicable attorney laws; in other cantons, such as Canton Zurich, no legal or law society barriers currently exist.[56]

Medium-sized law firms in Switzerland will typically have from around eight to fifteen attorneys.[57] In recent years, more and more Zurich and Geneva firms have merged with one another to achieve a nation-wide presence. Only a few Swiss firms have foreign offices, although this number, too, has increased in recent years.[58]

ATTORNEY CAPACITIES

In Switzerland, the legal adviser may serve in a number of various capacities. The Swiss legal adviser may engage exclusively in traditional legal activities, acting as an advocate in court proceedings and providing legal advice outside the courtroom. On the other hand, however, because of Switzerland's leading financial marketplaces and its attractiveness to investors, Swiss legal advisers are also called upon by their clients to serve from time to time as board members, trustees, asset managers or business agents, escrow agents, custodians or intermediaries in financial or other business transactions.

According to the Swiss Federal Supreme Court, information acquired by lawyers through the provision of services typically engaged in by banks, asset managers or trustee companies, such as acting as a director, asset manager or investor, will not enjoy the protections of attorney secrecy under the Swiss Penal Code[59] to the extent that such services are not tied up with a traditional legal activity, such as an estate distribution.[60]

55. Brunner, *Die Anwaltsgemeinschaft* (Arlesheim, 1977), pp. 448–450.

56. Teitler, "Formen der Zusammenarbeit unter Rechtsanwälten", 119 (1989), *Der Schweizer Anwalt*, p. 17.

57. "Will Swiss Lawyers Miss the European Boat?", *International Financial Law Review*, December 1992, pp. 9, 11.

58. "Will Swiss Lawyers Miss the European Boat?", *International Financial Law Review*, December 1992, p. 11; "The Discrete Charm of the Swiss Lawyer", *International Financial Law Review*, November 1986, pp. 7, 9.

59. See below.

60. BGE 112 Ib 606, 608–609, Judgement of the First Public Law Division of 29 December 1986.

On the other hand, an attorney who engages in a non-traditional activity at a client's request continues as a rule to be subject to normally-applicable professional duties.[61]

Since needy parties in Switzerland have a right determined by cantonal law to legal representation in civil, criminal and administrative proceedings free of charge, Swiss private practitioners also serve, on a rotation basis, in the capacity of State-appointed and State-compensated "attorneys for the needy".[62] In certain cases, defendants in Swiss criminal proceedings have the right to an "official defender" free of charge, irrespective of their ability to pay.[63] Official defenders are also private practitioners appointed in rotation and paid by the State, except in Cantons Glarus, Lucerne and St. Gallen, where individual public defenders are appointed to serve for a term in office.[64] The State-appointed attorney is, *vis-à-vis* his client, held to the same standard of care and efforts that applies to Swiss attorneys in connection with private mandates.[65]

GENERAL DUTIES AND THEIR SOURCES

Professional duties under attorney laws

As already discussed, differing attorney laws and differing law society rules for professional conduct exist in nearly all of Switzerland's cantons. Some of the more important professional duties to which Swiss licensed attorneys may be subject as a matter of attorney law in the various cantons are discussed below.

Duty of attorney confidentiality

The duty of confidentiality is typically set forth in both the cantonal attorney laws and the rules for professional conduct.[66] Pursuant to this duty, which is also prescribed under the Swiss Penal Code, a Swiss attorney is required to preserve the confidentiality of non-public facts which are entrusted to him on the basis of, or of which he became aware

61. Wegmann, *Handbuch über die Berufspflichten des Rechtsanwalts im Kanton Zürich* (Zurich, 1988), pp. 16–17.
62. Wolffers, *Der Rechtsanwalt in der Schweiz* (Zurich, 1986), p. 42.
63. Wolffers, *Der Rechtsanwalt in der Schweiz* (Zurich, 1986), pp. 45–46.
64. Wolffers, *Der Rechtsanwalt in der Schweiz* (Zurich, 1986), p. 48.
65. Wolffers, *Der Rechtsanwalt in der Schweiz* (Zurich, 1986), p. 46.
66. Wolffers, *Der Rechtsanwalt in der Schweiz* (Zurich, 1986), p. 133.

in the exercise of, his profession.[67] There are various grounds justifying disclosure of a client's secret known to the attorney; in addition to those also mentioned in the Swiss Penal Code, such as the client's consent or written consent of the competent official or authority, some cantonal attorney laws list further justifications, e.g., the existence of a "higher interest".[68] Such additional grounds will only be relevant, however, with respect to disciplinary, and not criminal, punishment.[69]

Duty to relieve the strain on the judiciary

The duty to relieve the strain on the judiciary means that, depending on the canton, the attorney may be under a duty to promote the out-of-court settlement of disputes.[70] He is normally prohibited under cantonal attorney laws and rules of civil procedure from engaging in pointless, malicious or dilatory litigation[71] and/or is required to restrain his clients from engaging in the same.[72]

Duty to assist in the search for justice

The Swiss attorney is also required to assist in the search for justice.[73] For this reason, he is required as a matter of cantonal attorney law to accept State appointments as an attorney for the needy and as an official defender, unless there is a convincing reason for his refusal. Such reason might be an existing bias, inadequate experience in the particular legal area, work overload or client wishes.[74] In addition, most cantonal attorney laws prescribe a duty to create clear legal relationships and to restrain

67. Wolffers, *Der Rechtsanwalt in der Schweiz* (Zurich, 1986), p. 134.

68. Wolffers, *Der Rechtsanwalt in der Schweiz* (Zurich, 1986), p. 138.

69. Wolffers, *Der Rechtsanwalt in der Schweiz* (Zurich, 1986), p. 139.

70. Wolffers, *Der Rechtsanwalt in der Schweiz* (Zurich, 1986), p. 41; Wegmann, *Handbuch über die Berufspflichten des Rechtsanwalts im Kanton Zürich* (Zurich, 1988), p. 68.

71. Wegmann, *Handbuch über die Berufspflichten des Rechtsanwalts im Kanton Zürich* (Zurich, 1988), p. 68.

72. Wegmann, *Handbuch über die Berufspflichten des Rechtsanwalts im Kanton Zürich* (Zurich, 1988), p. 73; Wolffers, *Der Rechtsanwalt in der Schweiz* (Zurich, 1986), p. 41.

73. Wolffers, *Der Rechtsanwalt in der Schweiz* (Zurich, 1986), p. 38; Wegmann, *Handbuch über die Berufspflichten des Rechtsanwalts im Kanton Zürich* (Zurich, 1988), p. 123; Judgement of the Second Public Law Division dated 22 February 1980, BGE 106 Ia 100, 104.

74. Wegmann, *Handbuch über die Berufspflichten des Rechtsanwalts im Kanton Zürich* (Zurich, 1988), pp. 47–49.

from hindering the pursuit of justice through, for example, asserting a fact known to be untrue, influencing witnesses, destroying evidence or submitting false evidence.[75]

Duty of loyalty and due care to the client

In addition to the duty of loyalty and due care to the client imposed as a matter of civil law, many of the various duties imposed under attorney laws are also intended to ensure that a special relationship of trust and loyalty to the client prevails.[76] This duty has several aspects.

REPRESENTATION OF OPPOSING INTERESTS

Most attorney laws expressly prohibit the representation of opposing interests in the same litigation matter.[77] An attorney also may not represent a client in litigation if the attorney has a personal interest conflicting with the litigation goals of the client.[78] Litigation against a former client is not permitted to the extent that the attorney might knowingly or unknowingly apply knowledge derived from the former client's mandate to the disadvantage of the former client.[79]

SUCCESS-ORIENTED FEE ARRANGEMENTS

To prevent the attorney from having a personal interest in the outcome of litigation possibly divergent from that of the client's, Swiss attorneys are generally forbidden under the cantonal attorney laws from accepting contingent fees, success premiums or the assignment of rights in an asset which is the subject of the litigation.[80]

75. Wegmann, *Handbuch über die Berufspflichten des Rechtsanwalts im Kanton Zürich* (Zurich, 1988), p. 131; Wolffers, *Der Rechtsanwalt in der Schweiz* (Zurich, 1986), at pp. 34–35.

76. Wolffers, *Der Rechtsanwalt in der Schweiz* (Zurich, 1986), p. 141.

77. Wolffers, *Der Rechtsanwalt in der Schweiz* (Zurich, 1986), p. 141; advice provided outside of litigation is normally not affected by this prohibition.

78. Wolffers, *Der Rechtsanwalt in der Schweiz* (Zurich, 1986), p. 142.

79. Wegmann, *Handbuch über die Berufspflichten des Rechtsanwalts im Kanton Zürich* (Zurich, 1988), p. 136.

80. Wegmann, *Handbuch über die Berufspflichten des Rechtsanwalts im Kanton Zürich* (Zurich, 1988), pp. 153–155; Wolffers, *Der Rechtsanwalt in der Schweiz* (Zurich, 1986), p. 165.

CLIENT'S INSTRUCTIONS

The attorney is basically required to comply with the instructions of his client. Exceptions may be available under certain limited circumstances, for instance, if the instructions are irrelevant, impermissible or ineffective or the attorney is required to take immediate action under changed circumstances.[81]

UNREASONABLE DELAYS AND MISSED DEADLINES

The attorney is also generally under a duty to avoid unreasonable delays in attending to the client's affairs and to take ordinary preventative measures to ensure that filing or other deadlines are met.[82]

UNTIMELY WITHDRAWAL FROM MANDATE

It is generally recognised as part of the duty of loyalty to the client that an attorney may not withdraw from a mandate on an untimely basis.[83] A withdrawal will generally be impermissible if, for instance, it were to occur shortly prior to a hearing or the expiration of a filing deadline, with little possibility of timely instructing a new attorney.[84]

ADEQUATELY INFORMING THE CLIENT

An attorney is required to adequately inform the client as to important matters, such as the issuance of important court orders, expected delays or settlement proposals, and to obtain instructions whenever circumstances arise making this necessary.[85]

Advertisement

Finally, most cantonal attorney laws, especially the newer laws and those in urban areas, contain provisions limiting the extent to which attorneys

81. Wegmann, *Handbuch über die Berufspflichten des Rechtsanwalts im Kanton Zürich* (Zurich, 1988), p. 89.

82. Wegmann, *Handbuch über die Berufspflichten des Rechtsanwalts im Kanton Zürich* (Zurich, 1988), pp. 84–85.

83. Wolffers, *Der Rechtsanwalt in der Schweiz* (Zurich, 1986), pp. 143–144.

84. Wegmann, *Handbuch über die Berufspflichten des Rechtsanwalts im Kanton Zürich* (Zurich, 1988), p. 126.

85. Wegmann, *Handbuch über die Berufspflichten des Rechtsanwalts im Kanton Zürich* (Zurich, 1988), p. 160.

may engage in advertising.[86] The limitations are typically formulated in broad terms. thus prohibited advertising measures may be those which involve "insistent advertising", "insistent recommendation" or "any type of unethical extolling," with the exact boundaries of the prohibited advertising activities being defined under the law society rules for professional conduct.[87]

Duties under Swiss Civil Law

As discussed above, Chapter 13 of the Swiss Federal Code of Obligations[88] primarily determines the scope of the civil law duties imposed on Swiss legal advisers, including non-licensed attorneys, based on the attorney/client relationship.

Pursuant to Article 398(2) of the Code of Obligations, agents under an ordinary mandate are subject to a duty of due care and loyalty to their clients in carrying out the mandate. The duty of due care and loyalty of Swiss attorneys must be viewed within the framework of the professional duties imposed on the Swiss attorney as a matter of public law.[89] The duty of due care, on the one hand, requires lawyers to exercise the amount of due care in fulfilling the mandate which may in good faith be expected from members of the legal profession.[90]

The duty of loyalty, on the other hand, requires the lawyer to refrain from acting to the detriment of his client in performing the mandate and, further, as a result of the ties to the client, subjects him to a certain permanent behaviour after conclusion of the mandate.[91] This duty encompasses, but is not limited to, the duty to maintain attorney secrecy, to refrain from (simultaneously or successively) representing clients with opposing interests, to refrain from engaging in disloyal management, to reject clearly hopeless mandates and to refrain from withdrawing from the mandate on an untimely basis.[92]

Article 397(1) of the Code of Obligations requires that the mandate be performed in accordance with the client's instructions unless client permission is not, under the circumstances, necessary and, furthermore, one could assume that the client would have granted permission had he been familiar with the situation.

86. Wolffers, *Der Rechtsanwalt in der Schweiz* (Zurich, 1986), p. 145.
87. Wolffers, *Der Rechtsanwalt in der Schweiz* (Zurich, 1986), p. 145.
88. Code of Obligations, Articles 394 *et seq.*
89. Schwander, "Einige Gedanken zur Anwaltshaftung", 104 (1986), *SLF Bulletin*, p. 8.
90. Brunner, *Die Anwaltsgemeinschaft* (Arlesheim, 1977), pp. 409–410.
91. Brunner, *Die Anwaltsgemeinschaft* (Arlesheim, 1977), pp. 358–360.
92. Brunner, *Die Anwaltsgemeinschaft* (Arlesheim, 1977), pp. 359, 364.

Unless authorised to do so or when permissible as a matter of common usage, an attorney is prohibited under Article 398(3) of the Code of Obligations from assigning performance of the mandate to a third party. This prohibition applies only to the assignment of the mandate in whole or part to a third party (so-called "substitution"), and not to the mere delegation to assistants working under the attorney's guidance and supervision.[93]

Finally, pursuant to Article 400 of the Code of Obligations, a legal adviser is subject to a far-reaching duty to provide an accounting to his client. This means that the lawyer must accurately and completely inform the client on a timely basis as to all facts which would be of importance to the client.[94] Further, the attorney must promptly hand over to the client, at the latter's request, all documents and/or assets which the lawyer received from the client or a third party during performance of the mandate.[95]

Duties under the Swiss Penal Code

The main duty imposed on legal advisers under Swiss criminal law is the obligation to maintain attorney secrecy pursuant to Article 321 of the Swiss Penal Code (*Strafgesetzbuch* — StGB). Assuming that information obtained in the course of executing a client mandate is non-public, the legal adviser may disclose such information only in certain situations prescribed by the Penal Code: with the consent of the client, former client or other party entitled to confidentiality, pursuant to written permission of the competent supervisory authority or official,[96] or, in the absence of express permission, if justified on the basis of self-defence,[97] a state of distress[98] or one of the other justification grounds described in Articles 32 *et seq.* of the Penal Code. Criminal charges for violating attorney secrecy will only be pursued at the request of an affected party.

Because of the significant criminal law sanctions to which a lawyer may be subject for wilfully or intentionally disclosing an attorney secret (imprisonment of up to three years and/or a fine of up to SFr. 40,000), all cantonal codes of procedure include provisions granting legal advisers certain rights to refuse to testify and/or produce documents.[99]

93. Weber, *Praxis zum Auftragsrecht und zu den besonderen Auftragsarten* (Berne 1970), p. 77.

94. Weber, *Praxis zum Auftragsrecht und zu den besonderen Auftragsarten* (Berne 1970), p. 91.

95. Weber, *Praxis zum Auftragsrecht und zu den besonderen Auftragsarten* (Berne 1970), p. 93; Judgement of the First Civil Division of 5 October 1965, BGE 91 II 442, 451.

96. StGB, Article 321(2).

97. StGB, Article 33.

98. StGB, Article 34.

99. Wolffers, *Der Rechtsanwalt in der Schweiz* (Zurich, 1986), pp.136–137.

Attorney secrecy is not the only aspect of the attorney's civil law duty of loyalty which is simultaneously regulated in the Swiss Penal Code. Other violations of the duty of loyalty which may, depending upon the circumstances, be subject to criminal punishment include misappropriation of assets[100] and disloyal management.[101] As a rule, if the representation of clients with opposing interests results in financial damages, the elements of the crime of disloyal management will be satisfied.[102]

Another provision of the Swiss Penal Code potentially applicable to legal advisers is Article 181, which prohibits coercion through force or the threat of serious detriment. Thus, a legal adviser who, in attempting to enforce a claim, threatens to file criminal charges in order to lend emphasis to his endeavours may, depending upon the circumstances, subject himself to criminal punishment. According to leading case law, Article 181 of the Penal Code is violated if the coercion applied is illegal or represents a violation of common decency.[103] Generally, if an attorney threatens, e.g., to denounce someone for tax evasion in connection with an unrelated matter, the elements of prohibited coercion will be fulfilled.[104]

CIVIL LIABILITY

The civil liability of legal advisers is a relatively new topic in Switzerland and one which is only infrequently dealt with under Swiss case law and in the legal commentaries.[105]

Basis for civil liability

The attorney/client relationship in Switzerland is primarily governed by the rules on the ordinary mandate.[106] If a lawyer fails to exercise the required amount of due care in connection with a mandate and this leads to the non-performance or improper performance of the mandate, the attorney is liable for the interest in proper fulfilment of the mandate

100. StGB, Articles 140 and 142.

101. StGB, Article 159.

102. Gautschi, "Der einfache Auftrag", in: *Berner Kommentar zum Schweizerischen Zivilgesetzbuch, Das Obligationenrecht*, Part II, Vol. 4 (3rd ed., Berne, 1971), p. 359.

103. Schwander, "Einige Gedanken zur Anwaltshaftung", 104 (1986), *SLF Bulletin*, p. 5.

104. Schwander, "Einige Gedanken zur Anwaltshaftung", 104 (1986), *SLF Bulletin*, p. 6.

105. Christe, "Die zivilrechtliche Haftung des Anwaltes", 136 (1992), *Der Schweizer Anwalt*, p. 12.

106. Code of Obligations, Articles 394 *et seq.*

pursuant to Article 97(1) of the Code of Obligations.[107] This provision provides that a debtor who fails to carry out a contractual obligation or who does not fulfil it properly is liable for damages, unless he proves that there was no fault on his part.

In the case of liability based on an unjustified failure to comply with the client's instructions,[108] a special rule in Article 397(2) of the Code of Obligations provides that the mandate will nonetheless be viewed as having been properly performed if the agent (attorney) assumes the damages thereby incurred, for example, by absorbing the excess legal fees if the attorney has disregarded a fee ceiling.[109] However, if a subsequent payment by the agent cannot effect proper performance of the mandate, liability will be determined in accordance with Article 97(1) of the Code of Obligations.[110]

Although a violation of the civil law duty of loyalty represents a violation of the mandate, it does not necessarily constitute non-performance or improper performance within the meaning of Article 97(1) of the Code of Obligations.[111] A violation of attorney secrecy, for example, may have no impact whatsoever on the attorney's performance under the mandate or may occur after the mandate has been carried out. Liability will, therefore, not exist for the interest in proper performance of the mandate but, rather, for damages determined under Article 398 Code of Obligations and Article 8 of the Swiss Civil Code.[112]

In instances where mandate negotiations occurred during which legal advice was given or representations were made, liability on the part of the lawyer may arise on the basis of *culpa in contrahendo* regardless of whether or not a mandate relationship was subsequently entered into. Namely, parties to negotiations are subject to a trust relationship during the course of the negotiations, a breach of which results in a duty to compensate.[113] It is controversial whether *culpa in contrahendo* liability is based on Article 1 of the Code of Obligations or Article 2(1) of the Civil Code. A party may, therefore, be required during negotiations to reveal facts to the opposing party which may be of decisive value in reaching a decision but which are not recognisable to the opposing party and to

107. Gautschi, "Der einfache Auftrag", in *Berner Kommentar zum Schweizerischen Zivilgesetzbuch, Das Obligationenrecht*, Part II, Vol. 4 (3rd ed., Berne, 1971), p. 351.

108. Code of Obligations, Article 397(1).

109. Weber, *Praxis zum Auftragsrecht und zu den besonderenAuftragsarten* (Berne 1970), p. 83.

110. Gautschi, "Der einfache Auftrag", in *Berner Kommentar zum Schweizerischen Zivilgesetzbuch, Das Obligationenrecht*, Part II, Vol. 4 (3rd ed., Berne, 1971), p. 338.

111. Gautschi, "Der einfache Auftrag", in *Berner Kommentar zum Schweizerischen Zivilgesetzbuch, Das Obligationenrecht*, Part II, Vol. 4 (3rd ed., Berne, 1971), p. 364.

112. Gautschi, "Der einfache Auftrag", in *Berner Kommentar zum Schweizerischen Zivilgesetzbuch, Das Obligationenrecht*, Part II, Vol. 4 (3rd ed., Berne, 1971), p. 365.

113. Brunner, *Die Anwaltsgemeinschaft* (Arlesheim, 1977), p. 439.

provide objectively correct information.[114] In particular, liability may arise for making false representations during negotiations which cause the opposing party to take action, resulting in damages.[115]

Swiss tort law, Articles 41 *et seq*. of the Code of Obligations, provides that whoever unlawfully causes damage to another, whether wilfully or negligently, shall be liable for such damages.[116] One of the prerequisites for a cause of action in torts under Swiss law is the existence of a wrongful act.[117]

Certain attorney conduct may give rise to criminal liability under the Penal Code. Such conduct could include disloyal management, misappropriation or breach of attorney secrecy. If the conduct is adjudged to have violated the Swiss Penal Code and is hence deemed "wrongful", civil liability in tort pursuant to Articles 41 *et seq*. of the Code of Obligations may arise, independent of potential civil liability under the contractual duty of loyalty of Article 398 (2) of the Code of Obligations.[118] The Swiss Federal Supreme Court has expressly approved the cumulation of claims for compensation as a matter of both contract (mandate) and tort law,[119] so that a claim may be based on both causes of action cumulatively or alternatively.

With respect to the civil liability of notaries, a distinction is drawn between official acts reserved for notaries and non-official legal activities. With respect to the former, notaries are not subject to liability under the provisions of mandate law but, rather, are subject to Article 61 of the Code of Obligations, allowing cantons to adopt special laws governing the civil liability of notaries for damages caused by their official acts.[120] To the extent that a particular canton has not adopted such a law, the civil liability for official notary acts will be governed by the tort rules in Articles 41 *et seq*. of the Code of Obligations.[121] With respect to non-official acts, notaries may be subject to civil liability under special cantonal notary laws or, in the absence thereof, under the provisions of mandate law.[122]

114. Brunner, *Die Anwaltsgemeinschaft* (Arlesheim, 1977), p. 439.

115. Judgement of the First Civil Division of 7 October 1942, BGE 68 II 295, 303.

116. Code of Obligations, Article 41(1).

117. See Judgement of the Second Civil Division of 5 May 1967, BGE 93 II 170, 183: There was no cause of action under the Code of Obligations, Article 41 because there had been no wrongful act; Judgement of the Second Civil Division of 6 September 1962, BGE 88 II 276, 280–281: same reasoning.

118. Brunner, *Die Anwaltsgemeinschaft* (Arlesheim, 1977), at p. 443.

119. Judgement of the First Civil Division of 25 May 1938, BGE 64 II 254, 259; Judgement of the First Civil Division of 22 May 1945, BGE 71 II 107, 113; Judgement of 2 April 1965, BGE 91 I 223, 239.

120. Judgement of the First Civil Division of 6 October 1964, BGE 90 II 274, 278.

121. Judgement of the First Civil Division of 6 October 1964, BGE 90 II 274, 278.

122. Judgement of the First Civil Division of 6 October 1964, BGE 90 II 274, 278; Judgement of the First Civil Division of 13 November 1944, BGE 70 II 221, 223.

Standards

The standard against which the attorney's behavior is measured is of especial importance with respect to the civil law duty of due care. Pursuant to controlling case law and commentary, the legal adviser is required to comply with an "objective" due care standard: the amount of due care which one may in good faith demand from representatives of the legal profession.[123]

The civil law duty of due care is basically satisfied if the legal adviser acts with the amount of knowledge which in the ordinary course of matters may lead to possible success.[124] Assuming this is the case, the client must then accept a false assessment of the legal situation or a mistake in litigation tactics.[125] The commissioned attorney may only be held liable for his failure to succeed on behalf of the client to the extent that such failure is based on a lack of due care.[126] As a rule, liability for lack of due care will arise from professional errors only if the attorney takes a stance clearly contrary to case law and legal commentary; a false but defensible legal interpretation of the ruling law will not generally give rise to liability.[127] In the context of litigation, the attorney is required as a matter of due care to be familiar with all formal prerequisites of procedural law and comply with the deadlines and periods prescribed thereunder.[128]

The standard of loyalty owed under Article 398(2) Code of Obligations, on the other hand, cannot be defined abstractly, as in the case of the duty of due care, but varies from case to case, depending on the concrete set of facts at hand.[129]

Burden of proof

Swiss law basically assumes that members of professions required to meet governmental qualification and licensing requirements are in compliance

123. Brunner, *Die Anwaltsgemeinschaft* (Arlesheim, 1977), pp. 409–410.

124. Brunner, *Die Anwaltsgemeinschaft* (Arlesheim, 1977), p. 352, citing Gautschi, "Der einfache Auftrag", in *Berner Kommentar zum Schweizerischen Zivilgesetzbuch, Das Obligationenrecht*, Part II, Vol. 4 (3rd ed., Berne, 1971), p. 376.

125. Schwander, "Einige Gedanken zur Anwaltshaftung" (1986), p. 104, *SLF Bulletin*, p. 8.

126. Brunner, *Die Anwaltsgemeinschaft* (Arlesheim, 1977), p. 351.

127. Brunner, *Die Anwaltsgemeinschaft* (Arlesheim, 1977), p. 351.

128. Judgement of the First Civil Division of 19 September 1934, BGE 60 II 352; Judgement of the First Civil Division of 22 December 1937, BGE 63 II 422, 423; Judgement of the Second Civil Division of 13 February 1959, BGE 85 II 46.

129. Gautschi, "Der einfache Auftrag", in *Berner Kommentar zum Schweizerischen Zivilgesetzbuch, Das Obligationenrecht*, Part II, Vol. 4 (3rd ed., Berne, 1971), p. 365.

with their professional duties.[130] Thus, in a civil law claim based on a violation of Swiss mandate law, the burden of proof is on the plaintiff to prove three elements:[131]

(1) The damages suffered;
(2) The breach of a duty under mandate law; and
(3) Proximate cause between the breach of duty and the damages.

In certain cases, it may be difficult for the plaintiff to prove the required causal link between an attorney's breach of his duty of due care and the damages suffered by the plaintiff. This will particularly be the case in the context of litigation if an attorney's lack of due care results in the client's loss of his right to litigate, submit evidence to the court or take an appeal, for example, through missing a filing deadline. According to the Swiss Supreme Court, the plaintiff's burden of proof in such instances as to causation will be satisfied if the judge is able to reach the conclusion that the client would have in all probability won the lawsuit had the attorney not committed the alleged mistake.[132] As a practical matter, this means that a "mini-trial" of the original proceeding will have to take place.[133]

With respect to a claim against a legal adviser under Swiss tort law, the burden of proving that each of the various tort prerequisites are fulfilled — wrongful act, damages and proximate cause — similarly rests with the party claiming compensation.[134] However, in some cases, an injured client may have a choice between, on the one hand, bringing a civil lawsuit based on violation of the contractual (mandate) duty of loyalty or, on the other hand, bringing criminal charges and a derivative civil lawsuit based on tort law. In such cases, the client may prefer the latter alternative, since the criminal authorities will then be required to investigate the situation *ex officio* and, depending on the results of their investigation, the client may be relieved of the burden of proving a "wrongful act" in a subsequent proceeding in tort.[135]

130. Gautschi, "Der einfache Auftrag", in *Berner Kommentar zum Schweizerischen Zivilgesetzbuch, Das Obligationenrecht*, Part II, Vol. 4 (3rd ed., Berne, 1971), p. 379.

131. Civil Code, Article 8; see Brunner, *Die Anwaltsgemeinschaft* (Arlesheim, 1977), p. 414.

132. Judgement of the Second Civil Division of 12 December 1961, BGE 87 II 364, 372; see Christe, "Die zivilrechtliche Haftung des Anwalts" (1992), p. 136, *Der Schweizer Anwalt*, p. 14.

133. Schwander, "Einige Gedanken zur Anwaltshaftung" (1986), p. 104, *SLF Bulletin*, p. 10.

134. Civil Code, Article 8; Code of Obligations, Article 42(1).

135. Brunner, *Die Anwaltsgemeinschaft* (Arlesheim, 1977), p. 444.

Damages recoverable

The damages recoverable for claims based on a breach of a contractual (mandate) duty are, pursuant to Article 99 (3) of the Code of Obligations, governed by the rules for damages in tort.[136] Pursuant to these rules, damages are limited to the difference between the current financial condition and the financial condition that would have existed if the event giving rise to the damages had not occurred.[137] This includes, however, costs for determination of the amount of damages suffered, e.g., through expert opinions, attorney fees and court fees.[138]

If an alleged attorney error did, indeed, result in the client's defeat in the original proceeding but such defeat did not inflict on the client any actual monetary damage (for example, in the case of a custody proceeding), damages may be awarded in the amount of the attorney fees, court costs and other costs and fees related to the original proceeding.[139]

In addition to tangible monetary damages, Swiss civil law also recognises the right of an injured party to receive, in certain cases, what is known as "satisfaction", i.e., payment in compensation for intangible injustices which have been suffered.[140] Claims to satisfaction are only available in the case of injuries to life or limb[141] or injuries to inherent individual rights,[142] including slander and libel. Thus, a client might in some cases be entitled to satisfaction as a result of an attorney's violation of a civil law duty, e.g., attorney secrecy.

Under Swiss law, however, as in most statutory law jurisdictions, the Anglo-Saxon concept of punitive damages does not exist.[143] In fact, the "prohibition on enrichment", a long-established doctrine under Swiss law, limits claims for compensation under Swiss civil law to the sum of the effective damage, regardless of the nature of the cause of action, in order to prevent the injured party from being unjustly enriched:

136. Code of Obligations, Articles 41 *et seq.*

137. Christe, "Die zivilrechtliche Haftung des Anwalts", 136 (1992) *Der Schweizer Anwalt*, p. 12.

138. Brunner, *Die Anwaltsgemeinschaft* (Arlesheim, 1977), p. 418.

139. Schwander, "Einige Gedanken zur Anwaltshaftung", 104 (1986), *SLF Bulletin*, p. 10.

140. Drolshammer and Schaerer, "Die Verletzung des materiellen ordre public als Verweigerungsgrund bei der Vollstreckung eines US-amerikanischen 'punitive damages-Urteils'", 82 *Schweizerische Juristenzeitung* (1986), p. 316.

141. Code of Obligations, Article 47.

142. Code of Obligations, Article 49.

143. See *CCH Europe Business Law Guide to Switzerland* (Zurich, 1991), p. 101.

"Swiss civil law views compensation for damages as compensation for an economically determinable diminishment of assets. [. . .] The effective damage suffered therefore places an upper ceiling on the duty to compensate."[144]

If the damages are not ascertainable by calculation, e.g., in the case of a breach of attorney secrecy, it is up to the judge, at his discretion and with a view toward "the ordinary course of events and the measures taken by the damaged party", to determine the exact amount of damages.[145]

Defences and time bars

If no criminal liability arises with respect to the disclosure of an attorney secret because one of the exceptions under Article 321 of the Swiss Penal Code applies, the existence of such exception will simultaneously constitute a valid defence to a civil complaint under Article 398(11) of the Code of Obligations alleging violation of attorney secrecy.[146]

Assuming that it has been proven that an attorney failed to meet the objective standard of due care required in executing the mandate, Article 97(1) of the Code of Obligations permits the attorney to exculpate himself from civil liability by proof that, based on the concrete circumstances, he was not subjectively at fault for the objective lack of due care.[147] While an objectively incorrect assessment or action by the attorney may qualify as a lack of due care, the attorney may exculpate himself by proving that the lack of due care was not, under the circumstances, caused by any lack of ability or desire on his part.[148]

The consent of a client not versed in Swiss law will not exculpate a lawyer from compliance with the duty of due care applicable to members of the Swiss legal profession.[149]

The statute of limitations for civil claims based on violations of mandate law expires 10 years after the claim arises.[150] In the case of a breach

144. Order dated 1 October 1982 of the District Court President of Sargans, cited in Drolshammer and Schaerer, "Die Verletzung des materiellen ordre public als Verweigerungsgrund bei der Vollstreckung eines US-amerikanischen 'punitive damages-Urteils'", 82 *Schweizerische Juristenzeitung*, p. 310 (1986).

145. Code of Obligations, Article 42(2).

146. Brunner, *Die Anwaltsgemeinschaft* (Arlesheim, 1977), p. 362; Gautschi, "Der einfache Auftrag", in *Berner Kommentar zum Schweizerischen Zivilgesetzbuch, Das Obligationenrecht*, Part II, Vol. 4 (3rd ed., Berne, 1971), at p. 374.

147. Judgement of the First Civil Division of 10 October 1944, BGE 70 II 207, 211; Gautschi, "Der einfache Auftrag", in *Berner Kommentar zum Schweizerischen Zivilgesetzbuch, Das Obligationenrecht*, Part II, Vol. 4 (3rd ed., Berne, 1971), at pp. 378–379.

148. Gautschi, "Der einfache Auftrag", in *Berner Kommentar zum Schweizerischen Zivilgesetzbuch, Das Obligationenrecht*, Part II, Vol. 4 (3rd ed., Berne, 1971), at pp. 378–379.

149. 9 *Schweizerische Juristenzeitung,* p. 344 (1963), (Lawyers Chamber of Lucerne).

150. Code of Obligations, Article 127 *et seq.*

of mandate, the claim normally arises at the time of the act, and not at the time the plaintiff learns of the act.[151] In the case of the duty to provide an accounting to the client, the claim arises on termination of the mandate.[152]

The statute of limitations period applicable to criminal prosecutions of conduct by attorneys is 10 years after the last act of misappropriation has been committed, in the case of disloyal management,[153] and five years after the last act of disloyal management or the last violation of attorney secrecy has occurred.[154] For claims in tort law which are derivative of criminal acts, the corresponding statute of limitations period under the Penal Code applies to the extent that the such period is longer than the statute of limitations period for tort claims.[155]

Contours of relevant case law

The duty of due care under mandate law in connection with litigation represent the most common basis for civil lawsuits against attorneys in Switzerland.[156]

The Swiss attorney will not generally be held liable for mistakes in the choice of litigation tactics or for his taking an incorrect (but tenable) position with respect to a question of law.[157] pp. 89, 107 (1945) (Waadt Cantonal Court); ZR 36 (1937) 321 Number 168: liability denied where attorney failed to draft bank guarantee to provide for non-applicability of provision of law concerning ability to sue guarantor.

On the other hand, it may be generally said that procedural mistakes on the part of an attorney, such as the missing of deadlines or errors as to form, will be subject to a form of strict liability.[158] Thus, an attorney who missed a deadline for filing a paternity complaint was held to have violated his civil duty of due care to the former client and was required

151. Weber, *Praxis zum Auftragsrecht und zu den besonderen Auftragsarten* (Berne 1970), p. 134; see Judgement of the First Civil Division of 19 September 1961, BGE 87 II 155, 158.

152. Weber, *Praxis zum Auftragsrecht und zu den besonderen Auftragsarten* (Berne 1970), p. 134.

153. *Strafgesetzbuch*, Articles 7 *et seq.* and Article 140.

154. *Strafgesetzbuch*, Articles 70 *et seq.*, 159 and 321; see Brunner, *Die Anwaltsgemeinschaft* (Arlesheim, 1977), p. 444.

155. Code of Obligations, Article 60(2).

156. Christe, "Die zivilrechtliche Haftung des Anwalts", 136 (1992) *Der Schweizer Anwalt*, p. 12.

157. Gautschi, "Der einfache Auftrag", in *Berner Kommentar zum Schweizerischen Zivilgesetzbuch, Das Obligationenrecht*, Part II, Vol. 4 (3rd ed., Berne, 1971), p. 400; cf. 41 *Schweizerische Juristenzeitung*

158. Gautschi, "Der einfache Auftrag", in *Berner Kommentar zum Schweizerischen Zivilgesetzbuch, Das Obligationenrecht*, Part II, Vol. 4 (3rd ed., Berne, 1971), p. 400.

to compensate the mother for child maintenance and support payments which would presumably have been awarded to the plaintiff had the complaint been filed.[159]

The six-month filing period triggered by the permission to file suit expired around the time that the attorney was appointed by the State to assist the needy mother; although the attorney argued that the permission to file was undated and, further, that he assumed in good faith that the relevant filing period was first triggered by his appointment as attorney for the needy, the Supreme Court rejected these arguments, stating that the attorney violated his duty of due care by not filing the complaint or requesting permission for a settlement hearing prior to expiration of the six-month deadline.[160]

Outside the context of litigation, civil liability most frequently arises on the basis of official acts of authentication by notaries;[161] and, in some cases, on the basis of private, non-official legal services provided by notaries.[162]

Taken as a whole, where civil liability has been upheld based on attorney misconduct, the Swiss attorney will seldom be required to replace the entire judgement (or, contractual) interest but will, instead, regularly be required to forfeit and/or pay fees, out-of-pocket expenses, court costs and litigation compensation to the opposing party.[163]

CIVIL LIABILITY FOR PARTNERS AND ASSISTANTS

Partners

Generally, members of a law firm in the form of a simple or general partnership will be subject under Swiss law to joint and several liability

159. BGE 87 II 367–368.

160. BGE 87 II 369; see also Judgement of the First Civil Division of 15 September 1980, BGE 106 II 173, 174; BGE 85 II 48: attorney has duty to organise his office such that deadlines can be met; Judgement of the Second Civil Division of 27 September 1934, BGE 60 II 353, 354: attorney has duty to ensure that appeal is correctly addressed; SJ 65 (1943) 23: liability based on attorney's unawareness of important case law concerning procedural law of canton in which the attorney practised.

161. See, e.g., BGE 90 II 284: knowing authentication of incorrect information; Judgement of the Second Civil Division of 6 March 1924, BGE 50 II 46, 48–50: failure to notify widow that orally dictated will was required to be immediately filed with court; REP 78 (1945) 373 (*Tribunale di Appello*, Ticino): failure to authenticate document; ZBGR 25 (1944) 301 (Court of Appeals Lucerne).

162. See, e.g., BGE 70 II 224: failure to adequately review financial risks of share purchase, including insolvency of seller.

163. Gautschi, "Der einfache Auftrag", in *Berner Kommentar zum Schweizerischen Zivilgesetzbuch, Das Obligationenrecht*, Part II, Vol. 4 (3rd ed., Berne, 1971),p. 499; Judgement of the First Civil Division of 13 November 1961, BGE 87 II 290, 293.

with respect to mandates taken on by the partnership or in the name of all partners.[164] One of the most typical and prevalent types of law practice in Switzerland, however, is the office-sharing arrangement pursuant to which two or more attorneys join together to share a common infrastructure (office premises, telephone, acceptance of mail, office equipment and, as the case may be, office staff, accounting, costs and letterhead), but nonetheless handle client matters and represent the interests of their clients essentially alone.[165] It is controverted whether or not members of a shared-office law firm will be viewed as a simple or general partnership giving rise to joint and several liability on the part of all firm members.

According to many Swiss commentators, for purposes of liability for the activities of a law firm's members, the firm's presentation of itself as a unity *vis-à-vis* the public, e.g., through the use of a common firm name, joint letterhead, etc., may suffice to give rise to a presumption as to the existence of a simple partnership.[166] This presumption may be rebutted through evidence as to the lack of a common goal to be attained through joint effort characteristic of a simple partnership[167] and/or through evidence that it was made unmistakably clear to the client that the mandate was not being taken on by the partnership but, rather, by the attorney alone, as a sole agent.[168] According to these authors, such evidence might include, for instance, use of a power of attorney which does not list the other law firm members by name, though possibly granting the named attorney the right of substitution.[169]

On the other hand, the view has been presented that the typical shared office arrangement will only constitute a partnership (resulting in joint and several liability of all firm members) with respect to transactions regarding the office's infrastructure, not with respect to the client's mandates themselves.[170] This view is based, first, on the fact that members of

164. See Meier-Hayoz and Forstmoser, *Grundriss des Schweizerischen Gesellschaftsrechts* (7th ed., Berne 1993), pp. 208, 222 .

165. Oesch, "Gegenseitige Haftung von Partnern in einem Anwaltsbüro und Auswirkungen auf die Berufshaftpflichtversicherung", 142 *Der Schweizer Anwalt*, 16 (1993).

166. See, e.g., Oesch, "Gegenseitige Haftung von Partnern in einem Anwaltsbüro und Auswirkungen auf die Berufshaftpflichtversicherung", 142 *Der Schweizer Anwalt*, 16 (1993), p. 16; Steiger, "Haftung des in Gemeinschaften tätigen Anwalts", 142 *Der Schweizer Anwalt*, 18 (1993); 96 SAV Bulletin 15 (1985) (excerpt from expert opinion of Reymond for Law Society of Geneva).

167. Code of Obligations, Article 530(1).

168. Oesch, "Gegenseitige Haftung von Partnern in einem Anwaltsbüro und Auswirkungen auf die Berufshaftpflichtversicherung", 142 *Der Schweizer Anwalt*, 16 (1993), p. 16, citing Reymond; Steiger, "Haftung des in Gemeinschaften tätigen Anwalts", 142 *Der Schweizer Anwalt*, 18 (1993), p. 19.

169. 6 *SAV Bulletin* 16 (1985); Steiger, "Haftung des in Gemeinschaften tätigen Anwalts", 142 *Der Schweizer Anwalt*, 18 (1993), p. 19.

170. Simonius, "Solidarishe Haftung der Mitglieder einer Bürogemeinschaft", 144 *Der Schweizer Anwalt*, (1993) pp. 29–32.

a shared-office law firm generally do not agree to handle client mandates together, sharing full responsibility therefor, such that the definition of a simple partnership under Article 530 (1) of the Code of Obligations of a "joint goal to be attained through joint effort or joint means" is not satisfied.[171] Further, it is argued that a general partnership cannot exist in such case because a general partnership requires action to be taken in the name of the partnership or on behalf of all partners, which requirement is not satisfied through the mere use of law firm letterhead, absent a signature in the name of all firm members.[172]

Finally, it is argued that, in light of prevailing Swiss commercial usage with respect to legal entities and partnerships, a client would not be justified in assuming that he was dealing with a partnership based solely on the law firm's use of a joint office plaque and joint letterhead, absent a signature being given in the name of the law firm itself.[173] Assistance rendered by firm members in connection with the mandate of another firm member will typically be limited to the supervision of incoming post and, in some cases, assistance with meeting deadlines in the absence of the other attorney due to military service, illness or vacation and should therefore not, it is argued, lead to joint and several liability; rather, the firm members should be viewed as in such cases as "assistants" within the meaning of Article 101(1) of the Code of Obligations, working under the supervision and responsibility of their colleague.[174]

Assuming that a partnership does exist, whether or not a new partner will be exposed to liability arising from the prior acts of firm members will depend on whether the partnership constitutes a simple or general partnership. In the case of the simple partnership, the new partner cannot be sued by third parties for existing debts, although the new partner may be jointly liable for such debts *vis-à-vis* other firm members, depending on the nature of agreement reached with the other firm members.[175] On the other hand, in a general partnership, the new partner will, pursuant to Article 569 of the Code of Obligations, be subject to unlimited liability to third parties for debts in existence at the time of his joinder.[176]

171. Simonius, "Solidarishe Haftung der Mitglieder einer Bürogemeinschaft", 144 *Der Schweizer Anwalt* (1993), p. 30.

172. Simonius, "Solidarishe Haftung der Mitglieder einer Bürogemeinschaft", 144 *Der Schweizer Anwalt* (1993), p. 31; *see* Code of Obligations, Article 564 (1).

173. Simonius, "Solidarishe Haftung der Mitglieder einer Bürogemeinschaft", 144 *Der Schweizer Anwalt* (1993), p. 31.

174. Simonius, "Solidarishe Haftung der Mitglieder einer Bürogemeinschaft", 144 *Der Schweizer Anwalt* (1993), pp. 31, 32.

175. Brunner, *Die Anwaltsgemeinschaft* (Arlesheim, 1977), p. 436.

176. Brunner, *Die Anwaltsgemeinschaft* (Arlesheim, 1977), p. 436.

Assistants

Pursuant to Article 101(1) of the Code of Obligations, a person who has carried out an obligation or exercised a right arising out of a legal relationship through an assistant, such as a fellow-tenant or employee, is liable to compensate for any damages caused by the assistant in the performance of his functions, even if use of the assistant was expressly authorised. The concept of "assistant" within the meaning of Article 101 of the Code of Obligations is not limited to employees (e.g. associates, secretaries) but, rather, includes any type of person whose assistance is sought in connection with an obligation.[177]

According to the Swiss Federal Supreme Court, an agent in a mandate relationship may be held liable to the client under Article 101 of the Code of Obligations for actions of an assistant falling below the standard of expert knowledge, loyalty and due care which could be expected of the agent himself.[178] Thus, the scope of the liability of a lawyer for his assistants under Article 101 of the Code of Obligations is defined by the duty of due care and loyalty under Article 398(2) of the Code of Obligations.[179] The lawyer will be held responsible for the assistant's conduct if such conduct falls below the standard applicable to the lawyer himself, even if the assistant acted contrary to clear instructions provided by the lawyer.[180]

With respect to a law firm, Article 101(3) of the Code of Obligations permits liability for slight negligence of assistants to be precluded in advance through agreement with the clients. However, such a limitation of liability might, in the case of attorneys, violate applicable law society rules.[181]

PROFESSIONAL LIABILITY INSURANCE

Today, most Swiss attorneys carry professional liability insurance.[182] There is a relatively low incidence of professional malpractice suits in

177. Judgement of the Court of Cassations of 1 September 1981, BGE 107 Ia 168, 169–70: insurance company employee held to be "assistant" to lawyer.

178. Judgement of the First Civil Division of 23 November 1927, BGE 53 II 419, 425; Judgement of the First Civil Division of 26 April 1920, BGE 46 II 128, 130.

179. Brunner, *Die Anwaltsgemeinschaft* (Arlesheim, 1977), p. 431; see BGE 107 Ia, p. 169: failure of insurance company employee to pay advance on court costs prior to deadline.

180. Brunner, *Die Anwaltsgemeinschaft* (Arlesheim, 1977), p. 431; see BGE 107 Ia, pp. 170–171.

181. Brunner, *Die Anwaltsgemeinschaft* (Arlesheim, 1977), p. 421; cf. ZBJV 105 (1969) p. 372: clause limiting liability of attorney to gross negligence contrary to attorney duty of due care and violation of rules for professional conduct.

182. *10 Schriftenreihe SAV, Die Berufshaftpflicht des Rechtsanwalts*, p. 11 (1992).

Switzerland, and premiums for professional liability insurance are felt to be clearly lower than in other countries.[183]

The professional liability policies offered in Switzerland typically encompass not only the traditional lawyer activities of legal advice and assistance in litigation, but also the usual secondary activities, such as administrator, trustee in bankruptcy, testamentary executor, guardian and arbitral judge.[184] The exact activities covered are expressly mentioned under the liability policy. Except subject to special agreement and the payment of additional premiums, the policy will not cover liability for activities as a board member of a stock corporation or co-operative society, liquidator or auditor of enterprises and foundations or trustee under foreign trust arrangements.[185] No liability coverage is provided for the provision of investment advice and similar purely financial services, nor for the loss of money, securities and valuable assets.[186]

It is currently usual to agree on a liability ceiling of SFr. 2-million per incident of liability.[187] It is possible for members of a law partnership to jointly enter into a liability policy, in which case the maximum coverage ceiling must be high enough to cover multiple incidents of liability.[188] Some, but not all, policies in Switzerland exclude coverage for claims based on the joint and several liability of one partner for the other partner's acts,[189] while coverage extends, as a rule, to personal liability for assistants.[190]

INTERNATIONAL PRIVATE LAW ASPECTS

Swiss attorneys in Switzerland

Typically, the form of power of attorney used by Swiss attorneys will expressly subject the mandate to Swiss law and provide for jurisdiction as to disputes at the Swiss courts at the defendant's place of domicile.

The Swiss Federal Code on International Private Law allows the law chosen by the parties to govern a contract, provided that the choice of law is express or clearly evident from the contract or circumstances.[191] Thus, in theory, a Swiss attorney accepting a mandate from a foreign

183. *10 Schriftenreihe SAV, Die Berufshaftpflicht des Rechtsanwalts* (1992), p. 21.
184. *10 Schriftenreihe SAV, Die Berufshaftpflicht des Rechtsanwalts* (1992), p. 13.
185. *10 Schriftenreihe SAV, Die Berufshaftpflicht des Rechtsanwalts* (1992), p. 13.
186. *10 Schriftenreihe SAV, Die Berufshaftpflicht des Rechtsanwalts* (1992), p. 17.
187. *10 Schriftenreihe SAV, Die Berufshaftpflicht des Rechtsanwalts* (1992), p. 15.
188. De Maddalena, "Deckung der Berufshaftpflichtversicherung", 142 *Der Schweizer Anwalt*, p. 20 (1993).
189. De Maddalena, "Deckung der Berufshaftpflichtversicherung", 142 *Der Schweizer Anwalt*, p. 20 (1993).
190. Brunner, *Die Anwaltsgemeinschaft* (Arlesheim, 1977), p. 434.
191. Code on International Private Law, Article 116.

client could stipulate the law of a foreign country to govern civil disputes arising under the mandate. However, it is questionable whether such a choice of foreign law would be permissible as a matter of cantonal attorney law and/or applicable rules for professional conduct. In the absence of an express choice of law, Swiss law provides that the law of the State where the service is to be performed shall govern civil disputes under a mandate.[192]

Under the Code on International Private Law, suit may be filed on the basis of a contract (mandate) at the Swiss courts at the defendant's place of domicile or, in the absence of a Swiss domicile, at his place of habitual residence in Switzerland or, if the suit arises from the defendant's place of business in Switzerland, at such place of business.[193] Otherwise, suit may also be brought in Switzerland at the place of performance of the contractual obligation.[194] If, in the concrete case, Swiss law were to provide for jurisdiction in Switzerland and the laws of a foreign country provided for jurisdiction in the foreign country, the rules of the Lugano Convention on the Jurisdiction and Enforcement of Court Decisions in Civil and Commercial Matters of 16 September 1988, or one of the other State treaties on jurisdiction in civil matters ratified by Switzerland would be applied to resolve the conflict of law.

Foreign legal advisers in Switzerland

As foreign attorneys in Switzerland are not generally allowed to take the Swiss attorney licensing examination and obtain a license, they are not permitted to join the cantonal law societies and are hence not subject to the law societies' rules for professional conduct. Furthermore, because the cantonal attorney laws are limited in application to the legal areas subject to the cantonal attorney monopoly, foreign legal advisers without attorney licenses are not subject to the duties and standards specified under attorney law. However, the foreign legal adviser will be subject to the codes of ethic of the foreign bar association of which the foreign attorney is a member and will, in any case, be subject to Swiss (contractual) mandate law in the absence of an express choice of foreign law to govern civil disputes arising under a particular mandate.

Foreign lawyers outside Switzerland

Foreign attorneys engaged in providing legal services outside Switzerland will similarly not be subject to duties or standards as a matter of Swiss

192. Code on International Private Law, Article 117(3)(c).
193. Code on International Private Law, Article 112.
194. Code on International Private Law, Article 113.

attorney law or under the law society rules for professional conduct. With respect to civil disputes arising under a mandate, a foreign attorney domiciled abroad with no habitual residence or place of business in Switzerland could not as a matter of Swiss law be sued in Switzerland on the basis of his legal activities on behalf of a Swiss client, unless the mandate were required to be performed in Switzerland.[195]

An express choice of Swiss law to govern a mandate by a foreign lawyer outside Switzerland will be upheld by Swiss courts.[196]

CONCLUSION

While there has been an increasing tendency in recent years to hold Swiss attorneys responsible for their conduct as a matter of civil law,[197] such lawsuits nonetheless remain relatively rare.

One ground for the scarcity of case law in the area of attorney malpractice could be that, in many cases, potential civil lawsuits will often be settled out-of-court by the insurance provider. However, if this were the main reason, Swiss attorney liability insurance premiums would not, presumably, continue to be inexpensive in comparison with other countries.

The rules and standards applicable to attorneys under Swiss mandate law overlap to a large extent with the applicable rules and standards under cantonal attorney law and law society rules for professional conduct, and investigations and/or disciplinary proceedings brought against Swiss attorneys under cantonal attorney law or law society rules are, unlike civil lawsuits, not rare. This fact serves in and of itself to suggest a further ground for the scarcity of civil lawsuits against Swiss attorneys. Swiss mandate law presumes that professionals, such as attorneys, are in compliance with their professional duties and thus requires the plaintiff to bear the burden of proof in demonstrating attorney misconduct. The potential plaintiff — typically, the ex-client — may be likely to have little knowledge in the field of law and will hesitate to commence a lawsuit unless he is certain, as in the case of a missed deadline or glaring mistake as to form, that the attorney has committed an error. As in most European countries, Swiss civil procedural law provides that the losing party must bear court costs and pay attorney compensation to the winning party. However, in a disciplinary proceeding, the client will have nothing to lose by bringing charges against his ex-attorney, and the burden of

195. Code on International Private Law, Articles 112 and 113.

196. Code on International Private Law, Article 116.

197. Christe, "Die zivilrechtliche Haftung des Anwaltes", *Der Schweizer Anwalt* 136 (1992), p. 12.

investigating whether or not the relevant attorney has violated a professional duty or standard will rest with the disciplinary instance rather than the client.

Last but not least, one could also suggest a general compliance by Swiss attorneys with applicable standards under mandate law as a possible explanation for the relatively low incidence of civil lawsuits against Swiss attorneys in Switzerland. In this regard, the existence of extensive and, in large part, overlapping regulation of attorney conduct at the cantonal, federal and law society level may serve an important role in deterring attorney misconduct in Switzerland.

Note: The author would like to thank Dr. jur. Robert Umbricht and lic. jur. Thomas Hippele, also of Umbricht Badertscher & Roesle, for their helpful comments and kind assistance.

CHAPTER 14

UNITED STATES

MICHAEL R. GOLDMAN AND SCOTT A. SEMENEK
Rudnick & Wolfe
Chicago, Illinois

INTRODUCTION

"A lawyer is a representative of clients, an officer of the legal system, and a public citizen having special responsibility for the quality of justice . . . ."[1]

In the United States, the legal profession is quite enigmatic. Some view lawyers as champions of justice who are to be held to a higher code of moral responsibility than members of other professions. Others view lawyers as hired guns who are paid to advance their clients' interests using whatever means necessary. The body of law concerning professional responsibility for lawyers practising in the United States reflects both views. While this body of law espouses the idealistic notion of a lawyer as a champion of justice, it is drafted in a pragmatic manner that acknowledges the adversarial nature of the profession.

This chapter is intended to give the reader a brief overview of the types of prohibited behaviour, the penalties that can be imposed, and the enforcement mechanisms utilised. It will become apparent that professional responsibility is taken quite seriously in the United States. Stiff penalties are levied for a wide variety of improper acts, and there are numerous overlapping ethical codes and enforcement bodies. This chapter should serve as an introduction to issues that should weigh heavily on each lawyer's mind as he practises law in the United States.

REGULATORY FRAMEWORK OF THE PROFESSION

To appreciate the importance of professional responsibility in the United States, one must first examine the highly complex framework within which ethical rules are promulgated and enforced. The body of law regulating the behaviour of American lawyers comes from many sources: statutes, administrative regulations, rules of evidence and procedure and, most prominently, ethical codes.

1. Preamble to the Model Rules of Professional Conduct.

The role of the American Bar Association

The American Bar Association (ABA), was founded in 1878 and consists of more than 362,000 lawyers, judges, court administrators, educators, law students, legal assistants, criminal justice professionals, government officials, and business executives, plus state and local bar associations and law-related organisations. It is the largest and most vocal of several national legal organisations and purports to speak as the national voice of the legal profession. To help develop a uniform national standard of professional conduct, the ABA promulgates ethical rules that utilise models when promulgating enforceable codes. The ABA itself does not have the power to discipline attorneys or enforce its own rules.[2]

States follow one of two sets of ethical rules that were developed by the ABA. The first, the Model Code of Professional Responsibility (Model Code), was promulgated in 1969. In the Model Code, mandatory rules are called Disciplinary Rules (DR) while advisory rules are denominated as Ethical Considerations (EC). Within a few years of its promulgation, all but one state had adopted the Model Code in some form without significant variations. California, however, rejected or substantially revised many of the DRs and deleted all of the ECs.

The second set of ethical rules, the Model Rules of Professional Conduct (Model Rules), was adopted in 1983 and amended in 1987 and 1989. The Model Rules consist of black letter rules and explanatory comments which are amended periodically. The Model Rules' mandatory regulations are expressed in terms of conduct which an attorney "shall" or "shall not" pursue. The advisory rules are expressed in terms of what an attorney "may" do. The Preamble and Comments to the Model Rules express desirable standards of conduct that lawyers "should" but are not required to follow.

Following the adoption of the Model Rules, states had to choose whether to adopt the Model Rules or retain the Model Code. A few of the Model Rules, particularly those relating to confidentiality and client fraud, were highly controversial. Most states have adopted the Model Rules,[3] although a number of states have significantly altered many controversial provisions. Some states retained the Model Code but are now considering whether to switch to the Model Rules.

State regulation

As previously noted, the ABA does not have the power to enforce its ethical rules. That duty is left to the individual states. Each state established

2. See *Paul E. Iacono Structural Eng., Inc.* v. *Humphrey*, 722 F2d 435, cert. denied, 464 United States 851.

3. See, e.g., *Virgin Islands Bar Ass'n* v. *Boyd-Richards*, 765 F Supp. 263.

its own set of rules governing lawyers' conduct. In all but a few states, these ethical rules are closely patterned after either the Model Code or the Model Rules. Each state also has a body of case law concerning lawyers' rights and duties. As the reader will learn in this chapter, states regulate virtually every aspect of a lawyer's career.

Admission to practise law

To practise law, most states require bar applicants to be of a certain age, to have graduated from an accredited law school, to have passed the state's bar examination, and to have good moral character.[4] Each state has its own "bar", or roster of lawyers, admitted to practice. Being admitted to one state's bar does not automatically entitle a person to practise law in another state.

Each state has an association of lawyers commonly called the state bar association. Many states have an "integrated" bar system, wherein each lawyer admitted to practise in the state must be a member of the state bar association. State bar associations administer the state bar examination, provide continuing education programmes for practising lawyers, and assist state courts in regulating and imposing professional discipline on lawyers.

Professional discipline

"Professional discipline" is imposed on a lawyer when he or she has broken a rule of professional ethics. In most states, the state's bar association provides the procedural mechanism for professional discipline. It is the state court's responsibility to supervise the members of its bar, and it may raise professional ethics questions on its own initiative.[5] In a typical case, the state bar receives a complaint about a lawyer, investigates the allegations and, if the complaint appears to have some merit, the bar holds a hearing. Typically, such a hearing is held before volunteer lawyers from the community who receive evidence and make a recommendation about what discipline, if any, is appropriate. In some cases, state courts review disciplinary cases. Disciplinary actions that may be imposed include:

(1) Censure or public or private reprimand;[6]
(2) Suspension from practice;[7] and
(3) Disbarment.[8]

4. See, e.g., *Salibra* v. *Supreme Court of Ohio*, 730 F2d 1059.
5. See *Duca* v. *Raymark*, Indus, 663 F Supp. 184.
6. See *In re Disciplinary Action Boucher*, 850 F2d 597.
7. See *Polydoroff* v. *Interstate Commerce Comm.*, 773 F2d 372.
8. See *Matter of Sassower*, 700 F Supp. 100, aff'd, 875 F2d 856.

Some states allow a disbarred lawyer to apply for re-admission under certain circumstances.[9]

Additionally, as will be explained in more detail later in this chapter, a lawyer may be directly liable to those individuals harmed by such lawyer's violation of his or her ethical duties. The threat of legal malpractice liability helps to ensure proper conduct on the behalf of lawyers.

PRACTICE STRUCTURE

The legal profession expanded greatly after the Second World War.[10] As the profession grew, the proportion of lawyers practising as sole practitioners declined and the proportion of lawyers practising in firms, governmental positions and/or professional corporations increased.[11]

In a law firm, attorneys are classified in a variety of categories. These categories include partners who share in the firm's profits and losses, salaried associates who work toward becoming partners, and permanently salaried lawyers "of counsel" to the firm. Both the Model Code and the Model Rules provide guidelines regarding these classifications, impose duties upon partners concerning the supervision of associates as well as non-lawyer employees, and outline the potential liability that can result from violating these guidelines. For example, a lawyer may be designated "of counsel" on a letterhead only if he has a continuing relationship, other than as a partner or associate, with a lawyer or law firm.[12] In addition, a lawyer or a law firm may be designated as "general counsel" of a particular client only if he or the firm devotes a substantial amount of professional time representing that client. Finally, lawyers may not be designated as members of a firm when this is not the case.[13]

GENERAL DUTIES OF LAWYERS

All lawyers have general duties to uphold while representing their clients. Attorneys must also meet various standards developed by the legal profession. These standards have been developed over time to provide the public with competent legal services.

9. See *In re Fleischman*, 553 NE2d 352.

10. See Curran, "American Lawyers in 1980s: A Profession in Transition", 20 *Law & Soc. Rev.* 19.

11. See Curran, "American Lawyers in 1980s: A Profession in Transition", 20 *Law & Soc. Rev.* 19.

12. DR 2–102(A)(4).

13. Model Rule 7.5(d); *In re Weiss, Healy & Rea*, 536 A2d 266; *Attorney Grievance Comm'n* v. *Crowther*, 453 A2d 140.

Duty of competence

Lawyers should provide competent representation. Lawyers should have the legal knowledge, skill, thoroughness and preparation reasonably necessary for such representation.[14] Every attorney should be familiar with the requisite knowledge of legal principles, procedure, court rules, and basic research. Each attorney also should be able to draft pleadings and documents, manage a law practice efficiently, be familiar with the federal pleadings rules, and be able to investigate a client's matter.

Duty of diligence

Lawyers should be diligent in all aspects of the representation of their clients' matters and should not neglect legal matters entrusted to them.[15] A lawyer should pursue a client's matter to its conclusion despite any opposition or personal inconvenience to the lawyer and should periodically communicate the status of the matter to the client. *In the Matter of Maloney*,[16] an attorney was publicly censured for repeatedly failing to answer his client's letters concerning important legal matters. The client became distressed and frustrated, and his legal position was potentially weakened.

Duty to keep client informed

Communication is an essential element in the attorney-client relationship. A failure to communicate creates an impression of attorney neglect and leads to client discontent. As such, an attorney should keep a client reasonably informed about the status of a matter and promptly comply with reasonable requests for information.[17] Additionally, the attorney should explain a matter to the extent reasonably necessary to permit the client to make informed decisions regarding the representation. For example, in *State Bar of Nevada* v. *Schreiber*,[18] an attorney failed to make timely replies to his clients' inquiries and failed to co-operate in the investigation of the alleged professional misconduct. The court publicly reprimanded the attorney for failing to communicate with his clients and refusing to co-operate with the disciplinary inquiry.[19]

14. Model Rule 1.1.
15. DR 6–101(A)(3).
16. 620 SW2d 361.
17. Model Rule 1.4.
18. 653 P2d, at p. 151.
19. 653 P2d, at p. 151.

Duty of loyalty to the client

An attorney's loyalty to a client is essential to an attorney-client relationship. As the "Conflicts of Interest" section of this chapter demonstrates in greater detail, a lawyer cannot represent a client if doing so would conflict with his representation of a previous or current client.

Duty to report professional misconduct

Because the legal profession is self-regulating, attorneys are bound to report the misconduct of others, under certain circumstances.[20] When an attorney discovers a possible ethical violation concerning a matter before a court, he is obligated to bring the issue to the court's attention.[21] Furthermore, an attorney must report judicial misconduct. Judges are similarly bound by the duty to report lawyer misconduct.[22]

ADVISOR, INTERMEDIARY, ADVOCATE, CUSTODIAN

A lawyer's job is multifaceted — he can advise, mediate, and advocate. The ethical rules to which he is subject often depend on what role he is playing.

Lawyer as advisor

Duty to render candid advice

Even though imparting advice may require revealing unpleasant facts and alternatives that a client may not like to hear, the lawyer must give the client a candid opinion.[23] A lawyer is allowed to boost his client's morale by putting his advice in as favourable a light as honesty permits.[24] However, a lawyer cannot be deterred from giving candid advice because his client may find such advice unpalatable. Further, a lawyer may not render advice that would encourage a client to engage in fraudulent or illegal conduct. In *Wright* v. *Roberts*,[25] for example, a lawyer was suspended for advising his client to violate a restraining order. On the other

20. See Model Rule 1.8.
21. *In re Matter of Gopman*, 531 F2d, at p. 262.
22. *In re Order as to Sanctions*, 495 So2d, at p. 187.
23. Model Rule 2.1(a).
24. Comment to Model Rule 2.1.
25. 573 SW2d 468.

hand, if the client insists that the lawyer engage in conduct that is contrary to the advice and judgement of the lawyer, the lawyer may withdraw from representation.[26]

Giving advice beyond the law

The resolution of a legal problem may involve non-legal considerations such as social responsibility, morality, ethical consideration and economic, political or emotional consequences.[27] It is often difficult for a lawyer to limit advice to the narrow confines of legal issues. As such, lawyers should give advice that apprises the client of the full implications of a proposed course of action. However, the client, not the lawyer, ultimately must make the final decision, regardless of whether the lawyer's advice is based on legal or non-legal considerations.

Volunteering advice

In general, a lawyer is not expected to give advice unless the client requests it. However, when a lawyer knows his client's proposed course of action is likely to result in a substantial, adverse legal consequence, he may be required to offer advice.[28]

Lawyer as intermediary between clients

Functions of an intermediary

A lawyer acts as an intermediary when he represents two or more parties with potentially conflicting interests.[29] In his role as intermediary, the lawyer seeks to resolve the potentially conflicting interests by developing the parties' mutual interests on an amicable and mutually advantageous basis.

Because clients often desire mediation to save costs and time, it is common practice, for example, for attorneys to act for both partners in drafting the articles of a partnership, both the grantor and grantee in the sale of real property, and both the lender and borrower in a loan transaction.[30] The alternative can be that each party may have to obtain separate representation, incurring additional costs, complications, and possibly

26. Model Rule 1.16(b)(3).
27. Comment to Model Rule 2.1.
28. Model Rule 1.4.
29. Model Rule 2.2.
30. *Lessing* v. *Gibbons,* 45 P2d 258, at p. 261.

even litigation. However, in considering whether to act as intermediary between clients, a lawyer should be aware that if intermediation fails, additional costs, embarrassment and recrimination may result.[31]

When intermediation is proper

Model Rule 2.2(a) states three preconditions for a proper and successful mediation. The first requirement is consultation, which means explaining frankly both the advantages and risks involved so that both clients can make their own informed judgement about how to proceed. The lawyer should also be convinced that the potential gains to the clients outweigh the risks, and likewise, he must be independently satisfied that he can play his role without compromising other responsibilities to the clients.

A particularly important factor in determining the appropriateness of intermediation is its effect on client-lawyer confidentiality and the attorney-client privilege. He must keep each client adequately informed and maintain client confidentiality relating to the representation.[32] If this balance cannot be maintained, then common representation becomes improper.

Consultation and confidentiality

When a lawyer acts as an intermediary between clients, the clients must give knowing consent and assume greater responsibility for decisions than when each is independently represented. The clients should understand that the lawyer will not act in a partisan role on behalf of one of the clients to the detriment of the other. Additionally, each of the clients should be warned that the evidentiary attorney-client privilege does not apply to parties who have shared a lawyer, so that if the parties were later to litigate against each other over the subject of the failed mediation, the mediating lawyer could be called as a witness and forced to testify.

Withdrawal

When an actual conflict of interest arises, a lawyer must withdraw from representation. The court in *Klemm* v. *Superior Court*[33] required the lawyer to withdraw from dual representation of litigants who had adverse interests at a contested hearing. The court reasoned that such dual representation would be *per se* inconsistent with the lawyer's role as advocate

31. Comment to Model Rule 2.2.
32. See Model Rules 1.4 and 1.6.
33. 42 Cal. Rptr. 509.

in the litigation. Similarly, in *In re Robertson*,[34] the lawyer was disciplined for failing to obtain consent for common representation in a real estate purchase and sale. After withdrawal, the lawyer should not represent any of the clients concerning the matter being mediated.[35]

Lawyer as advocate

When a lawyer acts as an advocate, he must temper his desire for victory by recognising and abiding by the rules of fair play contained in the overlapping ethical codes to which he is subject.

Duty to expedite litigation

In today's judicial system, it may take years for a case to go to trial. The effects of delays can breed frustration with the legal system and, ultimately, disrespect for the law. Advocates should attempt to expedite all phases of the litigation process, including filing pleadings, propounding and complying with discovery requests, such as written interrogatories, producing documents and depositions, and the actual trial and appeals.

Unnecessary delays in litigation caused by an attorney can lead to sanctions by the court.[36] In *Mungo* v. *UTA French Airlines*,[37] for example, the appellant's attorney was fined US $500 for lack of preparedness for trial. The attorney had 18 months' notice of the trial date, but did not arrange to have the key witness ready to appear. *In re Darby*,[38] a lawyer was suspended for not less than one year and liable for the costs of the disciplinary proceeding for repeatedly misrepresenting his calendar to the court to avoid scheduled court appearances. The issue is whether a competent lawyer acting in good faith would regard the course of action as having some substantial purpose other than delay.

Duty of candour toward the tribunal

LAW APPLICABLE TO THE CASE

An attorney must apply the proper law to a case and reveal legal authority which may be relevant and material — even if the law and facts are adverse to the client's position. This rule does not require the lawyer to

34. 624 P2d 603
35. Model Rule 2.2(c).
36. Model Rule 3.2; Federal Rules of Civil Procedure 11.
37. 212 Cal. Rptr., at p. 369.
38. 403 NE2d, at 1074.

make a disinterested exposition of the law. However, the lawyer should not fail to disclose pertinent, adverse authority in the controlling jurisdiction. In *In re Greenberg*,[39] the court limited this disclosure duty to decisions of the courts of the state involved and, with respect to federal questions, to decisions of the courts of the United States.

CANDOUR ABOUT THE FACTS OF THE CASE

The temptation to misrepresent facts or fail to disclose certain material facts is a serious problem in the legal profession, as attorneys are faced with a constant conflict between the vigorous pursuit of a client's interest and the adherence to various ethical codes. An attorney is responsible for the veracity of pleadings and the authenticity of evidence used in litigation. An attorney who knows statements in the pleadings are false should inform the tribunal.[40] In one case, an attorney was disbarred because of his continuous and ongoing deceit and dishonesty towards his clients, other attorneys, and judges.[41] In *Breen*, the attorney misrepresented facts, made fraudulent statements on behalf of his client, offered false evidence, and failed to comply with court orders.[42] In *In the Matter of Edson*,[43] an attorney was disbarred for deliberately creating false facts to support a defence and personally lying to a prosecuting attorney.

FALSE EVIDENCE

A lawyer does not violate his duty to represent a client diligently if he refuses to offer evidence the lawyer has reason to believe is false. In *Nix* v. *Whiteside*,[44] the Supreme Court held that there was no violation of the Sixth Amendment right to effective counsel when a lawyer refused to present perjured evidence at trial. In that case, the lawyer informed the defendant that if he committed perjury, the lawyer would have to advise the court of the tainted testimony and would seek to withdraw from further representation. In another case, *Florida Bar* v. *Lopez*,[45] an attorney was suspended for one year for advising clients and witnesses to

39. 104 A2d 46, at p. 49.
40. Model Rule 3.3.
41. *In the Matter of Breen*, 552 A2d, at p. 119.
42. 552 A2d, at p. 109.
43. 530 A2d, at p. 1246.
44. 475 US 157.
45. 406 So2d, at p. 1100.

testify falsely. Any obligation to disclose evidence is strictly limited to the case where the lawyer knows that the client committed perjury.[46] A lawyer's suspicions are not enough to trigger the obligation.

Duty of fairness to opposing counsel

OPPONENTS ACCESS TO EVIDENCE

To establish a claim or defence, it is often essential for an attorney to have access to documents and other items of evidence. An attorney should not unlawfully obstruct another party's access to evidence or unlawfully alter, destroy or conceal a document or other material having potential evidentiary value. In *Price* v. *State Bar of California*,[47] for example, a prosecutor was suspended for five years from the practice of law for altering evidence in a criminal trial and attempting to prevent discovery of his misconduct. Another attorney was suspended for five years from the practice of law for falsifying documentary evidence for use on his own behalf in pending civil litigation and for falsely affirming the authenticity of such documents while under oath.[48] These principles apply whether the lawyer is involved in litigation or negotiations.

PAYING WITNESSES

Although it is improper to bribe a witness, not all compensation to a witness is forbidden. Because appearing as a witness may be very timeconsuming and costly, it may be acceptable to pay reasonable compensation for the loss of work time and other expenses to a witness. Such payments are often necessary to obtain the testimony of certain expert witnesses. However, it is improper to make compensation of a witness contingent upon the content of his testimony or the outcome of the case.[49]

ABUSING DISCOVERY PROCEDURES

An attorney should not, in pre-trial procedure, make a frivolous discovery request or fail to make a reasonably diligent effort to comply with a legally proper discovery request by an opposing party. Additionally, Model Rule 3.4(c) prohibits a lawyer from disobeying or advising his

46. ABA Formal Op. 87–353.
47. 179 Cal. Rptr., at p. 915.
48. *In the Matter of Stump*, 621 P2d, at p. 263.
49. Model Rule 3.4(b).

client to disobey a court order regarding pre-trial discovery or other obligations. In *People* v. *Young*,[50] for example, a lawyer was censured for disregarding an order to furnish documents to opposing counsel and for ignoring subsequent enforcement orders.

Duty to preserve the impartiality and decorum of the tribunal

The purpose of a judicial system is to utilise the services of an impartial third person to resolve the conflicts of others. To prevent corruption within the judicial system, a lawyer must not seek to influence a judge, juror, prospective juror or other official by means prohibited by law, communicate *ex parte* with them except as permitted by law, or engage in conduct intended to disrupt a tribunal.[51] For example, an attorney received a one-year suspension from the practice of law for personally loaning a judge $2500.[52] In another case, *In the Matter of Holman*,[53] an attorney representing a defendant was disbarred for communicating with the jury *ex parte*.

Trial publicity

There is often an inherent conflict between the right to a fair trial and the right of free speech. The dissemination of information to the public about a pending case may be curtailed to preserve a party's right to a fair trial — especially if the proceeding is a jury trial. Since information given to the public may unduly influence the jurors, a lawyer should avoid making extra-judicial statements to the public that would materially prejudice an adjudicative proceeding.[54] In *United States* v. *Bingham*,[55] for example, lawyers representing defendants in a highly-publicised criminal case were investigated by the court after making statements on the eve of jury selection which criticised the judge's decision to empanel an anonymous jury.

Trial counsel as a witness

A lawyer attempting to combine the roles of attorney and witness can prejudice the opposing party and create a conflict of interest between

50. 599 P2d 257.
51. Model Rule 3.5.
52. *In re Lane*, 535 NE2d, at p. 866.
53. 286 SE2d, at p. 148.
54. Model Rule 3.6.
55. 769 F Supp. 1039.

himself and his client.[56] Therefore, a lawyer should not act as an advocate at a trial in which he is likely to be called as a necessary witness, unless:

(1) His testimony relates to an uncontested issue or the value of legal services rendered; or
(2) His disqualification would cause substantial hardship to his client.

In *Nebraska State Bar Ass'n.* v. *Neumeister*,[57] for example, an attorney received a one-year suspension for representing his client in a guardianship case, testifying about substantive matters, and submitting personal affidavits pertaining to those issues.

CIVIL AND ADMINISTRATIVE LIABILITIES

Civil liabilities

The rights and interests of a client involved in litigation or business negotiations are usually in conflict with those of another party. Only rarely can a client receive everything he wants from such a situation. This inability to produce completely satisfactory results tends to produce more dissatisfaction with attorneys than with other professionals.

Causes of action

NEGLIGENCE

Legal malpractice actions are most commonly based on the lawyer's negligence. The cause of action for legal malpractice involves the routine elements of any negligence action: a duty of due care, a breach of that duty, proximate cause and damages.

Duty of due care

To establish the existence of an attorney's duty to exercise due care and diligence in the exercise of services, a plaintiff must first show either the existence of an attorney-client relationship or that the plaintiff was an intended beneficiary of the attorney's services. As a professional, the attorney is recognised as having knowledge and skill superior to that of the ordinary person and, thus, is held to a higher standard of care. The

56. Model Rule 3.7.
57. 449 NW2d, at 17.

standard of care for a general practitioner is the degree of care, skill, prudence and knowledge possessed by similarly situated general practitioners of ordinary skill and capacity.

With the growth of certified or self-designated specialists in the law, and with the increasing use of advertising of specialists to the public, an attorney who purports to be an expert in a certain field of law risks the application of the more stringent standard of care met by other attorneys practising in that speciality. A New Mexico court stated that a lawyer who held himself out to be a specialist in workers' compensation law was appropriately held to the higher standard of care imposed on lawyers who so specialised.[58] A growing number of states recognise the existence of specialities by providing that attorneys may be certified by the state bar as specialists in a certain area. For example, California certifies specialities in criminal law, taxation and workers' compensation.[59]

Breach

An attorney does not insure or guarantee the correctness of his work or the results which will be attained. To be actionable, a breach of due care must be something more than an honest mistake or a mere error in judgement by the attorney.[60] Liability can attach for ignorance or non-observance of statutes, court rules or court decisions that are applicable to a client's case.

Proximate cause

In an action for professional negligence against an attorney, the client has the burden to plead and prove not only that the attorney was negligent, but also that the lawyer's negligence was the proximate cause of his injury. In order to prove proximate cause, the client must show that "but for" the attorney's misconduct, the injury would not have been suffered. In order to plead and prove proximate cause in the context of litigation, the client must demonstrate that, but for the alleged negligence of the attorney, the client would have been more successful in the prosecution or defence of the lawsuit. For example, in *Gillion* v. *Tieman*,[61] the court held that a client had to prove that her appeal would have been successful in order to prevail in a malpractice claim based on her attorney's failure to file a timely Notice of Appeal. Thus, a plaintiff must prove that the

58. *Rodriguez* v. *Horton*, 622 P2d 261, at pp. 264–265.

59. "Final Report of the Committee on Specialization of the State Bar of California", 44 *Cal.St.BJ* 493.

60. *Lynn* v. *Lynn*, 480 P2d 789.

61. 407 NE2d 1146, at pp. 1148–1149.

underlying claim was valid, that it would have resulted in a favourable decision had it not been for the attorney's error, and that the judgement was collectible.

Damages

In an action for professional negligence against an attorney, the client bears the burden of proving that damages actually resulted. The extent of damages must be affirmatively shown because an attorney is liable only for the actual damages his client has sustained. In general, nominal damages or the mere threat of future harm will not suffice.

The amount of damages recoverable against an attorney for misconduct is governed by the rules of the jurisdiction in which the suit is brought. An attorney is always liable for direct damages and may be liable for foreseeable consequential damages as well. Where the injury alleged is the loss of a judgement that would have been recovered against a defendant, the insolvency of the defendant will absolve an attorney from liability. No liability will be imposed because the judgement lost would not have been collectible anyway.

Recovery for special damages, such as punitive damages, or attorneys' fees incurred in prosecuting a malpractice action, varies among jurisdictions. Some jurisdictions have statutes which provide for special damage awards where the defendant is an attorney, while other jurisdictions have statutes which expressly disallow any punitive, exemplary, vindictive or aggravated damages.

BREACH OF CONTRACT

Since an attorney often performs duties pursuant to a contract with his client, his failure to exercise the requisite skill and care can be deemed a breach of an expressed or implied contract. If an attorney warrants that he will render a specific service, will provide services of a special quality, or will achieve a specific result, the attorney may be liable for his failure to do so. In *Gunn* v. *Mahoney*,[62] the court held that the client stated a viable cause of action for malpractice where the attorney promised to incorporate the client's business, failed to do so, and the client suffered damages as a result of such failure. However, merely agreeing to represent a client does not imply an agreement to produce a particular result.

In order to recover on the basis of breach of contract, a client must establish the existence of the attorney-client agreement, a breach of duty by the attorney, and injury to the client resulting from the breach. The

62. 408 NYS2d 896, at p. 900.

existence of the attorney-client relationship creates an implied warranty that the attorney will use the knowledge, skill, and ability ordinarily possessed and exercised by members of the legal profession in similar circumstances.[63] An attorney who contracts to render legal services warrants himself to be bound by this standard. The attorney's obligations to his client are enforceable in the absence of consideration. In fact, the attorney may even be found liable for gratuitous advice.

INTENTIONAL TORTS

Although negligence and breach of contract are the most common forms of liability for legal malpractice, liability to clients may also be predicated on intentional misconduct. Courts have recognised the existence of causes of action based on fraud, malicious prosecution, breach of fiduciary duty, defamation, false imprisonment, misuse of funds, and invasion of privacy. The rules concerning malpractice liability based on intentional torts are generally no different than the general rules for such intentional torts.

Fraud is one of the most readily available actions to redress the intentional misconduct of an attorney. The elements are generally the same in the case of an attorney as in the case of a non-professional:

(1) There must be a misrepresentation of a material fact;
(2) With knowledge or reckless disregard of its falsity;
(3) To a party with the intention that he rely on it; and
(4) That the believing party relies upon and is injured thereby.

However, the misrepresentation element is somewhat different in the case of an attorney. A representation of the state of the law is regarded as a statement of opinion, as opposed to a fact, when made by a layman. However, when a representation concerning the state of the law is made by an attorney, it can be considered a statement of fact and may form the basis of an action for fraud.[64] Thus, an attorney's advice or opinion, if knowingly false, may constitute fraud.[65]

BREACH OF FIDUCIARY DUTIES

An attorney acting as a fiduciary for his client owes the client all of the customary duties a fiduciary generally owes. An attorney's fiduciary duties require him to deal with his client with the utmost fidelity, honesty

63. *Hughes* v. *Klein*, 427 A2d 353.
64. *Lawson* v. *Cagle*, 504 So2d 226, at p. 227.
65. *Lietz* v. *Primock*, 327 P2d 288.

and good faith, to preserve the client's confidences, to make full disclosure of all facts bearing on the attorney's representation of the client, to zealously represent the client in accordance with the codes of professional ethics, to promptly account for any funds of the client which come into the attorney's possession, and to refrain from acquiring interests adverse to the client. Generally, to recover damages for breach of a fiduciary duty, the client must plead and prove the identical elements for a cause of action based on negligence.

STATUTORY LIABILITY

Various statutes provide remedies to third persons against attorneys. Some of these statutes create a cause of action unknown at Common Law. Other statutes merely expand various Common Law rights and remedies. The statutes most often used in legal malpractice actions are highlighted below.

Civil rights act

The federal Civil Rights Act concerns the deprivation of civil rights by one acting under "colour of law".[66] Ordinarily, courts have held that a private attorney performing services on behalf of a client in litigation does not act under colour of law. However, an attorney who is a wilful participant in a joint activity with a state official may be liable under the Act. In *Sparkman* v. *McFarlin*,[67] the court held that an attorney may be liable under the Civil Rights Act if he conspired with a state judge performing a judicial act to deprive a plaintiff of a constitutional right.

Consumer protection statutes

Various states have enacted legislation, commonly referred to as the "consumer fraud acts", to protect consumers. Recently, lawyers have begun to find themselves named as defendants in such actions filed by both clients and non-clients. For example, in *Bourland* v. *State*,[68] an attorney was held liable under the Texas Deceptive Trade Practices Act as a result of his involvement in a conspiracy to obtain property.

66. 42 USC 1983.
67. 601 F2d 261, at p. 268.
68. 528 SW2d 350, at pp. 355–58.

Securities acts

An attorney may be liable to a person other than a client because of an error made in connection with a securities transaction. Liability may be predicated on the Securities Act of 1933, the Securities and Exchange Act of 1934, or similar state statutes.

Claimants

Generally, attorneys are not liable to non-clients for professional malpractice unless fraud or other malicious or intentional acts have been committed. However, there are situations where a lawyer is obliged to protect a non-client's interests. In most jurisdictions, a third party beneficiary, such as an intended beneficiary of a will, can recover from a lawyer if that lawyer did not draft a document properly.[69] However, proving that a third party is an intended beneficiary of the attorney-client "contract" is not a simple task. Even when the attorney and client do intend to benefit the third party, the existence of another purpose of the contract, superior to that of benefiting the third party, may cause a denial of recovery to the third party.

Litigation conduct

FRIVOLOUS CLAIMS

Lawyers are prohibited from bringing claims, asserting defences or pursuing appeals that are frivolous or that are meant to harass or maliciously injure another person or entity.[70] A claim, defence or appeal is not considered frivolous if it is based either on existing law or on a good faith argument for the extension, modification, or reversal of existing law. An infraction of the rules concerning a frivolous claim can result in professional discipline ranging from a reprimand to disbarment.

In addition to professional discipline, attorneys who pursue frivolous claims may be directly liable to those who were the targets of such litigation. In order to institute a successful claim for malicious prosecution, a plaintiff must plead and prove that the attorney filed an unsuccessful action on behalf of a client without probable cause to do so and with malicious intent. Since such actions are not favoured by law, the essential requirements for malicious prosecution actions are strictly construed.

69. *McLane* v. *Russell*, 546 NE2d 499, at pp. 503–4.
70. See, e.g., Federal Rules of Civil Procedure 11.

REGULATORY AND COURT-IMPOSED SANCTIONS

Another way in which lawyers who engage in groundless litigation are subject to discipline and monetary penalties is through the various statutes, court rules and inherent powers of the court, including:

(1) Rule 11 of the Federal Rules of Civil Procedure (Rule 11) (and any corresponding state rule), which requires lawyers to make sure a pleading states an arguable claim before signing it and to refrain from filing court papers for harassment or delay;
(2) 28 USC 1927, which penalises attorneys who "unreasonably and vexatiously" multiply litigation;
(3) Fed.RApp.P 38, which addresses the problem of frivolous appeals; and
(4) The inherent power of federal and state court judges to impose fines and other sanctions on attorneys who act in bad faith in order to abuse the judicial process.

RULE 11

Rule 11 requires that every pleading, motion or other paper of a party be signed by the attorney representing the party, or by the party himself if he has no attorney. The signature constitutes a guarantee that the pleading, motion or other paper is well-grounded in fact and is not interposed for an improper purpose. If the pleading contains a misstatement of the facts or of the law, then the court may impose sanctions on the signatory. The court, however, may not use Rule 11 to sanction the signer's law firm, even if the pleading was signed by the individual attorney "on behalf of" the law firm.[71]

Depending upon the situation, the court has discretion to impose sanctions on either the lawyer, the client, or both of them.[72] A client was sanctioned where he misled the lawyer, causing him to file a meritless claim in *Blake* v. *National Casualty Co.*[73] However, because lawyers have an affirmative duty to investigate the viability of a pleading prior to filing it, the court in *Borowski* v. *DePuy, Inc.*[74] imposed sanctions solely on the lawyer when a groundless pleading was found to be legally insufficient. Rule 11 states that an appropriate sanction may include an order to pay the other party's expenses incurred by the frivolous pleading, including attorneys' fees. However, the Supreme Court has clearly emphasised that Rule 11 is not a fee-shifting statute and was not meant to pawn off

71. *Pavelic & LeFlore* v. *Marvel Entertainment Group*, 493 US 120.
72. *Business Guides, Inc.* v. *Chromatic Communications Enterprises*, 111 SCt. 922.
73. 607 F Supp 189.
74. 850 F2d 297.

expenses on adversaries.[75] Instead, the central purpose of the rule is to deter baseless filings in the district court to streamline the administration and procedure of the federal judicial system.[76]

The United States Supreme Court recently adopted revisions to Rule 11, effective 1 December 1993, which should eviscerate the bite of the former rule. First, the amended Rule 11 would require motions for sanctions to be served on the opposing party and not filed with the court unless the opposing party withdraws or corrects the challenged pleading. Second, the amendments would impose sanctions jointly against the offending lawyer and his law firm. Third, the amendments would give courts the option not to impose sanctions despite finding a violation of the rule.

CONFLICTS OF INTEREST

Conflicts generally

As noted earlier, an attorney owes an undivided loyalty to his client. After he has been retained, an attorney cannot act for both the client and for one whose interests are adverse to those of the client without obtaining the client's informed consent. Additionally, the client is entitled to expect to receive the undivided loyalty of his attorney. When an attorney represents a client without being completely loyal to his client's interests, he may be reprimanded in several ways: He may be disqualified from representing the client further; he may be subject to disciplinary or disbarment proceedings; and if the attorney's actions have resulted in damage to the client, the client may sue for malpractice.

Present clients

Potential conflicts between two clients

A "conflict of interest" is most commonly defined as a situation in which the lawyer has to contend for one client that which his duty to another client requires him to oppose. A classic example is the case of *Alayo I Carreras* v. *Cable West Corp*.[77] In that case, a lawyer who represented the plaintiff corporation, the creditors, and the co-defendant, who was a debtor in a derivative shareholder suit, was held to have acted improperly.

75. *Cooter & Gell* v. *Hartmarx Corp.*, 110 SCt. 2447.
76. *Cooter & Gell* v. *Hartmarx Corp.*, 110 SCt. 2447.
77. 624 F Supp. 1167.

Present actual conflict between two clients

Quite often, a lawyer is called upon to represent two or more clients in the same matter. For example, he may be asked to represent several clients incorporating a single business, multiple personal injury plaintiffs, or multiple criminal defendants. Such a relationship tends to reduce fees and save time. On the other hand, these arrangements increase the potential for conflict. A lawyer must weigh carefully the probability that his judgement may be impaired or his loyalty divided if he accepts or continues such employment. A lawyer may represent more than one client in a particular matter where the lawyer reasonably believes that he or she can adequately represent the interest of each client if all the clients consent to the representation after full disclosure of the implications of the multiple representation.[78]

However, there are some situations in which an "unwaiveable" conflict of interest arises. The reasoning underlying this concept is that no rational client, having been properly informed of the implications, would consent to waive the conflict, and thus any purported waiver is invalid. This emerging doctrine has been applied in such situations as where an attorney seeks to represent both the buyer and the seller of a parcel of real estate.

Opposing a client in another case

Absent consent following consultation, a lawyer may not represent a client in one case and oppose that same client in a simultaneously pending case, even when the two cases are unrelated to each other. For example, a lawyer could not bring suit on behalf of a subcontractor against a general contractor he was already representing in another matter.[79] This rule is designed to prevent the client from having to treat an attorney as friend and adversary at the same time.

Representing clients with inconsistent legal positions

Absent consent following consultation, an attorney must not represent two clients whose positions on a point of law in separate cases are inconsistent if either client would be disadvantaged. Ordinarily, an attorney may take inconsistent legal positions in two cases pending in different trial courts; however, it may be improper to take inconsistent legal positions in two cases pending in the same appellate court.[80]

78. Model Rule 1.7.
79. *Unified Sewerage Agency* v. *Jelco, Inc.*, 646 F2d 1339, at p. 1351.
80. Comment to Model Rule 1.7.

Former clients

Continuing duty of confidentiality

An attorney's duty to preserve client confidences extends beyond the termination of his representation.[81] The attorney has a continuing obligation to preserve confidences obtained during the agency relationship. Discharge from representation does not free a lawyer from these duties to a former client.[82] However, if the former client is fully informed about the possible consequences of such a situation, these protections can be waived.[83]

Opposing former client

When an attorney has obtained confidential information from a former client, the lawyer cannot oppose that former client in any matter to which the confidential information would be relevant, unless the client consents after consultation.[84] In fact, an attorney is always prohibited from using any such confidential information to the former client's disadvantage unless that client consents after consultation. A client must feel assured that any information he gives his lawyer during the representation will not later be disclosed or used against him. Without such assurances, clients would be reluctant to confide completely in their attorneys.[85]

Opposing former client in substantially related matter

An attorney also is prohibited from opposing a former client in a matter that is substantially related to the matter he handled for the former client.[86] This rule applies even in situations where the former client is unable to establish that the attorney possesses any confidential information. The scope of a "related matter" depends on the facts of a particular situation or transaction. When a lawyer has been directly involved in a particular transaction, he cannot oppose the former client in a matter concerning that same transaction.[87] On the other hand, a lawyer who routinely handled a certain type of problem for a former client may later oppose that client in a wholly different matter of the same general type.

81. Model Rule 1.9.
82. *Greene* v. *Greene*, 418 NYS2d 379, at p. 382.
83. *Melamed.* v. *ITT Continental Banking Co.*, 592 F2d 290, at p. 294.
84. Model Rule 1.9(a)–(c).
85. *In re Corn Derivatives Antitrust Litigation*, 748 F2d 157, at p. 161.
86. Model Rule 1.9(a).
87. See *Metromedia Co.* v. *Fugazy*, 753 F Supp. 93.

That was the situation in *Kaminski Brothers, Inc.* v. *Detroit Diesel Allison*.[88] In that case, the court held that a firm's representation of General Motors in 15 cases involving cars and light trucks did not disqualify the firm from representing an adversary in a case involving heavy equipment manufactured by General Motors.

Imputed Disqualification

General rule

In the context of a law firm, a true conflict of interest between clients simultaneously represented by the firm is not resolved by assigning the representation to different attorneys in the firm. Imputed disqualification occurs when a lawyer who, considered alone, could handle a matter is associated with another lawyer who is barred from that representation because of a conflict of interest.[89] Since client confidences are shared among law firm members, this rule prevents a lawyer from circumventing professional standards through partners, associates and other employees.

The general rule of imputed disqualification applies to lawyers within a "firm". For purposes of the rule, a "firm" includes lawyers in a private firm, lawyers employed in a corporate legal department, or lawyers employed by any other legal service organisation. A firm might attempt to screen a disqualified lawyer from any participation in the client's representation through the use of a "Chinese Wall". Such screening involves isolating the disqualified lawyer from other lawyers in a firm in an effort to rebut the presumption of shared confidences.[90] Under this approach, the firm would argue that, although it had a technical conflict of interest, no actual conflict existed because the flow of confidential information concerning the client was barred by the "Chinese Wall". In order to successfully create a "Chinese Wall". courts require the law firm to establish specific institutional mechanisms, including:

(1) Attorneys at the firm must be instructed to have no discussions regarding the matter with the screened attorney;
(2) The screened attorney must not discuss the matter with any attorney in the new firm;
(3) No documents concerning the matter may be shown to the screened attorney; and
(4) Client files with respect to the matter should be kept away from the screened attorney with a prominent notice to that effect.[91]

88. 638 F Supp. 414, at pp. 415–417.
89. Model Rule 1.10.
90. *Schiessle* v. *Stephens*, 717 F2d 417, at p. 421.
91. *Manning* v. *Waring, Cox, James, Sklar & Allen*, 849 F2d 222, at pp. 225–227.

The use of a "Chinese Wall" does not guarantee that the firm will not be disqualified. It merely constitutes evidence that client confidences were not disclosed.

When lawyers change firms

In today's mobile legal market, it is common for lawyers to change jobs several times during their careers. In such situations, there are several competing considerations. On one hand, the client previously represented by the former firm should be able to count on the continued protection of its confidential information. On the other hand, the rule should not hamper lawyers from forming new associations.

DISQUALIFICATION OF A LAWYER'S NEW FIRM

A lawyer cannot represent a client in the same or a substantially related matter if that lawyer was formerly associated with a firm that previously represented an individual:

(1) Whose interests are materially adverse to the client; and
(2) About whom the lawyer had acquired confidential information that is material to that matter.[92]

This rule may be waived if the individual consents after consultation.

DISQUALIFICATION OF A LAWYER'S FORMER FIRM

Model Rule 1.10(b) states the obligations of a lawyer's former firm. Under this rule, when a lawyer has terminated an association with a firm, the firm is not thereafter prohibited from representing a person with interests materially adverse to those of a client represented by the formerly associated lawyer, unless:

(1) The matter is the same or substantially related to that in which the formerly associated lawyer represented the client; and
(2) Any lawyer remaining in the firm has confidential information that is material to the matter.

92. Model Rule 1.9(b).

SUCCESSIVE GOVERNMENT AND PRIVATE EMPLOYMENT

When an attorney serves the government for a period of time and then enters the private practise of law, the government has a right to expect that its confidential information will be safeguarded from future use against it or third parties. Moreover, there exists a risk that an unfair advantage could accrue by reason of the lawyer's access to confidential governmental information about the client's adversary. To solve this problem, Model Rule 1.11 provides that, except where expressly permitted by law, a lawyer who leaves government service and enters private practise must not represent a private client in any matter in which the lawyer participated personally and substantially while in government service, unless the government agency consents after consultation.

REPRESENTING AN ORGANISATION

While an organisational client is a separate legal entity, it cannot act except through its officers, directors, employees, shareholders and constituents. Because the organisation itself is the client, the attorney owes his obligations to the organisation rather than to its individual constituents. When the organisation's interests may be adverse to one or more of its constituents, the lawyer should advise the constituent that he represents the organisation, and that said individual constituent may wish to obtain independent counsel.[93]

Questionable transactions

Business transactions with client

As a general rule, business transactions with clients are greatly disfavoured, although not absolutely prohibited. If a lawyer engages in a business transaction with a client, such transaction should be fair and reasonable to the client. Model Rule 1.8 provides mandatory safeguards designed to protect the client. These safeguards include requirements that:

(1) Such transactions be objectively fair to the client;
(2) The client be given a written explanation of the terms;
(3) The client be given an opportunity to consult independent counsel; and
(4) The client consent to the arrangement in writing.

93. Model Rule 1.13.

Soliciting investment funds from a client is a common illustration of an improper business transaction. *In re Harris*,[94] for example, the court found that a lawyer who persuaded his client to invest in the purchase and rental of property without disclosing that the property was to be managed by the lawyer's corporation had acted improperly. Moreover, a lawyer need not intend to defraud a client in order to violate the restrictions on business dealings with clients. However, a lawyer's lack of intent to harm his client may serve to mitigate the discipline he might receive for entering into the transaction.

Use of confidential information to client's disadvantage

A lawyer is absolutely prohibited from using a client's confidential information to such client's disadvantage, absent the client's consent. Model Rule 1.8(b) prevents a lawyer from exploiting, for his own benefit, information relating to his representation of a client.

Gifts from clients

A lawyer may accept a gift from a client if the transaction meets general standards of fairness. For example, a simple gift, such as a present given on a holiday or as a token of appreciation, is permissible. However, a lawyer is prohibited from drafting instruments on behalf of a client if the lawyer is to receive a substantial gift through such instrument.[95] For example, it is improper for a lawyer to draft a will and trust under which he stands to benefit.[96] The primary concern is that the lawyer drafting the instrument could exert undue influence over the client.

Publication and media rights

An agreement by which a lawyer acquires literary or media rights concerning his representation creates a conflict between the interests of his client and the personal interests of the lawyer.[97] Measures appropriate in the representation of the client may detract from the publication value of the account of such representation. Therefore, a lawyer is prohibited from acquiring literary or media rights to a story concerning the representation of a client. Under this prohibition, a client's covenant with his

94. 741 P2d 890, at p. 893.
95. Model Rule 1.8(c).
96. *In re Anderson*, 287 NE2d 682, at p. 684.
97. Model Rule 1.8(d).

lawyer to refrain from publishing her own account was held to be improper.[98] However, a lawyer may acquire such rights after his representation of the client is terminated.

Financial assistance to client in litigation

An attorney is prohibited from advancing financial aid to a client in connection with pending or contemplated litigation.[99] The major concern underlying this rule is that a lawyer's financial assistance could encourage a client to pursue lawsuits that might otherwise be forsaken, thereby adding to the public cost of administering justice. Additionally, the rule was designed to prevent impairment of the lawyer's judgement due to any desire to protect his investment in the outcome of the lawsuit.

The most common violation of this rule occurs when an attorney advances living expenses to a client while litigation is pending.[100] An attorney may advance court costs and litigation expenses on the client's behalf if the client remains ultimately liable for these costs and expenses. Courts have become increasingly dissatisfied with such a rigid rule and have allowed lawyers to provide financial assistance to clients even though a client's financial situation makes reimbursement unlikely.[101] An attorney is, however, permitted to assume responsibility for court costs and expenses on behalf of indigent clients.

Compensation from a third party

An attorney is prohibited from accepting compensation from a third person for representing a client unless:

(1) The client consents after consultation;
(2) The attorney's independent judgement is not impaired; and
(3) The arrangement does not compromise the client's confidential information.[102]

Prohibited conflicts may arise when fee payments are made to the lawyer by a third person whose interest may be adverse to the client's. The most prevalent example of a situation in which a third party might offer

98. *United States* v. *Hearst*, 638 F2d 1190.
99. Model Rule 1.8(e).
100. *In re Stewart*, 589 P2d 886, at p. 888.
101. *In re Ruffalo*, 249 F Supp. 432, at p. 443.
102. Model Rule 1.8(f).

to compensate a lawyer for services rendered to another party occurs when an insurance company offers to pay the legal fees associated with defending a suit against a party it has insured.[103]

Opposing counsel who are related to each other

Absent client consent, when two attorneys are closely related, they are prohibited from representing clients whose interests are directly adverse.[104] Such a rule seeks to prevent the inadvertent disclosure of client confidences by closely related lawyers. Unlike other conflicts, this type of conflict is not imputed to other lawyers within a law firm.

Proprietary interest in subject of litigation

Generally, an attorney may not acquire a proprietary interest in the client's cause of action or the subject matter of litigation.[105] The rule is intended to prevent conflicts of interest that might interfere with the lawyer's exercise of independent judgement. Despite this rule, an attorney may enter into contingent fee arrangements with clients in civil matters. Additionally, an attorney is permitted to acquire certain liens to secure payment of legal fees and expenses.

DEFENCES, EXCLUSIONS, AND STATUTES OF LIMITATION

There are many possible defences to an action for legal malpractice, including expiration of the statute of limitations, contributory negligence, estoppel and *res judicata*. Each defence operates much in the same way it operates in actions at Common Law. Some of the defences have aspects unique to legal malpractice actions and are discussed in more detail below.

Statutes of limitations

The statute of limitations has been one of the most effective defences to legal malpractice actions. Statutes of limitations applicable to actions against attorneys vary widely among jurisdictions, and may be dependent upon fact patterns or the particular cause of action asserted against the

103. *Parsons* v. *Continental Nat's Am. Group*, 550 P2d 94, at pp. 97–99.
104. Model Rule 1.8(i).
105. Model Rule 1.8(j).

attorney. Some jurisdictions have enacted statutes which establish a limitations period specifically for legal malpractice actions. Several jurisdictions have applied general professional malpractice statutes to legal malpractice cases. In other jurisdictions, the applicable statute of limitations varies according to the cause of action alleged. Since legal malpractice actions may sound in either tort or contract, one must look at the essence of the claim in order to determine the applicable statute of limitations in such jurisdictions.

To properly analyse a statute of limitations, it is essential to determine exactly when the client's cause of action accrues. Under the "occurrence rule", a cause of action accrues on the date the attorney's allegedly wrongful act occurred, regardless of the client's knowledge of or injury resulting from the act.[106] The "damage rule" provides that a client's cause of action does not accrue until a client has been injured as a result of the attorney's act.[107] The "discovery rule" states that the limitations period does not begin until the client knows or reasonably should know the facts giving rise to his cause of action.[108] Additionally, under the "continuous representation" doctrine, a client's cause of action does not accrue until the lawyer's representation concerning a matter is terminated.[109] Each statute of limitations utilises one of the above rules to determine when the cause accrues.

Contributory negligence

Contributory negligence may be a successful defence to a malpractice action when the client fails to provide an attorney with information and data essential to the case or when the client misrepresents facts to the attorney. Additionally, clients have been barred from recovery against their attorney for their failure to follow instructions or heed the advice of their attorney.

Res judicata and collateral estoppel

If the issue of the lawyer's degree of skill was adjudicated previously in another suit in the attorney's favour, that issue should not be re-litigated in a malpractice suit. For example, in *Felger* v. *Nichols*,[110] the court had previously found that an attorney properly performed his services and

106. *Glamm* v. *Allen*, 439 NE2d 390, at p. 393.
107. *McClung* v. *Johnson*, 620 SW2d 644, at p. 647.
108. *Hendrickson* v. *Sears*, 495 F2d 513, at p. 514.
109. *Glamm* v. *Allen*, 439 NE2d, 390, at p. 393.
110. 370 A2d 141, at p. 144.

was entitled to payment from a client in a suit to collect fees. In a subsequent suit by the client for malpractice, the court ruled that the adequacy of the lawyer's representation had already been adjudicated in the suit over fees.

VICARIOUS LIABILITY

A question central to many professional liability cases is "who can be held liable for an individual attorney's misconduct?" The effects of malpractice can extend far beyond the individual whose misconduct is at issue.

Partners

When a client retains one partner of a law firm, that client actually retains the entire firm.[111] A legal partnership and its members are liable for a tortious wrong or contractual breach committed within the actual or apparent scope of authority of one of its members.[112]

The scope of apparent authority, and thus the scope of liability, is limited to the normal business of a law firm. Partners are not liable for the personal actions or debts of other partners. For example, in *Safeco Insurance Co.* v. *McGrath*,[113] a law firm was found to be not liable for the conduct of one of its partners who, after a business meeting, shot a patron in a bar. Also, in *McGarity* v. *Craighill, Rendleman, Ingle & Blythe, P.A.*,[114] the firm was found to be not liable when one of its partners lost property given to him to invest by a client.

In general, a firm and its innocent partners will not be vicariously liable for the punitive damages incurred by another partner. In *Husted* v. *McCloud*,[115] the court held that the rationale behind punitive damages was not to compensate the plaintiff but rather to punish wrongdoers and to deter others from engaging in similar conduct in the future; therefore, the court reasoned, punitive damages should not be imposed on attorneys who are personally innocent of any wrongdoing.

The termination of a partnership may not relieve partners of liabilities that arose during its existence.[116] An individual may remain liable for those partnership liabilities that arose when he was a member of the

111. *Burton by Burton* v. *Estrada*, 501 NE2d 254.

112. See, e.g., *Tri-Growth Centre City, Ltd.* v. *Silldorf, Burdman, Duigman & Eisenberg*, 265 Cal. Rptr. 330; *American Casualty Co.* v. *Costello*, 435 NW2d 760.

113. 749 P2d 178.

114. 349 SE2d 311.

115. 450 NE2d 491.

116. *Ellerby* v. *Spiezer*, 485 NE2d 413.

partnership, but an incoming partner may not be liable for those liabilities that arose before he joined the partnership.

Professional corporations

Unlike the law of legal partnerships, the courts of individual states do not address the issue of vicarious liability for shareholders of professional corporations in a uniform manner. There are four basic legislative approaches to assessing the liability of officers and shareholders of a professional corporation.

The first approach follows the principle that a change to the corporate form does not alter the existing rules concerning liability; therefore, rules for shareholder liability are no different than those imposed on partners in a partnership setting. States following this approach include Arizona,[117] Maine[118] and Wisconsin.[119]

The second approach holds that personal liability for shareholders exists only if the misconduct at issue involves the rendition of professional services. States following this approach include New York.[120]

The third approach holds only the tortfeasor and the corporation itself liable — not the individual shareholders. States following this approach include Pennsylvania,[121] Delaware,[122] Idaho,[123] Illinois,[124] Tennessee[125] and Georgia.[126]

The final approach limits liability to the tortfeasor and the corporation itself if and only if a statutorily required security for liability has been provided; otherwise individual shareholders will be personally liable. States following this approach include Rhode Island.[127]

It is important to note, however, that the Supreme Court of the State of Georgia held that its power to regulate the legal profession superseded the power of the state legislature to enact laws concerning professional

117. Ariz. Rev. Stat. tit. 10, ch. 9, §10–905.
118. Me. Rev. Stat. Ann. §708.
119. Wis. Stat. Ann. 180.99(8).
120. See *We're Associates Co.* v. *Cohen, Stracher & Bloom*, P.C., 480 NE2d 357.
121. 15 PS §2913(b).
122. Title 8 Del.Code §608.
123. Idaho Code §30–1306.
124. 805 ILCS 10/8.
125. Tenn. Code Ann. §§48–3–401 to 43–3–407.
126. Official Code Ga. Ann. §14–7–1 *et seq.*
127. *In re Rhode Island Bar Association*, 263 A2d 692.

corporations.[128] Thus, no matter how clear the language of a statute, the limits of vicarious liability for professional corporations cannot be considered completely settled.

Employees

Simply stated, an attorney is responsible for the conduct of his staff members. The Model Rules impose two types of duties on partners and other supervisory lawyers. The first type of duty is preventative. Model Rule 5.1(a) requires that a law firm partner "make reasonable efforts to ensure that the firm has in effect measures giving reasonable assurance that all lawyers in the firm conform to the Model Rules." Model Rule 5.1(b) imposes the duty to "make reasonable efforts to ensure that the other lawyer conforms to the Model Rules." The second type of duty is corrective. A partner or supervisory lawyer who learns of a subordinate's ethical violation will be equally culpable if he "knows of the conduct at a time when its consequences can be avoided or mitigated but fails to take reasonable remedial action."[129]

However, if the supervising attorney has no reason to suspect misconduct, he may not be vicariously liable. *In re Corace*[130] involved an associate who signed the name of an opposing party on a stipulation for adjournment, despite the senior partner's earlier explanation that it was firm practice never to sign another's name. The court held that a partner is not vicariously liable if he had no reason to suspect or guard against an associate's violation.

A lawyer may be liable in a disciplinary action for the violations of partners or associates he does not supervise if he knew of or reasonably should have suspected the misconduct.[131] The New York Appellate Division disbarred an attorney whose partner repeatedly submitted false insurance claims even though he did not personally or directly participate in many of the fraudulent and dishonest practices charged. However, the attorney continued practising law with his partner when he knew or should have known of such partner's fraudulent and unethical practices.[132]

Under Model Rule 5.2(a), a lawyer is bound by the Model Rules even if he acts pursuant to another person's direction. However, a subordinate lawyer does not violate the Model Rules when he acts according to a supervisory lawyer's reasonable resolution of an arguable question of

128. *First National Bank & Trust Co.* v. *Zagoria*, 302 SE2d 674.
129. Model Rule 5.1(c)(2).
130. 213 NW2d 124.
131. *In re Fata*, 22 AD2d 116, cert. denied, 382 US 917; *In re Brown*, 59 NE2d 855.
132. *In re Gladston*, 16 AD2d 512.

professional duty.[133] Although a lawyer is not relieved of responsibility for a violation simply because he acted pursuant to the supervisor's direction, such direction may be relevant in determining whether a lawyer had the requisite knowledge required to render conduct a violation of the Model Rules.[134] When lawyers in a supervisor-subordinate relationship encounter a matter involving professional judgement as to an ethical duty, the supervisor is responsible for making the judgement. If the question can reasonably be answered only one way, both lawyers are equally responsible for fulfilling the clear duty. However, if the answer is arguable, someone, generally the supervisor, has to decide on a course of action, and the subordinate may be guided accordingly.[135]

Under Model Rule 5.2, a subordinate is not immunised from his duty to act ethically simply because his actions are taken at another's directions. Unless the subordinate acts pursuant to a supervisor's "reasonable" resolution of an "arguable" point, the subordinate remains liable.[136]

Courts have held that, while a lawyer's inexperience does not excuse wrongdoing, it may mitigate punishment. In *Attorney Grievance Comm.* v. *Kahn*,[137] the court found that factors such as age and inexperience may influence the punishment imposed. Also, in *In re Warlick*,[138] the court disbarred a senior attorney who hired a private investigator to interview potential jurors. However, in *In re Rivers*,[139] the court only reprimanded an inexperienced partner who caused such private investigator to interview the potential jurors at the senior attorney's direction and in reliance upon his assurance that such practice was ethical.

The courts have interpreted the Model Code to impose a broad duty to supervise junior lawyers and staff alike. If an associate's action is the result of negligent supervision, such carelessness may violate the senior attorney's fiduciary responsibility to his client.[140] For example, the California court in *Moore* v. *State Bar*,[141] suspended a lawyer who failed to supervise his associate's work, while assuring the client that his pleadings were being properly filed. The court found that Moore's neglect amounted to a "sustained, deliberate and wilful dereliction of duty" approaching moral turpitude.

133. Comment to Rule 5.2.
134. Comment to Rule 5.2.
135. Comment to Rule 5.2.
136. See *In re Callahan*, 442 NE2d 1092; *Attorney Grievance Comm.* v. *Kahn*, 431 A2d 1336.
137. 431 A2d 1336.
138. 339 SE2d 110.
139. 331 SE2d 332.
140. *Vaughan* v. *State Bar*, 494 P2d 1257.
141. 396 P2d 577.

A lawyer's duty to supervise non-lawyer assistants generally parallels the duty regarding the supervision of subordinate lawyers. Lawyers often employ various assistants, including secretaries, investigators, law student interns and para-professionals. Such assistants, whether employees or independent contractors, act for the lawyer in rendering professional services. The lawyer should properly instruct and supervise these assistants concerning the ethical aspects of their employment, particularly the obligation not to disclose confidential client information.[142]

Lawyers may delegate certain duties to non-lawyer assistants.[143] However, the lawyer is responsible for his assistants' work product. The lawyer should impose measures that take into account his assistants' lack of legal training and relative immunity from professional discipline. A supervisory lawyer must make reasonable efforts to ensure that any non-lawyer assistant's conduct is compatible with the professional obligations of the lawyer. For example, in *Florida Bar* v. *Carter*,[144] a lawyer was disciplined for failing to supervise his non-lawyer personnel's record-keeping and work product. Also, in *Attorney Grievance Comm.* v. *Goldberg*,[145] the court found a lawyer liable for failing to supervise his office manager who neglected case files.

The attorney's estate

If the attorney's misconduct is discovered after he has died, his estate may be liable for the damage caused.[146] Many states have statutes that expressly provide for the survival of a cause of action beyond the lifetime of the attorney.[147]

LEGAL MALPRACTICE INSURANCE

Background

Unlike certain other nations, the United States does not require its attorneys to carry legal malpractice insurance. However, because legal malpractice poses such a constant and potentially devastating threat to both

142. Comment to Rule 5.3.

143. See, e.g., *In re Corace*, 213 NW2d 124.

144. 502 So2d 904.

145. 441 A2d 338.

146. *Loveman* v. *Hamilton*, 420 NE2d 1007; *Brown* v. *Kelly*, 437 A2d 1103; *McGill* v. *Lazzaro*, 379 NE2d 16.

147. *Fazio* v. *Hayhurst*, 55 Cal. Rptr. 370; *Connors* v. *Newton National Bank*, 147 NE2d 185.

the sole practitioner and the large law firm, many attorneys in the United States reduce their risk by obtaining such insurance. Numerous institutions provide legal malpractice insurance. Commercial insurance carriers are the largest institutions and have the lowest risk of insolvency. Risk retention groups, facilitated by the Federal Risk Retention Act of 1986,[148] usually insure entities with similar risks and liability exposures. Offshore insurers, such as the Attorneys' Liability Assurance Society, Ltd., offer certain tax advantages to their members and typically insure large law firms. Regardless of the provider, the specific provisions of the resulting policy are determined by an analysis of various factors, such as:

(1) The risk and financial exposure of the particular matters handled by the firm or the attorney;
(2) The assets of the applicant;
(3) The number of attorneys to be covered by the policy; and
(4) The experience and reputation of the applicant.

Individuals covered

Attorneys obtaining malpractice insurance have great latitude to decide who is to be covered by the policy. Policies typically cover specifically designated (named) individuals as well as "additional insureds" who are covered by the nature of their relationship with the named individuals. An attorney's policy may cover his partners, associates, paralegals, secretaries, spouse and former partners.

Liability or indemnification

Malpractice insurance policies can be distinguished by the nature of the event that triggers the insurer's payment. "Liability" policies, which are the most common type available, provide coverage for "legal liability" regardless of whether the policyholder has actually been required to pay any claimant. "Indemnification" policies provide that the insurer pays only after the policyholder has defended and disposed of the claim. Indemnification policies may allow the insurer to avoid some of its payment obligation if the insured becomes insolvent because of a claim.

148. 15 USC 3901–06.

Policy limits

There are generally two limits imposed upon each malpractice policy: the "occurrence" limit, and the "aggregate" limit. The occurrence limit caps the insurance company's exposure on a particular claim to an amount disclosed in the policy. The aggregate limit caps the insurance company's exposure for the total sum of claims made against the insured in a single policy period. While these two types of limits seem straightforward, courts in the United States often struggle when interpreting whether claims for damages exceed either or both limits.

In *Transamerica Insurance Co.* v. *Keown*,[149] the court analysed how to interpret a policy when a single negligent act by an attorney generates numerous substantial claims. Stating the majority rule, the court held that because there was only one improper act, there should have been only one claim. Furthermore, the court rejected the contention that the attorney's failure to correct the act somehow constituted a separate "claim". Many current policies attempt to eliminate this issue by including language which clearly states that multiple claims arising out of a single act shall be treated as a single claim.[150]

The effectiveness of a policy will be greatly influenced by whether the defence coverage costs are subtracted from the limits imposed on claims. Many policies provide that costs of defending a claim are to be subtracted from the limits; thus, much of an insurer's pay-out will go toward paying the costs of litigation rather than towards satisfying the actual claim.

Conduct insured

Coverage is typically written to cover the acts, omissions or errors of an attorney. The claimant need not be a client of the attorney, although coverage is usually limited to liabilities arising out of the insured's professional services as an attorney.[151] The question of what constitutes an attorney's "professional services" has been litigated frequently. The key factor is whether the purpose of the lawyer 's retention was to obtain the benefit of the attorney's knowledge, skills and experience in the law.[152]

However, a brief review of the case law in this area reveals that decisions are quite unpredictable. A lawyer received coverage for a claim

149. 451 F Supp. 397.

150. See *Village of Camp Point* v. *Continental Casualty Co.*, 578 NE2d 1363.

151. See, e.g., *Donnelly* v. *Transportation Insurance Co.*, 589 F2d 761; *Mann* v. *Mann*, 273 NE2d 40.

152. *General Accident Insurance Co.* v. *Namesnik*, 790 F2d 1397.

resulting from his investment of funds received for his client as a consequence of his representation.[153] A lawyer who was retained to solicit funds for investment was not entitled to coverage for his failure to repay funds to his client.[154] A law firm retained to negotiate on behalf of a company with that company's employees was held to have acted as a "labour relations consultant" rather than as lawyers, and thus a claim stemming from the negotiations was not covered by the firm's legal malpractice policy.[155] A lawyer was not entitled to coverage when his ex-wife sued him for the manner in which he handled his divorce action against her.[156]

Claims-made and occurrence policies

Two basic types of malpractice insurance policies are available to attorneys. "Claims-made" policies cover claims that are asserted (made) after the policy becomes effective but before the policy period expires. "Occurrence" policies cover claims that stem from conduct of the insured that occurred during the period stated in the policy. Occurrence policies are rarely issued today and are more expensive to acquire than claims-made policies, because the insurer may be forced to pay claims many years in the future at inflated dollar amounts. However, because a claimant may not discover an attorney's error until many years after it occurred, some old occurrence policies remain in effect today.

While claims-made policies dominate the field today, in *Brown-Spaulding* v. *International Surplus Lines Insurance Co.*,[157] one court adopted the minority view that such policies violate public policy by effectively precluding coverage near the end of the policy period. The court reasoned that the reporting requirement of such policies precludes coverage for those claims-made toward the end of a policy period that cannot be reasonably reported to the provider until after the expiration of the policy.[158]

Exclusions

Insurers are not required to pay every conceivable claim, but instead are entitled to certain contractual exclusions from coverage. The most common

153. *Continental Casualty Co.* v. *Burton*, 795 F2d 1187.
154. *Smith* v. *Travelers Indemnity Co.*, 343 F Supp. 605.
155. *Ellenstein* v. *Herman Body Co.*, 128 A2d 268.
156. *Mendelsohn* v. *CNA Insurance Co.*, 451 NE2d 919.
157. 254 Cal. Rptr. 192, at p. 195.
158. 254 Cal. Rptr. 192, at p. 195.

exclusion, the "fraud" exclusion, states that a policy will not apply to any dishonest, fraudulent, criminal or malicious act or omission by the insured, or any partner or employee of the insured.[159] Coverage has been denied for malpractice when an attorney misappropriated the assets of an estate,[160] and when an attorney converted his client's securities.[161] This common exclusion may leave the innocent victims of an attorney's misconduct without a solvent source of recovery should the attorney dispose of the fraudulently obtained assets.

Many policies exclude personal injury or damage to property. In the leading case, *McAlear* v. *Saint Paul Insurance*,[162] an attorney attempted to recover pursuant to his malpractice policy when the plane he was piloting on a business trip crashed into other planes on the runway. The court held that even though the trip was related to his legal practice, the damage to tangible property fell within the exclusion, and that a reasonable attorney would not expect his malpractice insurance carrier to defend him against property damage claims arising from an aeroplane accident. Some policies specifically exclude liabilities arising out of the use of any vehicle, aircraft, or watercraft. Thus, an attorney should consider obtaining an automobile liability policy and a comprehensive general liability policy to cover any gaps created by exclusions from his or her malpractice policy.

Insurers often seek to exclude coverage for claims arising from securities laws because violations of such can subject the insurer to thousands of claims totalling millions of dollars. Insurers also may exclude coverage for any business activities, other than the practicse of law, that the policy holder engages in. Finally, an attorney's activities as administrator, executor, guardian, conservator, or trustee often are excluded from coverage.

INTERNATIONAL ASPECTS

Foreign lawyers in the United States

United States citizenship cannot be required as a condition for admission to the bar because there is no constitutionally legitimate justification for such a requirement.[163] Similarly, citizenship of a particular state cannot

159. *See Continental Casualty Co.* v. *Burton*, 795 F2d 1187.
160. *St. Paul Fire & Marine Ins. Corp.* v. *Starr*, 651 SW2d 517.
161. *Rabideau* v. *Schmitt*, 404 So2d 519.
162. 493 P2d 331.
163. *In re Griffiths*, 413 US 717.

be a condition precedent to admission to that state's bar.[164] Foreign lawyers are entitled to practice law in the United States — if they pass the bar examination in the appropriate state.

However, only certain states permit graduates of law schools outside the United States to take the examination. Graduates of an accredited foreign law school who have completed a three-year programme of study equivalent to that of an American school may take the New York bar examination.[165] Pennsylvania permits foreign students to apply for the bar examination after they have successfully completed 24 semester hours of study at an American school of law.[166] Other states permit foreign lawyers to take the bar examination only if allowed by a panel who evaluates their educational and practical experience. Most states, however, allow only graduates of accredited American law schools to take their bar examinations and practise law.

Model Rule 8.5 states that ". . . a lawyer admitted to practise in this jurisdiction is subject to the disciplinary authority of this jurisdiction although engaged in practise elsewhere". Therefore, foreign attorneys who are admitted to practise law in the United States become subject to the myriad ethical rules that confront all other attorneys who practise in the United States.

One issue that has arisen with increasing frequency is "what constitutes the practice of law". Certainly, a state cannot expect every foreign attorney who comes to the United States to take that state's bar examination. In *El Gemayel* v. *Seaman*,[167] a Lebanese lawyer was held not to have engaged in the unlawful practise of law in New York when his only activities included telephone calls and visits to his New York client in an attempt to recover his fees. However, if the attorney's actions extend beyond fee collections to actual substantive legal work, many states will consider the attorney to be engaged in the practise of law in that state.

One option a foreign lawyer should consider is the possibility of obtaining the status of "foreign legal consultant". This status enables foreign lawyers in certain states to provide legal services relating to the law of a foreign jurisdiction once they have registered with that state's bar. A foreign legal consultant who has registered with the state bar is subject to the same ethical rules as his licensed American counterpart. States which permit foreign legal consultants include California, Florida and New York.

164. *Supreme Court of New Hampshire* v. *Piper*, 470 US 274.
165. NYCt. App. R, Part 520, Section 520.5.
166. Pa. R. Ct. 205.
167. 533 NE2d 245.

American lawyers in other countries

With the opening of borders to international commerce, increasing numbers of international transactions are inevitable. Many American law firms, including the authors' firm, have either opened offices in other nations or formed affiliations with foreign firms. The new opportunities provided by international transactions are accompanied, however, by an increased level of malpractice risk to the international practitioner.

Model Rule 8.5 provides that the ethical rules of an American lawyer's home state follow him wherever he may practise law. Thus, an attorney may be disciplined for violating ethical rules of his American jurisdiction even though his actions occurred in a foreign nation.[168] If the ethical rules of an attorney's home state conflict with the corresponding rules of the foreign jurisdiction, then the principles of conflicts of laws should be utilised to determine which rule applies.[169]

An American attorney conducting business in a foreign nation should be careful to ensure that his actions do not constitute the illegal practise of law in that nation. If there is any doubt as to whether his activities would be considered improper, the attorney should consider retaining local counsel. However, the retention of foreign local counsel does not relieve an American attorney of his responsibilities to his client. The American attorney should closely monitor and supervise the work of his foreign counterpart.

LIABILITY TRENDS AND RISK REDUCTION MEASURES

Liability trends

Legal malpractice suits are being brought with increasing frequency. In fact, in the first six years of the 1980s there were as many appellate decisions concerning legal malpractice published as there were in the entire decade of the 1970s.[170]

The area of general litigation is, by far, the most frequent source of these claims.[171] Attorneys in firms of two to five lawyers account for nearly 50 per cent more claims than their relative numbers would project, while sole practitioners account for 40 per cent fewer claims than their relative numbers.[172]

While many areas in the field of professional responsibility have been analysed in the past two decades, the area of conflicts of interest has

168. *In re Scallen*, 269 NW2d 834, at 839.
169. Model Rule 8.5.
170. Mallon & Smith, *Legal Malpractice*, Section 1.7 at p. 19.
171. Mallon & Smith, *Legal Malpractice*, Section 1.7 at p. 26.
172. Mallon & Smith, *Legal Malpractice*, Section 1.7 at pp. 27–28.

received unusually close scrutiny by the courts in recent years. In the landmark 1992 case, *Maritrans* v. *Pepper, Hamilton & Sheetz*,[173] the Pennsylvania Supreme Court held that a law firm was not permitted to represent the economic competitor of a former client, even in matters in which the former client was not involved. While the court expressly stated that it did not wish to establish a blanket rule prohibiting such representation, it held that such representation would be improper in factual settings where the danger of revelation of the confidences of a former client is great.[174]

Large firms across the country should take note of the *Maritrans* decision, as it may significantly impact the manner in which such firms build client bases. For instance, if a law firm handles General Motors patent applications, to what extent should that firm be banned from doing legal work for Ford? Does the decision in *Maritrans* indicate that a law firm that specialises in franchise law cannot perform unrelated legal work for both McDonald's and Burger King? The factual scenarios under which other states may follow *Maritrans*' restrictive view of conflicts of interest are not yet known; indeed, that case may prove to be an anomaly that is not followed except in the most extreme factual settings.

Some firms have attempted to circumvent the uncertainty posed by *Maritrans* through obtaining waivers that allow the firm to undertake matters adverse to present clients in the future. For instance, a firm that represents many real estate developers might take on a matter from a bank that has been referred to it by the bank's general counsel. However, such representation may be contingent upon obtaining the bank's agreement to allow the firm to represent its developer clients in any future litigation that may arise against the bank.

Such a waiver clause is permitted under Model Rule 1.7; but only if the waiver contemplates such future conflicts with sufficient clarity so that the client's consent can be viewed as having been fully informed when it was given.[175] Thus, to be effective, prospective waivers must correctly predict and state with a high degree of precision the particular circumstances that will necessitate invoking such waivers.

Risk reduction measures

A heightened appreciation of professional responsibility has accompanied the rising frequency of legal malpractice suits. Today, more than ever, lawyers are taking active steps to reduce their risk of liability. Some of the more prevalent measures are highlighted below.

173. 602 A2d 1277.
174. 602 A2d 1277, at pp. 1286–87.
175. ABA Formal Opinion 93–372.

Docket control systems

Because most malpractice claims stem from litigation activity such as missed filing deadlines, complex docket control systems have been developed to help litigators avoid many frequent causes of malpractice. An effective docket control system should be centralised and mandatory, so that all the members of a firm can note upcoming deadlines. The system should give anticipatory warnings of upcoming dates, rather than merely mark an event on the date it takes place; in this manner, the responsible lawyer will have sufficient time to respond.

Conflict searches

Before the firm agrees to represent a new client or handle a new matter, a thorough conflict search should be conducted. Such a search should utilise a computerised data bank to determine whether the firm represents a party which is adverse to the proposed client. Additionally, the firm should obtain all waivers necessary for such representation to go forward.

Billing practices

Lawyers should avoid fee disputes, as such a dispute gives a disgruntled client an incentive to bring an action for malpractice against an attorney as a defence to an action by the firm for the collection of its past due fees. Accordingly, a client's financial strength should be assessed before the firm agrees to represent it. Invoices should be sent to the client in regular and frequent intervals and account balances monitored constantly, so that the client does not fall behind in its payments. Finally, each invoice should be itemised, so the client may discern precisely what services were provided and how much time was necessary to perform each task.

Work product

A firm should ensure that its junior associates have adequate supervision for the tasks they are asked to perform. A senior associate or partner should review important documents or pleadings generated by the firm's younger lawyers. The firm may choose to avoid taking cases in speciality areas in which its attorneys have little experience; these areas, such as bankruptcy, have their own unique sets of rules and procedures that pose a heightened risk of malpractice to those who confront them only occasionally. Finally, a "professional responsibility" partner should be designated and allowed to devote a sufficient amount of his time to develop an expertise in this important but complex area.

CONCLUSION

As this chapter has shown, professional responsibility is taken very seriously in the United States. Lawyers are held to higher standards than are members of some other professions. Complex overlapping sets of ethical rules and enforcement systems influence the daily activities of American lawyers. Indeed, virtually every aspect of the practice of law is governed by these various rules of professional responsibility.

The privilege of practising law in the United States is greatly cherished. Those individuals fortunate enough to be members of the profession should not feel burdened by the ethical rules they are subject to; instead, they should appreciate this system of rules that helps maximise the quality of justice available to all.

INDEX